P9-DUI-565

An Introduction to

MATRICES, VECTORS,
and
LINEAR PROGRAMMING

The Appleton-Century Mathematics Series

Raymond W. Brink and John M. H. Olmsted, *Editors*

An Introduction to
MATRICES, VECTORS,
and
LINEAR PROGRAMMING

Hugh G. Campbell

VIRGINIA POLYTECHNIC INSTITUTE

APPLETON-CENTURY-CROFTS
EDUCATIONAL DIVISION
New York   MEREDITH CORPORATION

7110- 10

Library of Congress Card Number: 65-16820

PRINTED IN THE UNITED STATES OF AMERICA

390–16840–8

To my parents
Wendell and Margaret

Preface

Many individuals and study groups recently have advocated the introduction of matrices and vectors at a much earlier stage in the mathematical program than has been customary in the past. Also, the use of matrix algebra as a technique is expanding rapidly within the fields of business administration, economics, agriculture, and various branches of engineering. The increasing emphasis on quantitative methods in all of these fields and the adaptation of high-speed computers to matrix manipulations are two of the many reasons for this development. Consequently, there is an increasing demand for textbooks on matrix algebra which require only a limited mathematical background. There are very few books available today that are suitable for these needs. Such books should begin in a very elementary manner and attempt to elevate the student's mathematical maturity as rapidly and gently as possible.

With these needs in mind, the author has attempted to serve the following triple purpose in this text:

1. To introduce matrices and vectors to such an extent that they may be used in a study of systems of equations, and an introduction to linear programming;

2. To help the student gain an insight (probably for the first time) into the structure of mathematics;

3. To begin building a vocabulary to enable the student to read literature that uses the language of matrix algebra.

With these purposes in mind the author believes that this book is suitable for use in the following ways:

As a text for students of social science, engineering, or business administration which will introduce them to the language of matrices for later use in linear programming and other applications.

As an elementary reference book for students or professional people in fields where matrices are applied.

As a text in a freshman or sophomore course for those who may, or may not, later take a rigorous course in modern algebra.

For accelerated high school seniors in compliance with the recommendations of various study groups on high school mathematics curricula. The book is purposely compatible with the objectives and level of presentation of the sample text prepared by a panel of the School Mathematics Study Group (SMSG), and published by the Yale University Press, 1961.

For high school teacher training programs at the undergraduate or graduate level. Frequently it is difficult to find material on matrices and vectors that is worthy of college credit but, by its method of presentation, is brought within the range of these programs.

About six years ago the Industrial Engineering Department of Virginia Polytechnic Institute requested that the Mathematics Department offer a course expressly for them with essentially the same purposes as those listed previously. To suit these needs, this text has evolved because a suitable book was not available. Primarily, the engineers wanted an elementary mathematics course with the applications left to them to do at a later date. While some applications are mentioned in the way of motivation, this text does not pretend to reveal the many diverse uses of matrix algebra. If done correctly this would be a considerable second task. Rather, the text is designed to give the student a firm mathematical foundation in matrix algebra upon which he may base further study in his applied field.

This text has been tested in the classroom by engineering students during two academic years and by three groups of high ability high school students in summer science training programs sponsored by the National Science Foundation. Using the teaching experience and the results of a lengthy questionnaire given to the students, the text was then revised and put into its present form.

The book is purposely written in a brief concise manner because the author has found in his years of teaching that undergraduate students have a very short interest span when it comes to reading textbooks. They seem to grasp the material better when theorems are called theorems, when definitions are emphasized, and when there is an example to illustrate each new idea that is presented. The style adopted also has obvious advantages when the book is used for reference purposes. An attempt has been made to ease the students' pain with proofs by using the format of high school geometry. Throughout, a special effort has been made to interweave the concrete with the abstract.

This text differs from most introductory matrix algebra books in that: (1) it is more elementary than most; (2) it contains a chapter on mathematical systems which seems to promote abstract thinking by emphasizing how matrices and vectors fit into the structure of mathematics; and (3) it contains a chapter on linear programming which is rapidly becoming a useful tool in many fields.

The book may be adapted to many types of courses. Some alternatives are listed. If the discussion of the simplex method (sections 12.9 and 12.10) is left out, then chapters 9 and 10 can be omitted. (This is an alternative for a one-quarter course.) For those interested in techniques and not in the theoretical aspects, some or all of the proofs may be omitted along with sections 3.6, 3.7, and 3.8. For those interested only in matrix methods for solutions of systems of simultaneous equations, just the first eight chapters need to be considered.

It is assumed that the student has mastered elementary algebra and plane geometry. A knowledge of certain topics from elementary analytic geometry and trigonometry is assumed in a few parts of the book; these topics, however, can be explained sufficiently by the teacher if necessary.

The author wishes to express his sincere gratitude to his wife, Allen, for her help and encouragement. The author is also indebted to his friend and colleague, Robert E. Spencer for his invaluable advice and assistance throughout the preparation of this text; he deserves considerable credit for any success that this book may enjoy. Special appreciation is expressed to Dr. R. W. Brink for all of his efforts in the publication of this book.

H. G. C.

Blacksburg, Virginia

Contents

xi

Chapter 3

MATHEMATICAL SYSTEMS

Chapter 4

SPECIAL MATRICES

Chapter 5

OMIT

DETERMINANTS

Chapter 6

THE INVERSE MATRIX

Chapter 7

ELEMENTARY MATRIX TRANSFORMATIONS

Chapter 8

SYSTEMS OF LINEAR EQUATIONS

Chapter 9

VECTOR SPACES

Chapter 10

LINEAR TRANSFORMATIONS

Chapter 11

CONVEX SETS

Chapter 12

LINEAR PROGRAMMING

An Introduction to

MATRICES, VECTORS,
and
LINEAR PROGRAMMING

Introduction to Matrices

1.1 AN ORIENTATION

It is the purpose of this book to introduce to the student two new
mathematical systems — the algebra of matrices and the algebra of vectors.
The student is already acquainted with the algebra of complex numbers and
real numbers.   There will be many similarities between these old and new
systems, and there will be many differences.

Over the years, the "elements" found useful by mathematicians have
gradually been extended.   First there were the natural numbers or positive
integers $(1, 2, 3, \ldots)$.   They were needed to count objects.   Zero and the
negative integers $(0, -1, -2, -3, \ldots)$ were introduced in order to make it
possible to subtract any positive integer from any other.   The number sys-
tem was eventually expanded to include all rational numbers $(\frac{2}{3}, \frac{4}{5}, \frac{6}{5}, etc.)$.
This was made necessary by the advent of division.   The solution to certain
problems and equations led to irrational numbers such as $\sqrt{2}, \sqrt{3}, \sqrt[3]{5}, \pi,$
and to complex numbers like $2 + 3i,\ 0 - 4i,\ 7 + 0i.$ Historically, these
events probably did not occur in the order in which they are listed above.
In fact, fractions probably preceded negative numbers in most civilizations.
The set or collection of all irrational and rational numbers is called the set of
real numbers.

The sets of numbers discussed above are not the only mathematical "elements" in use today, and indeed the purpose of the first two chapters of
this book is to introduce two new kinds of elements — the matrix and the
vector.   As men increase their knowledge, they seek and find more and
more ways to express their ideas using the language of Mathematics.   This
trend has been quite apparent since the end of World War II.   For example,
certain problems in decision making which have faced business executives
for years are now resolved quickly by computers after a translation has been
made to the language of matrix algebra.   Such solutions have been conceived

only in the last few years.   Thus vectors and matrices are becoming increasingly important to scholars in all branches of social and natural sciences
and engineering.   The need is great for trained personnel who can bring
the power of matrix and vector methods to bear on problems in one or more
of these disciplines.

Actually the elements, vector and matrix, are not new to mankind.   The
notion of a matrix is about a hundred years old, but the recent technological
explosion and the advent of high-speed computers have caused a flurry of
interest in this element.

Three objectives of this text are that it will help the student: (1) To study
matrices and vectors to such an extent that they may be used in a study of
systems of equations and an introduction to linear programming (both of
these topics lead directly to many applied problems); (2) To begin to gain
an insight into the structure of mathematics; (3) To begin building a vocabulary to enable the student to read literature which uses the language of matrix
algebra.

It should be pointed out that this is not a text in applied matrix algebra;
however, a few of the many diverse applications will be pointed out along
the way.

EXERCISES

1. Given the numbers, 2, $\frac{3}{4}$, $2i$, π, $\sqrt{3}$, $\frac{2}{3}$, $2 + 3i$, $2 + \sqrt{3}$, -6, and $\sqrt{9}$, state:
(*a*) which are integers;
(*b*) which are real numbers;
(*c*) which are rational numbers;
(*d*) which are irrational numbers.

1.2 BASIC DEFINITIONS

Undoubtedly, the student frequently sees various types of data presented
in the form of rectangular arrays of numbers, such as the box score of a
baseball game, or the vital statistics of several movie stars.   Consider the
following price chart for a length of pipe of given diameters.

	2 in.	4 in.	6 in.
copper	50¢	65¢	75¢
tin	30¢	40¢	45¢

Such rectangular arrays when subject to certain operations are examples of
matrices.   They are usually designated by capital letters *A, B, C, etc.*

Definition. *A matrix A is a rectangular array of entries, denoted by*

$$A = \begin{bmatrix} a_{11} & a_{12} & \ldots & a_{1n} \\ a_{21} & a_{22} & \ldots & a_{2n} \\ \cdot & \cdot & \cdot & \cdot \\ a_{m1} & a_{m2} & \ldots & a_{mn} \end{bmatrix}.$$

The *entries* of a matrix often are called the *elements* of the matrix. One use of matrix notation is to enable us to manipulate large rectangular arrays of numbers as single entities. This frequently simplifies the statements of various operations and relationships.

Example 1. Let the matrix $A = \begin{bmatrix} 8 & 2 \\ 1 & 1 \\ 2 & 7 \end{bmatrix}$ represent the number of gadgets R, S, and T that factories P and Q can produce in a day, that is, matrix A represents the following production capacity.

	Factory P	Factory Q
Gadget R	8 per day	2 per day
Gadget S	1 per day	1 per day
Gadget T	2 per day	7 per day

Later in this book, using the entity "matrix A," we will extend this example to accomplish some very useful results. First, however, we must become familiar with the terminology and manipulations of matrix algebra.

In this text we shall assume unless it is stated otherwise that the entries of a matrix are *scalars*; the term "scalar" will be defined explicitly in Chapter III. In the meantime the student can interpret the word scalar as a complex number, a real number or a function thereof. Under certain conditions, the entries of a matrix may also be certain other matrices.

Example 2. The following are examples of matrices:

(a) $\begin{bmatrix} 2 & 1 & 2 \\ 4 & 0 & 1 \end{bmatrix}$; the entries are integers.

(b) $\begin{bmatrix} x^2 & 2 \\ 2x & x+2 \end{bmatrix}$; the entries are functions of x.

(c) $\begin{bmatrix} 2i & i \\ 3 & i-1 \end{bmatrix}$; the entries are complex numbers.

(d) $\begin{bmatrix} \pi \\ \frac{2}{3} \\ \sqrt{2} \end{bmatrix}$; the entries are real numbers.

(e) $\begin{bmatrix} \begin{bmatrix} 2 & 1 \\ 4 & 0 \\ [6 & 1] \end{bmatrix} \begin{bmatrix} 3 & 4 \\ 0 & 2 \\ [1 & 4] \end{bmatrix} \end{bmatrix}$; the entries are matrices.

If all the entries of a matrix are real numbers, it is called a **real matrix**, like Examples 2(a) and 2(d). If all of the entries of a matrix are zero, the matrix is called the **zero matrix** or **null matrix** and is denoted by **0**. Bold print will be used to distinguish the zero matrix from the zero scalar.

The horizontal lines of the array are called **rows**. The vertical lines are **columns**. Each entry is designated in general as a_{ij}, where i represents the row number and j is the column number; thus a_{31} is the entry in the third row and first column. The double subscript can be called the **address** of the entry.

The dimensions of the array (number of rows stated first) determine the **order** of the matrix, designated "m by n". Example 2(a) had a total of 2 rows and 3 columns of entries. We say that the order of this matrix is 2 by 3. The order of Example 2(d) is 3 by 1. Such a matrix with a single column is called a **column matrix**. When a matrix consists of a single row (that is, is of order 1 by n), it is called a **row matrix**. When the dimensions of a matrix are equal, it is called a **square matrix**. The **main diagonal** of a square matrix consists of the entries $a_{11}, a_{22}, a_{33}, \ldots, a_{nn}$.

Example 3. In this example the main diagonal of a square matrix is set in heavy type for emphasis.

$$\begin{bmatrix} \mathbf{3} & 4 & 7 \\ 0 & \mathbf{\sqrt{2}} & 6 \\ \pi & 0 & \mathbf{0} \end{bmatrix}$$

This 3 by 3 real matrix is said to be of order 3. In general an n by n matrix is said to be of order n.

Matrices are denoted in several different ways by different authors. Some use parentheses, some use double vertical lines. In this text, an m by n matrix will be written in any one of the three following ways.

$$A = \begin{bmatrix} a_{11} & a_{12} & \cdots & a_{1n} \\ a_{21} & a_{22} & \cdots & a_{2n} \\ \cdot & \cdot & \cdot & \cdot \\ a_{m1} & a_{m2} & \cdots & a_{mn} \end{bmatrix} = [a_{ij}]_{(m,n)}.$$

The last notation is an abbreviation that is frequently convenient. When we have a square n by n matrix, the notation A_n occasionally will be used.

EXERCISES

1. Is the number of rows of a given matrix always the same as the number of columns? Always greater than the number of columns?

2. Why is the following array not a matrix? $\begin{bmatrix} 2 & 1 & 3 \\ 0 & -2 \end{bmatrix}$.

3. If $A = \begin{bmatrix} 1 & 9 \\ 6 & 2 \\ -1 & 3 \end{bmatrix}$, what is the entry in the third row and second column?

What is the address of the entry 6?

4. If $[a_{ij}]_{(2,2)} = \begin{bmatrix} [-2 & 2] & [1 & 4] \\ [\ 0 & 1] & [9 & 8] \\ [\ 2 & 3] & [7 & 5] \end{bmatrix}$, what is a_{12}?   What is a_{21}?

5. Let $A = \begin{bmatrix} 2 & 1 & 6 \\ 3 & 4 & -7 \end{bmatrix}$.   Find:

(a) a_{13};   (b) a_{23}.   (c) Is a_{32} defined?

6. Display the matrix $[a_{ij}]_{(2,3)}$ with entries

$$a_{13} = 3,\ a_{22} = 4,\ a_{11} = 5,\ a_{23} = 6,\ a_{12} = 7,\ \text{and}\ a_{21} = 8.$$

7. State the order of each of the following matrices:

(a) $[3 \quad 5 \quad 6 \quad -2]$;   (b) $\begin{bmatrix} 1 \\ 4 \\ -i \end{bmatrix}$;

(c) $\begin{bmatrix} 2 & x+1 & 4 & -1 \\ 3 & 2x+1 & 0 & 1 \end{bmatrix}$;   (d) $[5]$;   (e) $[2 + 3 + 4]$.

8. Write the matrix denoted by 0_3.

1.3 EQUALITIES AND INEQUALITIES

Definition.   *Two matrices A and B are said to be* **equal** *when they are of the same order and all their corresponding entries are equal; that is,* $a_{ij} = b_{ij}$ *for all i and j.*

Example 1.

(a) $A = \begin{bmatrix} 2 & 1 \\ 4 & 0 \\ 3 & 2 \end{bmatrix}$, $B = \begin{bmatrix} 2 & 1 \\ 4 & 0 \\ 3 & 2 \end{bmatrix}$, $A = B$.

(b) $A = \begin{bmatrix} x & 2 \\ 4 & 1 \end{bmatrix}$, $B = \begin{bmatrix} 3 & 2 \\ 4 & 1 \end{bmatrix}$, $A = B$ only when $x = 3$.

(c) $A = \begin{bmatrix} 3 & 2 & 0 \\ 1 & 4 & 0 \end{bmatrix}$, $B = \begin{bmatrix} 3 & 2 \\ 1 & 4 \end{bmatrix}$, $A \neq B$,

because A and B do not have the same order.

Definition. *A real matrix A is said to be "greater than" (>) real matrix B of the same order when each of the entries of A is "greater than" each of the corresponding entries of B. (≥ or ≤ or < can be substituted for > with corresponding changes in meaning).*

It should be pointed out that matrices behave differently from real numbers with respect to inequalities. For two real numbers a and b you probably remember that $a > b$ or $a < b$ or $a = b$. This is not the case for real matrices of the same order.

Example 2.

$$A = \begin{bmatrix} 2 & 1 \\ 4 & 2 \end{bmatrix}, \qquad B = \begin{bmatrix} 1 & 0 \\ 2 & -1 \end{bmatrix}, \qquad C = \begin{bmatrix} 1 & 4 \\ 2 & 0 \end{bmatrix}.$$

$A > B$ because every entry of A is greater than the corresponding entry of B.

$C \geq B$ because every entry of C is either greater than or equal to the corresponding entry of B.

A is not greater than C because a_{12} is not greater than c_{12}. Neither is C greater than A, and certainly $A \neq C$.

EXERCISES

1. Find, if possible, all values for each unknown that will make each of the following true:

(a) $\begin{bmatrix} 2 & 4 \\ 5 & x \end{bmatrix} = \begin{bmatrix} 2 & 4 \\ 5 & 7 \end{bmatrix}$;

(b) $\begin{bmatrix} 2y-3 & 4 \\ 1 & -1 \end{bmatrix} = \begin{bmatrix} 2 & 4 \\ 1 & -1 \end{bmatrix}$;

(c) $\begin{bmatrix} w & 1 & 0 \\ 3 & 2 & 0 \end{bmatrix} = \begin{bmatrix} 5 & 1 \\ 3 & 2 \end{bmatrix}$;

(d) $\begin{bmatrix} 1 & 4 \\ x & y \\ 0 & 3 \end{bmatrix} = \begin{bmatrix} 1 & 4 \\ 2x+1 & 2y \\ 0 & 3 \end{bmatrix}$;

(e) $\begin{bmatrix} 1 & 4 \\ x & y \\ 0 & 3 \end{bmatrix} = \begin{bmatrix} 1 & 4 \\ 2y & 2x+1 \\ 0 & 3 \end{bmatrix}$;

(f) $\begin{bmatrix} t & 2 \\ 1 & 0 \end{bmatrix} = \begin{bmatrix} t & \sqrt{4} \\ 1 & 0 \end{bmatrix}$;

(g) $\begin{bmatrix} 2 & 3 \\ x & -1 \end{bmatrix} > \begin{bmatrix} 0 & 1 \\ 8 & -2 \end{bmatrix}$;

(h) $\begin{bmatrix} 2 & 3i \\ x & -1 \end{bmatrix} > \begin{bmatrix} 0 & i \\ 8 & -2 \end{bmatrix}$;

(i) $\begin{bmatrix} 2 & 0 \\ y & 0 \end{bmatrix} < \begin{bmatrix} 1 \\ 1 \end{bmatrix}$;

(j) $\begin{bmatrix} w & 3 \\ -5 & 1 \end{bmatrix} > \begin{bmatrix} 0 & 3 \\ -1 & 1 \end{bmatrix}$;

(k) $\begin{bmatrix} w & 3 \\ -3 & 1 \end{bmatrix} \geq \begin{bmatrix} 0 & 3 \\ -5 & 0 \end{bmatrix}$;

(l) $\begin{bmatrix} 0 & -3 \\ 7 & -2 \end{bmatrix} \leq \begin{bmatrix} x & -3 \\ 7 & 0 \end{bmatrix}$.

2. Make up an example of a 2 by 2 matrix with real entries which is not greater than, less than, or equal to $A = \begin{bmatrix} -1 & -2 \\ -3 & -4 \end{bmatrix}$.

1.4 MATRIX ADDITION

Matrix addition can be performed only when the two matrices to be added are of the same order. We say then that they are **conformable for addition.**

Definition. *Given matrices*

$$A = [a_{ij}]_{(m,n)} \quad and \quad B = [b_{ij}]_{(m,n)}.$$

Matrix addition is defined as

$$A + B = [a_{ij} + b_{ij}]_{(m,n)}.$$

In other words, if two matrices are of the same order they may be added by adding corresponding entries.

Example 1.

$$A = \begin{bmatrix} 2 & 1 \\ 4 & 0 \end{bmatrix}, \quad B = \begin{bmatrix} 3 & 2 \\ 1 & 4 \end{bmatrix},$$

$$A + B = \begin{bmatrix} (2+3) & (1+2) \\ (4+1) & (0+4) \end{bmatrix} = \begin{bmatrix} 5 & 3 \\ 5 & 4 \end{bmatrix}.$$

Example 2.

$$A = \begin{bmatrix} 2 & 1 \\ 4 & 0 \end{bmatrix}, \quad C = \begin{bmatrix} 4 & 2 & 4 \\ 1 & 6 & 0 \end{bmatrix},$$

$A + C$ does not exist because A and C are not conformable for addition.

Example 3. A manufacturer produces a certain metal. The costs of purchasing and transporting specific amounts of necessary raw materials from two different locations are given by the following matrices:

$$A = \begin{bmatrix} 16 & 20 \\ 10 & 16 \\ 9 & 4 \end{bmatrix} \begin{array}{l} \text{ore } R \\ \text{ore } S \\ \text{ore } T, \end{array}$$

with column headings: purchase cost, transportation cost

$$B = \begin{bmatrix} 12 & 10 \\ 14 & 14 \\ 12 & 10 \end{bmatrix} \begin{array}{l} \text{ore } R \\ \text{ore } S \\ \text{ore } T. \end{array}$$

Find the matrix representing the total purchase and transportation costs of each type of ore.

$$A + B = \begin{bmatrix} 28 & 30 \\ 24 & 30 \\ 21 & 14 \end{bmatrix}.$$

In a problem such as Example 3, where a large number of raw materials and costs enter in (which is frequently the case), computers may be programmed to accomplish the labor of adding the many entries. This use of computers points up one of the big reasons for the revived interest in matrix algebra in applied fields.

EXERCISES

1. Perform the addition $\begin{bmatrix} 1 & 2 \\ -3 & 0 \end{bmatrix} + \begin{bmatrix} 1 & -2 \\ 2 & -3 \end{bmatrix}$.

2. Calculate $A + B$ if $A = \begin{bmatrix} 1 & 3 & -2 \\ 0 & -1 & -3 \end{bmatrix}$ and $B = \begin{bmatrix} -2 & 1 & 0 \\ 3 & -3 & 5 \end{bmatrix}$.

3. Calculate, if possible, each of the following:

(a) $\begin{bmatrix} 2 & 1-i \\ 1+i & -2 \end{bmatrix} + \begin{bmatrix} 2-i & 5 \\ 3-2i & 3i \end{bmatrix}$;   (b) $[0 \quad 5 \quad 8] + \begin{bmatrix} 3 \\ -6 \\ 4 \end{bmatrix}$;

(c) $\begin{bmatrix} 1 & 4 & -3 \\ 2 & 7 & x \\ 3 & -1 & -1 \end{bmatrix} + \begin{bmatrix} 4 & \sqrt{2} & -2 \\ \pi & 2x & 1 \\ i & 0 & \frac{2}{3} \end{bmatrix}$;

(d) $\begin{bmatrix} [1 \quad 2] & [-1 \quad 3] \\ \begin{bmatrix} 5 \\ 7 \end{bmatrix} & \begin{bmatrix} -5 \\ 0 \end{bmatrix} \end{bmatrix} + \begin{bmatrix} [0 \quad -3] & [\frac{3}{4} \quad 8] \\ \begin{bmatrix} 66 \\ -2 \end{bmatrix} & \begin{bmatrix} -1 \\ -2 \end{bmatrix} \end{bmatrix}$;

(e) $\begin{bmatrix} 1 & 4 \\ 2 & 8 \end{bmatrix} + \begin{bmatrix} 2 & 5 \\ 0 & -1 \end{bmatrix} + \begin{bmatrix} 3 & -2 \\ -2 & -2 \end{bmatrix}$; (f) $\begin{bmatrix} 6 & 4 \\ 3 & 2 \end{bmatrix} + \begin{bmatrix} 0 & 0 \\ 0 & 0 \end{bmatrix}$.

4. If A is a 2 by 3 matrix and B is a 3 by 2 matrix, are A and B conformable for addition?

1.5 MULTIPLICATION BY A SCALAR

Now that addition of matrices has been considered, the question of multiplication naturally arises. First, we consider the multiplication of a scalar and a matrix, and then, in the next section, we will learn a method of multiplying two matrices.

Definition. *Given matrix* $A = [a_{ij}]_{(m,n)}$ *and scalar* c, *then*

$$cA = [ca_{ij}]_{(m,n)}.$$

In other words, a matrix may be multiplied by a scalar by multiplying every entry of the matrix by the scalar.

Example 1.

$$A = \begin{bmatrix} 3 & 2 & 4 \\ 1 & 0 & -2 \end{bmatrix} \quad \text{and} \quad c = 2,$$

$$cA = \begin{bmatrix} 2 \cdot 3 & 2 \cdot 2 & 2 \cdot 4 \\ 2 \cdot 1 & 2 \cdot 0 & 2 \cdot (-2) \end{bmatrix} = \begin{bmatrix} 6 & 4 & 8 \\ 2 & 0 & -4 \end{bmatrix}$$

Example 2.

$$B = \begin{bmatrix} 5 & 2 & 6 \\ 1 & 0 & 1 \end{bmatrix} \quad \text{and} \quad c = -1,$$

$$cB = (-1)B = -B = \begin{bmatrix} -5 & -2 & -6 \\ -1 & 0 & -1 \end{bmatrix}.$$

We are now in a position to handle matrix subtraction similarly to the way in which we perform scalar subtraction. Remember that

$$a - b = a + (-b) \quad \text{or} \quad 6 - 4 = 6 + (-4).$$

Likewise, for matrices, $A - B = A + (-B)$.

EXERCISES

1. Given $A = \begin{bmatrix} 2 & -1 \\ -3 & -4 \end{bmatrix}$ and $B = \begin{bmatrix} -2 & 0 \\ -1 & 3 \end{bmatrix}$

Calculate: (a) $3A$; (b) $-2B$; (c) $-A$; (d) $A + 3B$; (e) $\frac{1}{2}B - 2A$.
   (f) Find C if $B + C = A$. (g) Find D if $A - 2D = 2B$.

2. Given $A = \begin{bmatrix} 5 \\ 1 + i \\ 2i \end{bmatrix}$ and $B = \begin{bmatrix} -4 \\ 2 - 3i \\ 1 + 2i \end{bmatrix}$:

   (a) calculate λA for $\lambda = -\frac{1}{2}$;
   (b) calculate $\lambda A + \alpha B$ for $\lambda = 1$ and $\alpha = 2$;
   (c) calculate $B + (-A)$; \qquad (d) find C if $C = \frac{1}{2}(A - B)$.

3. Let $A = \begin{bmatrix} 5 & 10 & 20 \\ -65 & 15 & -10 \end{bmatrix}$. Find a matrix B which is a scalar multiple of A

and which has 2 as its entry in the first row and second column.

4. For what values of x is $2A - 3B > C$ if $A = \begin{bmatrix} 8 & -2 \\ 2 & x \end{bmatrix}$, $B = \begin{bmatrix} 3 & -5 \\ 1 & 4 \end{bmatrix}$,

and $C = \begin{bmatrix} 5 & 1 \\ -5 & 2 \end{bmatrix}$?

5. Two matrices can be added only when they are of the same order. Is there any restriction on the multiplication of a matrix by a scalar?

6. Consider the following definition:

$$Ac = [a_{ij}c]_{(m,n)}.$$

Making use of this definition show that $3A = A3$ where

$$A = \begin{bmatrix} 2 & 1 \\ 6 & 3 \end{bmatrix}.$$

1.6 MATRIX MULTIPLICATION

We now define a second kind of product — the product of two matrices. Before giving a general definition, however, we consider the method of multiplying a row matrix by a column matrix. (Here the row matrix precedes the column matrix.)

Definition. *Let A be a 1 by p matrix and B be a p by 1 matrix. The product $C = AB$ is a 1 by 1 matrix given by*

$$[a_{11}\ a_{12}\ \cdots\ a_{1p}]\begin{bmatrix} b_{11} \\ b_{21} \\ \cdot \\ \cdot \\ \cdot \\ b_{p1} \end{bmatrix} = [a_{11}b_{11} + a_{12}b_{21} + \cdots + a_{1p}b_{p1}].$$

For example, $[2 \quad 1 \quad 3]\begin{bmatrix} 0 \\ 4 \\ 2 \end{bmatrix} = [(2\cdot0) + (1\cdot4) + (3\cdot2)] = [10].$

Notice that the number of columns of A must equal the number of rows of B. One use of this operation may be forecast, if we observe that a linear equation may be expressed using a product of two matrices, that is,

$[2 \quad 3]\begin{bmatrix} x \\ y \end{bmatrix} = [3]$ means $[2x + 3y] = [3]$ and therefore $2x + 3y = 3$. Now

in order to express a system of equations such as

$$\begin{cases} 2x + 3y = 3, \\ x + 4y = 1, \end{cases}$$

using matrix notation, we will need the following definition. Here we are not restricted to a row matrix times a column matrix, although we will see that the multiplication simply requires a succession of the manipulations previously described.

Definition. *Let A be an m by p matrix and B be a p by n matrix. The product $C = AB$ is an m by n matrix where each entry c_{ij} of C is obtained by* *multiplying corresponding entries of the i*th *row of A by those of the j*th *column of B and then adding the results.*

The operation defined above can be illustrated in general by the following diagrams.

$$\begin{bmatrix} \boxed{\begin{matrix} a_{11} & a_{12} & \cdots & a_{1p} \end{matrix}} \\ a_{21} & a_{22} & \cdots & a_{2p} \\ \cdot & \cdot & & \cdot \\ a_{m1} & a_{m2} & \cdots & a_{mp} \end{bmatrix} \begin{bmatrix} \boxed{\begin{matrix} b_{11} \\ b_{21} \\ \cdot \\ b_{p1} \end{matrix}} & b_{12} & \cdots & b_{1n} \\ & b_{22} & \cdots & b_{2n} \\ & \cdot & & \cdot \\ & b_{p2} & \cdots & b_{pn} \end{bmatrix} = \begin{bmatrix} \boxed{c_{11}} & c_{12} & \cdots & c_{1n} \\ c_{21} & c_{22} & \cdots & c_{2n} \\ \cdot & \cdot & & \cdot \\ c_{m1} & c_{m2} & \cdots & c_{mn} \end{bmatrix},$$

where $c_{11} = a_{11}b_{11} + a_{12}b_{21} + \cdots + a_{1p}b_{p1}$.

$$\begin{bmatrix} a_{11} & \cdots & a_{1p} \\ \cdot & \cdot & \cdot \\ \boxed{\begin{matrix} a_{i1} & \cdots & a_{ip} \end{matrix}} \\ \cdot & \cdot & \cdot \\ a_{m1} & \cdots & a_{mp} \end{bmatrix} \begin{bmatrix} b_{11} & \cdots & \boxed{b_{1j}} & \cdots & b_{1n} \\ \cdot & \cdot & \cdot & \cdot & \cdot \\ \cdot & \cdot & \cdot & \cdot & \cdot \\ \cdot & \cdot & \cdot & \cdot & \cdot \\ b_{p1} & \cdots & \boxed{b_{pj}} & \cdots & b_{pn} \end{bmatrix} = \begin{bmatrix} c_{11} & \cdots & & c_{1n} \\ \cdot & & & \cdot \\ \cdot & & \boxed{c_{ij}} & \cdot \\ \cdot & & & \cdot \\ c_{m1} & \cdots & & c_{mn} \end{bmatrix},$$

where $c_{ij} = a_{i1}b_{1j} + a_{i2}b_{2j} + \cdots + a_{ip}b_{pj}$.

Example 1.

$$A = \begin{bmatrix} 1 & 2 \\ 1 & 0 \end{bmatrix}, \quad B = \begin{bmatrix} 3 & 0 & 1 \\ 0 & 1 & 1 \end{bmatrix}, \quad AB = \begin{bmatrix} 1 & 2 \\ 1 & 0 \end{bmatrix}\begin{bmatrix} 3 & 0 & 1 \\ 0 & 1 & 1 \end{bmatrix}.$$

From the definition note that here $m = 2$, $p = 2$, and $n = 3$.

$$AB = \begin{bmatrix} (1 \cdot 3 + 2 \cdot 0) & (1 \cdot 0 + 2 \cdot 1) & (1 \cdot 1 + 2 \cdot 1) \\ (1 \cdot 3 + 0 \cdot 0) & (1 \cdot 0 + 0 \cdot 1) & (1 \cdot 1 + 0 \cdot 1) \end{bmatrix}$$

$$= \begin{bmatrix} 3 & 2 & 3 \\ 3 & 0 & 1 \end{bmatrix}.$$

It is helpful to think of the first matrix in the above example in terms of its rows,

$$A = \begin{bmatrix} R_1 \\ R_2 \end{bmatrix},$$

the second in terms of its columns,

$$B = [C_1 \ C_2 \ C_3],$$

then the product

$$AB = \begin{bmatrix} R_1 \\ R_2 \end{bmatrix}[C_1 \ C_2 \ C_3] = \begin{bmatrix} R_1C_1 & R_1C_2 & R_1C_3 \\ R_2C_1 & R_2C_2 & R_2C_3 \end{bmatrix}.$$

Prior to our definition of matrix multiplication we implied that it could be used to express the system of equations

$$\begin{cases} 2x + 3y = 3, \\ x + 4y = 1. \end{cases}$$

Consider the following matrix equation.

$$\begin{bmatrix} 2 & 3 \\ 1 & 4 \end{bmatrix} \begin{bmatrix} x \\ y \end{bmatrix} = \begin{bmatrix} 3 \\ 1 \end{bmatrix}.$$

Perform the indicated matrix multiplication on the left side; there results

$$\begin{bmatrix} 2x + 3y \\ x + 4y \end{bmatrix} = \begin{bmatrix} 3 \\ 1 \end{bmatrix}.$$

By the definition of the equality of matrices in Section 1.3 we obtain our original system. Expressing systems of linear equations as matrix equations is very useful as we shall see later.

Other examples of matrix multiplication follow.

Example 2.

$$A = \begin{bmatrix} 2 & 1 \\ 3 & 2 \end{bmatrix}, \quad B = \begin{bmatrix} 0 & 4 \\ 1 & 3 \end{bmatrix},$$

$$AB = \begin{bmatrix} 2 & 1 \\ 3 & 2 \end{bmatrix} \begin{bmatrix} 0 & 4 \\ 1 & 3 \end{bmatrix} = \begin{bmatrix} (2 \cdot 0 + 1 \cdot 1) & (2 \cdot 4 + 1 \cdot 3) \\ (3 \cdot 0 + 2 \cdot 1) & (3 \cdot 4 + 2 \cdot 3) \end{bmatrix} = \begin{bmatrix} 1 & 11 \\ 2 & 18 \end{bmatrix},$$

whereas

$$BA = \begin{bmatrix} 0 & 4 \\ 1 & 3 \end{bmatrix} \begin{bmatrix} 2 & 1 \\ 3 & 2 \end{bmatrix} = \begin{bmatrix} (0 \cdot 2 + 4 \cdot 3) & (0 \cdot 1 + 4 \cdot 2) \\ (1 \cdot 2 + 3 \cdot 3) & (1 \cdot 1 + 3 \cdot 2) \end{bmatrix} = \begin{bmatrix} 12 & 8 \\ 11 & 7 \end{bmatrix}.$$

NOTE: $BA \neq AB$. This is quite different from scalar algebra where $ab = ba$ (that is, $2 \cdot 3 = 3 \cdot 2$). We shall emphasize this in Chapter 3. In the first part of Example 2 we say that B was *premultiplied* by A. In the second part we say that B was *postmultiplied* by A.

Example 3.

$$A = \begin{bmatrix} 2 & 1 \\ 4 & 6 \\ 3 & 2 \end{bmatrix}, \quad B = \begin{bmatrix} 3 \\ -2 \end{bmatrix},$$

$$AB = \begin{bmatrix} 2 & 1 \\ 4 & 6 \\ 3 & 2 \end{bmatrix} \begin{bmatrix} 3 \\ -2 \end{bmatrix} = \begin{bmatrix} 4 \\ 0 \\ 5 \end{bmatrix}.$$

NOTE: A is a 3 by 2 matrix. B is a 2 by 1 matrix. AB is a 3 by 1 matrix. Reconsider the definition and diagram and see why this is so.

In Examples 1 and 3, if the student should try to find BA, he would quickly find that this is impossible. This is because the number of columns of the left matrix does not equal the number of rows of the right matrix. In order for multiplication of matrices to be performed, the number of columns of the left matrix must equal the number of rows of the right matrix. We then say that the left matrix is *conformable for multiplication* to the right matrix.

We define positive integral powers of square matrices as we did for scalars

$$A^2 = AA,$$
$$A^3 = AAA,$$
$$\text{etc.}$$

In view of our discussion in the previous paragraph, the student should be quick to realize why A has to be square for A^n to exist (where n is 2 or more).

One illustration of how matrix multiplication may be used is given by the following example, a simple problem from the field of decision making.

Example 4. A certain fruit grower in Florida has a boxcar loaded with fruit ready to be shipped north. The load consists of 900 boxes of oranges, 700 boxes of grapefruit, and 400 boxes of tangerines. The market prices, per box, of the different types of fruit in various cities are given by the following chart.

	oranges	grapefruit	tangerines
New York	$4 per box	$2 per box	$3 per box
Cleveland	$5 per box	$1 per box	$2 per box
St. Louis	$4 per box	$3 per box	$2 per box
Oklahoma City	$3 per box	$2 per box	$5 per box

To which city should the carload of fruit be sent in order for the grower to get maximum gross receipts for his fruit?

Solution: Consider the chart above as the "price matrix," and form the "quantity

matrix" $\begin{bmatrix} 900 \text{ boxes} \\ 700 \text{ boxes} \\ 400 \text{ boxes} \end{bmatrix}$. The product of these matrices, as shown below, yields

an "income matrix" where each entry represents the total income from all the fruit at the respective cities.

$$\begin{bmatrix} 4 & 2 & 3 \\ 5 & 1 & 2 \\ 4 & 3 & 2 \\ 3 & 2 & 5 \end{bmatrix} \begin{bmatrix} 900 \\ 700 \\ 400 \end{bmatrix} = \begin{bmatrix} 3600 + 1400 + 1200 \\ 4500 + 700 + 800 \\ 3600 + 2100 + 800 \\ 2700 + 1400 + 2000 \end{bmatrix} = \begin{bmatrix} 6200 \\ 6000 \\ 6500 \\ 6100 \end{bmatrix}.$$

The largest entry in the income matrix is 6500, and therefore the greatest income will come from St. Louis.

EXERCISES

1. Multiply: $\begin{bmatrix} 2 & 1 \\ 3 & 4 \end{bmatrix} \begin{bmatrix} 0 & 1 \\ 2 & -1 \end{bmatrix}$.

2. Multiply: $\begin{bmatrix} 2 & 1 \\ 6 & 0 \end{bmatrix} \begin{bmatrix} -1 \\ 4 \end{bmatrix}$.

3. Multiply: $[2 \quad 1 \quad 0] \begin{bmatrix} 4 & 0 \\ 0 & 2 \\ -1 & 1 \end{bmatrix}$.

4. Postmultiply: $\begin{bmatrix} 4 & 2 \\ 3 & 1 \end{bmatrix}$ by $\begin{bmatrix} 1 & 0 \\ 0 & 1 \end{bmatrix}$.

5. Let $A = [a_{ij}]_{(3,t)}$ and $B = [b_{ij}]_{(4,5)}$.

(a) Under what conditions does AB exist?
(b) What is the order of AB?
(c) Under what conditions, if any, does BA exist?

6. Let $A = [a_{ij}]_{(m,n)}$ and $B = [b_{ij}]_{(r,t)}$.

(a) Under what conditions does AB exist?
(b) What is the order of AB?
(c) Under what conditions does BA exist?
(d) What is the order of BA?
(e) Under what conditions will the order of AB be the same as that of BA?

7. Let $A = \begin{bmatrix} 2 & 0 \\ 3 & 1 \end{bmatrix}$, $B = \begin{bmatrix} 4 & -1 \\ 0 & 2 \end{bmatrix}$, $I = \begin{bmatrix} 1 & 0 \\ 0 & 1 \end{bmatrix}$, $0 = \begin{bmatrix} 0 & 0 \\ 0 & 0 \end{bmatrix}$.

(a) Premultiply B by A.   (b) Postmultiply B by A.
(c) Find B^2.   (d) Find B^3.
(e) Find IB.   (f) Find $0B$.
(g) Find I^3.

8. Let $A = [a_{ij}]_{(m,p)}$. Under what conditions does A^n exist?

9. Multiply the following if possible. If it is not possible, state why.

(a) $\begin{bmatrix} 2 & 1 \\ 4 & 0 \end{bmatrix} [3 \quad 2]$;   (b) $\begin{bmatrix} 2 & 3 & 4 & 4 \\ 1 & 0 & -1 & 6 \\ 0 & 1 & 2 & 9 \end{bmatrix} \begin{bmatrix} 0 & 2 \\ 3 & 1 \\ 1 & 0 \\ 0 & -1 \end{bmatrix}$;

(c) $[3 \quad 1 \quad 3] \begin{bmatrix} 4 \\ 0 \\ 9 \end{bmatrix}$;   (d) $\begin{bmatrix} 9 & 6 & 2 \\ 4 & 3 & 1 \end{bmatrix} \begin{bmatrix} 2 & 4 \\ 0 & 0 \end{bmatrix}$;

(e) $\begin{bmatrix} 9 & 6 & 2 \\ 4 & 3 & 1 \end{bmatrix} \begin{bmatrix} 2 & 4 \\ 0 & 9 \\ 0 & 0 \end{bmatrix}$;   (f) $\begin{bmatrix} 2 \\ 0 \end{bmatrix} [3 \quad -1]$;

(g) $\begin{bmatrix} 2 & 1 \\ 4 & 3 \end{bmatrix}\begin{bmatrix} x \\ y \end{bmatrix}$.

10. Let the matrix $A = \begin{bmatrix} 2 & 1 \\ 4 & 3 \end{bmatrix}$ represent the number of gadgets R and S that factories P and Q can produce in a day, according to the table below.

	Factory P	Factory Q
Gadget R	2 per day	1 per day
Gadget S	4 per day	3 per day

Let $N = \begin{bmatrix} 5 \\ 6 \end{bmatrix}$ represent the number of days the two factories operate, that is, P operates 5 days per week and Q operates 6 days per week. Find AN and state what it represents.

1.7 SIGMA NOTATION omit

When matrix multiplication is discussed in general, the so-called "Σ notation" (read "sigma notation") is very helpful as we shall see later in the text. It will also be of assistance in our discussion of determinants. Σ is a letter from the Greek alphabet and in mathematics usually stands for "sum of." For example, the sum

$$1^2 + 2^2 + 3^2 + 4^2 + 5^2 = \sum_{k=1}^{5} k^2.$$

The preceding expression is read "the sum of k^2 where k ranges from 1 through 5." *k is called the index of summation.*

Example 1.

(a) $2 + 4 + 6 + 8 + \ldots + 98 + 100 = \sum_{k=1}^{50} 2k.$

(b) $x_1 + x_2 + x_3 + \ldots + x_{100} = \sum_{k=1}^{100} x_k.$

(c) $a_{i1} + a_{i2} + a_{i3} = \sum_{k=1}^{3} a_{ik}.$

(d) $a_{11}b_{11} + a_{12}b_{21} + a_{13}b_{31} = \sum_{k=1}^{3} a_{1k}b_{k1}.$

(e) $a_{i1}b_{1j} + a_{i2}b_{2j} + a_{i3}b_{3j} = \sum_{k=1}^{3} a_{ik}b_{kj}.$

Example 1(d) may be recognized as the entry in the first row and first column of the product

$$\begin{bmatrix} a_{11} & a_{12} & a_{13} \\ \cdot & \cdot & \cdot \\ \cdot & \cdot & \cdot \\ \cdot & \cdot & \cdot \\ a_{m1} & a_{m2} & a_{m3} \end{bmatrix} \begin{bmatrix} b_{11} & \cdots & b_{1n} \\ b_{21} & \cdots & b_{2n} \\ b_{31} & \cdots & b_{3n} \end{bmatrix} = C.$$

The result in Example 1(e) is then the entry c_{ij} in the above product.

Example 2. Express the product of two 2 by 2 matrices using $\sum$ notation.

$$\begin{bmatrix} a_{11} & a_{12} \\ a_{21} & a_{22} \end{bmatrix} \begin{bmatrix} b_{11} & b_{12} \\ b_{21} & b_{22} \end{bmatrix} = \begin{bmatrix} (a_{11}b_{11} + a_{12}b_{21}) & (a_{11}b_{12} + a_{12}b_{22}) \\ (a_{21}b_{11} + a_{22}b_{21}) & (a_{21}b_{12} + a_{22}b_{22}) \end{bmatrix}$$

$$= \begin{bmatrix} \sum_{k=1}^{2} a_{1k}b_{k1} & \sum_{k=1}^{2} a_{1k}b_{k2} \\ \sum_{k=1}^{2} a_{2k}b_{k1} & \sum_{k=1}^{2} a_{2k}b_{k2} \end{bmatrix} = \begin{bmatrix} \sum_{k=1}^{2} a_{ik}b_{kj} \end{bmatrix}_{(2,\,2)}.$$

Example 3. Suppose a buyer needs certain numbers of three items. Designate the numbers wanted by a_1, a_2, and a_3. When he gets to the market, the buyer finds that the items have unit costs designated b_1, b_2, and b_3. The buyer can then express his bill as the summation of the number of each item times the cost per item.

$$\text{Cost} = a_1b_1 + a_2b_2 + a_3b_3,$$

or

$$\text{Cost} = \sum_{i=1}^{3} a_i b_i.$$

It will be helpful to list some of the rules pertaining to the summation notation. First of all, any letter not used for a different purpose may be used as the index of summation, that is,

$$\sum_{k=1}^{5} k^2 = \sum_{i=1}^{5} i^2.$$

Also any factor not involving the index of summation may be moved in front of $\sum$, that is,

$$\sum_{k=1}^{n} cx_k = c \sum_{k=1}^{n} x_k.$$

Also,

$$\sum_{k=1}^{n} a_k + \sum_{k=1}^{n} b_k = \sum_{k=1}^{n} (a_k + b_k).$$

Double Summation (Optional)

Two summations may occur in succession. The notation

$$\sum_{k=1}^{n} \sum_{i=1}^{m} a_{ik} = \sum_{k=1}^{n} \left(\sum_{i=1}^{m} a_{ik} \right)$$

means that the summation using the index i is to be performed first, giving

$$\sum_{k=1}^{n} (a_{1k} + a_{2k} + a_{3k} + \cdots + a_{mk}).$$

Then the second summation is performed using the index k. We have

$$\sum_{k=1}^{n} \sum_{i=1}^{m} a_{ik} = a_{11} + a_{21} + a_{31} + \cdots + a_{m1}$$

$$+ a_{12} + a_{22} + a_{32} + \cdots + a_{m2}$$

$$\cdot \qquad \cdot \qquad \cdot \qquad \cdot \qquad \cdot$$

$$+ a_{1n} + a_{2n} + a_{3n} + \cdots + a_{mn}.$$

EXERCISES

Write the following without $\sum$ notation:

1. $\displaystyle\sum_{k=1}^{5} k$.

2. $\displaystyle\sum_{k=3}^{7} (k - 2)$.

3. $\displaystyle\sum_{i=1}^{3} i^3$.

4. $\displaystyle\sum_{k=1}^{4} a_k$.

5. $\displaystyle\sum_{k=1}^{3} a_{2k}a_{k3}$.

In Exercises 6 to 11, express the sums in $\sum$ notation:

6. $3 + 6 + 9 + 12$.

7. $a_{21} + a_{22} + a_{23} + a_{24} + a_{25}$.

8. $a_{21}b_{13} + a_{22}b_{23} + a_{23}b_{33}$.

9. $[a_{11} \ a_{12} \ a_{13}] \begin{bmatrix} b_{11} \\ b_{21} \\ b_{31} \end{bmatrix}$.

10. $\begin{bmatrix} a_{11} & a_{12} \\ a_{21} & a_{22} \end{bmatrix} \begin{bmatrix} b_{11} \\ b_{21} \end{bmatrix}$.

11. $\begin{bmatrix} a_{11} & a_{12} \\ a_{21} & a_{22} \end{bmatrix} \begin{bmatrix} b_{11} & b_{12} & b_{13} \\ b_{21} & b_{22} & b_{23} \end{bmatrix}$.

12. Does $c \displaystyle\sum_{i=1}^{n} (i + 4) = \sum_{k=1}^{n} c(k + 4)$?   Why?

13. Express $\displaystyle\sum_{k=1}^{2} \sum_{i=1}^{2} a_{ik}$ without $\sum$ notation.

14. Express $\displaystyle\sum_{k=1}^{2} \sum_{h=1}^{2} (a_{1h}b_{hk}c_{k1})$ without $\sum$ notation.

1.8 HISTORY AND APPLICATIONS OF MATRICES

The matrix notation was first introduced by the English mathematician Arthur Cayley in 1858. He used it as an abbreviated notation for expressing systems of linear equations. That is,

$$\begin{cases} a_{11}x_1 + a_{12}x_2 + \cdots + a_{1n}x_n = b_1, \\ a_{21}x_1 + a_{22}x_2 + \cdots + a_{2n}x_n = b_2, \\ \phantom{a_{21}x_1 + a_{22}x_2} \cdots \\ a_{m1}x_1 + a_{m2}x_2 + \cdots + a_{mn}x_n = b_m, \end{cases}$$

can be expressed as

$$AX = B,$$

where

$$A = \begin{bmatrix} a_{11} & a_{12} & \cdots & a_{1n} \\ a_{21} & a_{22} & \cdots & a_{2n} \\ & & \cdots & \\ a_{m1} & a_{m2} & \cdots & a_{mn} \end{bmatrix}, \quad X = \begin{bmatrix} x_1 \\ x_2 \\ \cdot \\ \cdot \\ \cdot \\ x_n \end{bmatrix}, \quad B = \begin{bmatrix} b_1 \\ b_2 \\ \cdot \\ \cdot \\ \cdot \\ b_m \end{bmatrix}.$$

Example 1. The system of linear equations

$$\begin{cases} 2x_1 + 3x_2 + 4x_3 = 6, \\ x_1 + 5x_2 - 9x_3 = 0, \\ x_1 + 2x_2 + 4x_3 = 2, \end{cases}$$

can be expressed as

$$AX = B,$$

where

$$A = \begin{bmatrix} 2 & 3 & 4 \\ 1 & 5 & -9 \\ 1 & 2 & 4 \end{bmatrix}, \quad X = \begin{bmatrix} x_1 \\ x_2 \\ x_3 \end{bmatrix}, \quad B = \begin{bmatrix} 6 \\ 0 \\ 2 \end{bmatrix}.$$

The student should verify this statement using his new-found knowledge of matrix multiplication, and the definition of equality of matrices.

Cayley's matrices were quite radical at the time of their invention. One reason was that this was a system where AB did not in general equal BA. Gradually matrices gained general acceptance especially in dealing with systems of linear equations, vectors, and other applications. For example, in 1925, W. Heisenberg recognized matrices as a tool he needed for his work in quantum mechanics. The recent advent of many high-speed computers to handle such laborious operations as the multiplication of matrices has added impetus to the application of matrices.

Over the years various fields of learning have found uses for matrices. Some examples are: Electric networks and circuit analysis in electrical engineering, aerodynamic stress and structure in aeronautical engineering, industrial management and operations research in industrial engineering, quantum mechanics and atomic structure in physics, multiple factor analysis in psychology, genetics in biology, numerous branches of statistics, and the construction of model economies in economics. Later in this book we will specifically show how matrices may be used in that part of mathematics called linear programming. No doubt the future will provide many new uses for matrices.

EXERCISES

1. Multiply:
$$\begin{bmatrix} 3 & 2 & 1 \\ 0 & 4 & 1 \\ 2 & 1 & 6 \end{bmatrix} \begin{bmatrix} x_1 \\ x_2 \\ x_3 \end{bmatrix}.$$

2. Express the system

$$\begin{cases} x_1 + x_2 + x_3 = 4, \\ x_1 - x_2 + 2x_3 = 9, \\ 2x_1 \quad\quad + x_3 = 6, \end{cases}$$

using matrices and stating what each matrix is.

3. Repeat the preceding problem for

$$\begin{cases} x_1 + x_2 + x_3 + x_4 = 4, \\ x_1 - x_2 - 2x_3 - x_4 = 6. \end{cases}$$

4. Write the system represented by

$$\begin{bmatrix} 2 & 0 \\ 1 & 3 \\ 4 & 2 \end{bmatrix} \begin{bmatrix} x_1 \\ x_2 \end{bmatrix} = \begin{bmatrix} 2 \\ 1 \\ 3 \end{bmatrix}.$$

5. In Exercise 10 of Section 1.6 suppose $N = \begin{bmatrix} x_1 \\ x_2 \end{bmatrix}$. What is the interpretation of

$$A \begin{bmatrix} x_1 \\ x_2 \end{bmatrix} \geqq \begin{bmatrix} 9 \\ 8 \end{bmatrix}?$$

NEW VOCABULARY

2

Introduction to Vectors

2.1 BASIC DEFINITIONS

Frequently there arises the need for expressing an idea by means of a set of numbers which are arranged in a specific order, for example, the transportation costs to four different cities ($40, $20, $30, $50), or the coordinates of a point in three-space (2, 3, 4). Such ordered sets of numbers when subject to certain operations are examples of "vectors" and will be designated with Greek letters α, β, γ, *etc.*

Definition. *A vector α of order n is an ordered set of n scalars, $(a_1, a_2, a_3, \cdots, a_n)$.*

Just as with matrices, an advantage of vector notation is that we can manipulate sets of numbers as single entities. Force is a concept which cannot be completely described as a number because it has both magnitude and direction. Yet it is advantageous to express a force acting on a particle as a single entity; this can be done by making use of vectors.

Referring back to the definition of a vector, the a_i's are called **components** of α, and for n components, we say that α is an **n-dimensional** vector. If all of the components are real numbers then we have a **real vector.** If all of the components are zero we have a **zero vector** or **null vector.**

The student should recognize that a 1 by n or an n by 1 matrix of scalars will satisfy this definition of a vector; in fact, such a matrix is frequently called the matrix form of a vector. Therefore the definitions of Sections 1.3, 1.4, and 1.5 can be applied to vectors. They will be restated for emphasis.

*Two vectors of the same dimension are **equal** if their corresponding components are equal.* For example, if $\alpha = (1, 3, 4)$ and $\beta = (x, 3, 4)$, then $\alpha = \beta$ when $x = 1$; $\alpha \neq \beta$ when $x \neq 1$.

21

*Vector α is said to be **greater than** vector β of the same dimension if the components of α and β are real numbers and if each component of α is greater than the corresponding component of β.*

*Two vectors of the same dimension may be **added** by adding corresponding components.   The result of adding two vectors is called their **resultant**.*   For example, if $\alpha = (1, 3, 2)$ and $\beta = (4, -2, 0)$, then

$$\alpha + \beta = (1 + 4, 3 + (-2), 2 + 0) = (5, 1, 2).$$

*A vector may be **multiplied by a scalar** by multiplying each component by the scalar.*

It should be emphasized that the number of components of a vector is not restricted.   Vectors of n dimensions have widespread application; for instance in listing the weights of various components of a machine, we should not want to be restricted in the number that we could have.   Because we live in a three-dimensional world, however, vectors of two and three dimensions are of extreme importance.   Therefore in the next section we will restrict ourselves temporarily to vectors of these types.

EXERCISES

1. Let $\alpha = (2, -3, 0, 4)$ and let $\beta = (2, -1, 3, x)$.

(a) Find $\alpha + \beta$.   (b) Find 3α.

(c) Is $\beta \geqq \alpha$?   Why?   (d) Find $2\alpha - 3\beta$.

(e) Find $2\alpha + 3\beta$.   (f) Let $0 = (0, 0, 0, 0)$.   Find $\alpha + 0$.

2.2 GEOMETRIC REPRESENTATION OF A VECTOR

In dealing with such physical quantities as force and velocity, it is necessary to be concerned with both magnitude and direction.   For this reason, it has proved useful to interpret real vectors of two or three dimensions geometrically.

Let (x_1, x_2, x_3) be a three-dimensional vector.   We can associate with this vector the point $P(x_1, x_2, x_3)$ whose coordinates are the same as the corresponding components of the vector.   Moreover, if $P(x_1, x_2, x_3)$ is any point, we can associate with P the vector (x_1, x_2, x_3).   Also, if the point P is not the origin, we can associate the vector (x_1, x_2, x_3) with the directed line segment OP which has both length (or magnitude) and direction.   Geometrically, a 1, 2, or 3-dimensional real vector can be identified with any given directed line segment in 1, 2, or 3 dimensions.   To make this identification, starting at the origin, draw the directed line segment OP having

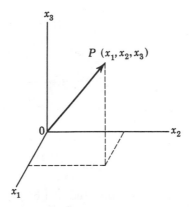

Figure 2.1

the desired length and direction (see Fig. 2.1). Then if (x_1, x_2, x_3) are the coordinates of the terminal point P, we identify the vector $\alpha = (x_1, x_2, x_3)$ with the given line segment. It is clear that the same vector is identified with any line segment having the same length and direction, and that the position of the initial point of the line segment is immaterial.

Example 1.

(a) $\alpha = (1, 2)$ may be thought of as an arrow drawn from the origin to the point $(1, 2)$ in the x_1x_2-plane (Fig. 2.2).

(b) A line segment drawn from the origin to the point $(2, 4, 3)$ in three-dimensional space represents $\beta = (2, 4, 3)$ (Fig. 2.3).

The length of a vector $\alpha = (x_1, x_2, x_3)$ is called the *magnitude* of α and is designated $|\alpha|$. For three dimensions this length can be calculated easily by applying the Pythagorean Theorem twice. Thus $|\alpha| = \sqrt{x_1^2 + x_2^2 + x_3^2}$.

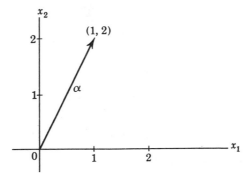

Figure 2.2

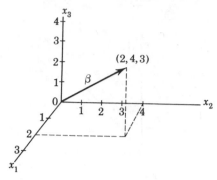

Figure 2.3

Direction is indicated by an arrow and can be expressed by the *cosines of the direction angles.* (The direction angles are the respective angles, equal to or less than 180°, between the vector and the positive direction of the coordinate axes, as shown in Fig. 2.4.)

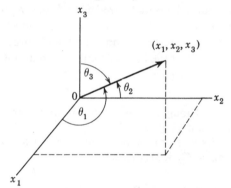

Figure 2.4

$$\cos \theta_1 = \frac{x_1}{\sqrt{x_1^2 + x_2^2 + x_3^2}},$$

$$\cos \theta_2 = \frac{x_2}{\sqrt{x_1^2 + x_2^2 + x_3^2}},$$

$$\cos \theta_3 = \frac{x_3}{\sqrt{x_1^2 + x_2^2 + x_3^2}},$$

The preceding formulas are easily justified by simple trigonometry.

Example 2. In Example 1 above

$$|\alpha| = \sqrt{1^2 + 2^2} = \sqrt{5}, \qquad |\beta| = \sqrt{2^2 + 4^2 + 3^2} = \sqrt{29},$$

and, for β, $\cos \theta_1 = \dfrac{2}{\sqrt{29}}$, $\cos \theta_2 = \dfrac{4}{\sqrt{29}}$, $\cos \theta_3 = \dfrac{3}{\sqrt{29}}$.

Now let us see what is meant geometrically by equality, addition, multiplication by a scalar, and subtraction of vectors. The following example illustrates equality of two vectors and the fact that vectors do not have to originate at the origin.

Example 3.

In Fig. 2.5, $\alpha = \beta$ because $|\alpha| = |\beta|$ and the directions are the same. The fact that they occupy different positions is immaterial. The student may wonder how to write vector β. It is done by simply subtracting the respective coordinates of the initial point from the coordinates of the terminal point, that is, $\beta = (2 - 1, 1 - 0) = (1, 1)$. Thus we see that this geometric concept of "equality of vectors" agrees with the definition in Section 2.1.

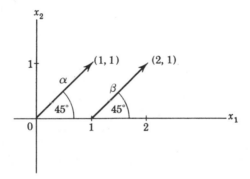

Figure 2.5

The addition of vectors geometrically is accomplished by drawing a parallelogram as shown in Fig. 2.6. It is helpful to think of the two vectors to be added as forces acting on a particle where the question is: In what direction is the particle going to move and under what net force? In Fig. 2.6, the vector γ is the resultant of α and β. The same idea can be extended to three dimensions. It should be noted that the results shown in the diagram agree with the definition of vector addition given in Section 2.1.

If a nonzero vector α is multiplied by the scalar $1/|\alpha|$, the result is called a *unit vector* because it has a magnitude of one unit. An important set of unit vectors in three-dimensional space is $i = (1, 0, 0)$, $j = (0, 1, 0)$, and $k = (0, 0, 1)$. Notice that their directions are the same as those of the coordinate axes. It is often convenient to express a vector $\alpha = (a_1, a_2, a_3)$ as $\alpha = a_1 i + a_2 j + a_3 k$.

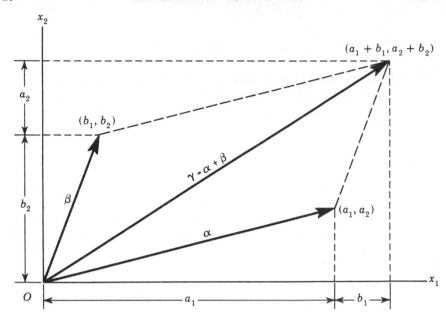

Figure 2.6

Example 4. Let $\alpha = (1, 4, 0) = i + 4j$,

$$\beta = (2, -3, 6) = 2i - 3j + 6k;$$

then $\alpha + \beta = (3, 1, 6) = 3i + j + 6k.$

Multiplying a vector by a positive scalar leaves the direction unchanged, while multiplying by a negative number reverses the direction. In both cases the change in magnitude depends upon the magnitude of the scalar multiple.

Example 5. Let $\alpha = (2, 1, 0) = 2i + j$ (Fig. 2.7); then $2\alpha = (4, 2, 0) = 4i + 2j$ (Fig. 2.8).

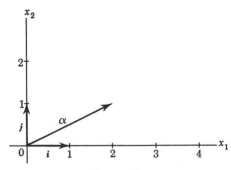

Figure 2.7

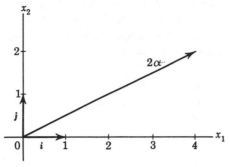

Figure 2.8

Subtraction of vectors can be accomplished as follows:

$$\alpha - \beta = \alpha + (-\beta) \text{ or by recalling that } \alpha = \beta + (\alpha - \beta).$$

Graphically, the subtraction can be performed in either of the two ways shown in Figures 2.9 and 2.10.

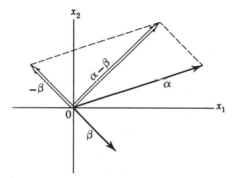

Figure 2.9

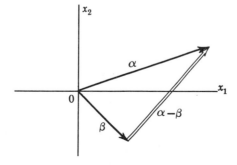

Figure 2.10

Notice in the last diagram that $\alpha - \beta$ is initiated at the terminal of β and terminates at the terminal of α. It might appear that $(\alpha - \beta)$ in the two diagrams are not equal since they occupy different positions. Not so! The directions and magnitudes are the same.

Example 6. Construct geometrically

$$2\alpha - 3\beta \text{ if } \alpha = i + 2j \quad \text{and} \quad \beta = -i + j.$$

(See Figures 2.11, 2.12, and 2.13.)

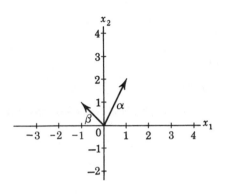

Figure 2.11

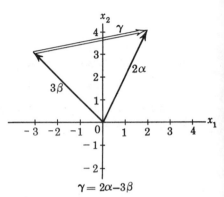

$$\gamma = 2\alpha - 3\beta$$

Figure 2.12

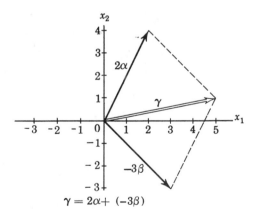

$$\gamma = 2\alpha + (-3\beta)$$

Figure 2.13

EXERCISES

1. Represent $\alpha = (3, -2)$ on a graph.
2. Represent $\beta = (2, 4, 3)$ on a graph.
3. Find the magnitudes of: $\alpha = (2, 3, 4)$; $\beta = (-1, 2)$; $\gamma = (4, 0, -1)$.
4. Let $\alpha = (1, 1, \sqrt{2})$.
(a) Find $|\alpha|$.

(*b*) Find the direction angles of α.

(*c*) Graph α, designating the direction angles and the magnitude.

5. Add $(2, 1)$ and $(1, 3)$ graphically.

6. Add $(-4i + j)$ and $(i + 2j)$ graphically.

7. Subtract $(4, 1)$ from $(0, 4)$ graphically.

8. Subtract $(2i - j)$ from $(-3i - j)$ graphically.

9. Find a unit vector in the direction of $(4, 3, 5)$.

10. Draw i, j, and a unit vector in the same direction with $4i + 3j$ on the same graph. (Make one unit very large on the graph paper.)

11. Graph $\alpha = i + j$ and 3α on adjacent graphs.

12. A force of 10 pounds pulls due north on an object while a force of $10\sqrt{3}$ pounds pulls due east on the same object. What is the magnitude of the resultant force acting on the object and in what direction does it act?

13. A helicopter pilot wishes to move due north. He has an airspeed of 50 miles per hour. A wind of $25\sqrt{2}$ miles per hour is blowing from the southeast. In what direction should the pilot point the helicopter, and with what speed will he move?

2.3 PRODUCTS OF VECTORS

In contrast to the usual method of multiplication of scalars, there are several ways of multiplying vectors that have proved useful. One method yields a scalar, one a vector, and another yields a matrix. The first and last types mentioned arise from matrix multiplication. The second method whose result is known as the vector or cross product will not be considered in this text, but the student may want to investigate it.

The first method, which will be our primary concern, yields what is known as the **scalar product,** the *inner product*, or the *dot product*. The operation is usually denoted by a dot.

Definition. *Let $\alpha = (a_1, a_2, \ldots, a_n)$ and $\beta = (b_1, b_2, \ldots, b_n)$. Then*

$$\alpha \cdot \beta = a_1b_1 + a_2b_2 + \cdots + a_nb_n$$

$$= \sum_{k=1}^{n} a_kb_k,$$

is called the scalar product of the vectors α and β.

Example 1. Let $\alpha = (3, 2, 0, 4)$ and $\beta = (1, 1, 2, 3)$. Then

$$\alpha \cdot \beta = 3 \cdot 1 + 2 \cdot 1 + 0 \cdot 2 + 4 \cdot 3,$$

$$= 3 + 2 + 0 + 12,$$

$$= 17.$$

The scalar product of two vectors α and β is related to the multiplication of matrices as follows: If α is written in matrix form as a 1 by n row matrix (frequently called a **row vector**) and β as an n by 1 column matrix (frequently called a **column vector**), we get

$$\alpha \cdot \beta = [a_1 a_2 \cdots a_n] \begin{bmatrix} b_1 \\ b_2 \\ \cdot \\ \cdot \\ \cdot \\ b_n \end{bmatrix} = [a_1 b_1 + a_2 b_2 + \cdots + a_n b_n],$$

which is a 1 by 1 matrix with a scalar entry. This entry is the dot product. On the other hand, suppose α is a 3 by 1 column vector and β is a 1 by 3 row vector. The resulting product $\alpha\beta$ is a 3 by 3 matrix.

$$\alpha\beta = \begin{bmatrix} a_1 \\ a_2 \\ a_3 \end{bmatrix} [b_1 \ b_2 \ b_3] = \begin{bmatrix} a_1 b_1 & a_1 b_2 & a_1 b_3 \\ a_2 b_1 & a_2 b_2 & a_2 b_3 \\ a_3 b_1 & a_3 b_2 & a_3 b_3 \end{bmatrix}.$$

This is the third method of multiplying vectors that was mentioned.

Applications of the scalar product are numerous. Two quite different types of applications will be indicated in Examples 2 and 3 which follow.

Example 2. An investment company decides to sell four of its stocks. In one transaction, 200 shares of stock A, 300 shares of stock B, 100 shares of stock C, and 200 shares of stock D were sold. The selling prices per share were $2, $3, $5, and $1 respectively. Let the quantity of stocks sold be represented by the vector $\alpha = (200, 300, 100, 200)$. Let the selling prices be denoted by the vector $\beta = (2, 3, 5, 1)$. The total receipts from the stock are then

$$\alpha \cdot \beta = (200, 300, 100, 200) \cdot (2, 3, 5, 1)$$

$$= 2{,}000 \text{ (dollars).}$$

We remind the student that vector methods become especially useful for problems of this type when the dimensions are much larger and computers are programmed to find the dot product.

Before proceeding to the next application, it will be helpful to obtain a geometric interpretation of the scalar product in two dimensions. The following theorem will aid in this endeavor.

Theorem 1. *If α and β are two nonzero vectors in the $x_1 x_2$-plane, then $\alpha \cdot \beta = |\alpha| \, |\beta| \cos \theta$ where θ is the smaller positive angle between α and β.*

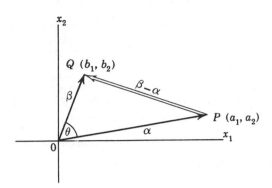

Figure 2.14

Proof (Refer to Fig. 2.14).

STATEMENT	REASON
(1) $2\lvert OP\rvert\,\lvert OQ\rvert\cos\theta = \lvert OP\rvert^2 + \lvert OQ\rvert^2 - \lvert PQ\rvert^2.$	(1) Law of Cosines.
(2) $\lvert OQ\rvert = \sqrt{b_1^2 + b_2^2} = \lvert\beta\rvert.$ $\lvert OP\rvert = \sqrt{a_1^2 + a_2^2} = \lvert\alpha\rvert.$ $\lvert PQ\rvert = \sqrt{(b_1 - a_1)^2 + (b_2 - a_2)^2} = \lvert\beta - \alpha\rvert.$	(2) Formula for magnitude of a two-dimensional vector.
(3) $2\lvert\alpha\rvert\,\lvert\beta\rvert\cos\theta = [a_1^2 + a_2^2] + [b_1^2 + b_2^2]$ $\qquad - [(b_1 - a_1)^2 + (b_2 - a_2)^2]$ $\qquad = 2(a_1b_1 + a_2b_2).$	(3) Substitution of (2) in (1) and collection of terms.
(4) $\lvert\alpha\rvert\,\lvert\beta\rvert\cos\theta = \alpha\cdot\beta.$	(4) Statement (3) and definition of scalar product.

The geometric interpretation of $\alpha\cdot\beta$ will require a knowledge of elementary trigonometry such as that shown in Fig. 2.15.

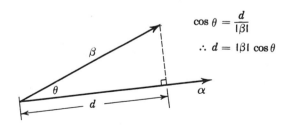

$$\cos\theta = \frac{d}{\lvert\beta\rvert}$$

$$\therefore\ d = \lvert\beta\rvert\cos\theta$$

Figure 2.15

Making use of these observations and the preceding theorem, we have $\alpha \cdot \beta = |\alpha|\,|\beta| \cos \theta = |\alpha|d$; hence geometrically $\alpha \cdot \beta$ is the projection of β on α (called d) times the length of α.

Example 3. In a study of elementary physics we learn that as a particle moves through a certain distance the work done on it by a constant force acting on it in the direction of its movement is given by the equation

$$\text{work} = (\text{force})(\text{distance}).$$

Suppose we are to find the work done in moving a particle along a path $\alpha = (3, 1)$ by a force $\beta = (1, 2)$ (See Fig. 2.16).

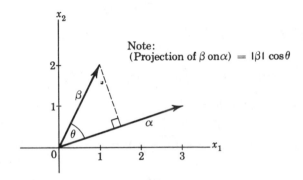

Figure 2.16

Since the force vector does not act directly in the direction of movement, some of it is wasted so far as moving the particle is concerned. We therefore are interested in the component of force β in the α direction. This, we have observed, is $|\beta| \cos \theta$. Now the distance the particle is moved is $|\alpha|$, therefore, the work is $|\alpha||\beta| \cos \theta$; but by Theorem 1, this is simply

$$\text{work} = \alpha \cdot \beta.$$

For the α and β that we were given, we have

$$\text{work} = (3, 1) \cdot (1, 2) = 3 + 2 = 5.$$

If the unit of distance is, say, a foot, and if the force is measured in pounds, then the work done is 5 foot-pounds.

EXERCISES

1. Evaluate each of the following products if a product exists. If it does not exist, state why it does not.

(a) $(2, 4, 0, 7) \cdot (0, -1, 6, 2)$;

(b) $(0, 2, 4) \cdot (6, 3, 1)$;

(c) $(0, 0, 0, 0) \cdot (3, 2, 1, 6)$;

(d) $(2, -1, -6, -1) \cdot (2, 3, 0, 1)$;

(e) $(2, 6, 3, 0) \cdot (2, 1, 2)$;

(f) $(2i + 3j - k) \cdot (i - j + k)$.

2. Solve for x:

(a) $(x, 1, 2, 0) \cdot (3, 2, 0, 1) = 4$;

(b) $(x, 1, 3, 2) \cdot (1, x, 0, x) = 4$.

3. Find the cosine of the angle between $\alpha = -2i + 2j$ and $\beta = 4i + 3j$. What is the significance of the negative answer? Draw a graph.

4. Find the angle between $\alpha = 2i - j$ and $\beta = 3i + 6j$.

5. Write an expression for $\alpha^2 = \alpha \cdot \alpha$.

6. In two-dimensional space prove the following theorem: If $\alpha \cdot \beta = 0$ and $\alpha \neq 0$ and $\beta \neq 0$, then α is perpendicular to β.

7. Determine x so that α is perpendicular to β where $\alpha = 2i + j$ and $\beta = xi + 2j$.

8. Find the projection of $\alpha = i + 2j$ on $\beta = 3i + j$.

9. Find the projection of $\beta = 3i - 2j$ on $\alpha = 2i + 4j$. What is the significance of the negative result?

10. Find a vector in the direction of $\alpha = 3i + 2j$ with magnitude equal to the projection of $\beta = i + j$ on α.

11. Find the work done by moving an object along a vector $2i + 6j$ if the force acting on the particle is $i + 2j$.

12. Find the work done by moving an object along a vector $4i - j$ by a force $2i + 2j$.

2.4 HISTORY AND APPLICATIONS

In this chapter we have introduced to the student the algebra of vectors of n dimensions. These concepts are important in various topics in higher mathematics, most of which are beyond the scope of this course. However, later on in Chapters 9 and 12 the need will arise for further consideration of the n-dimensional vector.

The algebra of vectors of n dimensions is rapidly becoming more useful in engineering and agriculture. Computers are playing a big part in this development. One application of vectors to the social sciences may be indicated partially by the following example.

Example 1. Suppose we construct a simple model economy in which there are three industries; the crude oil industry, the refining industry which produces gasoline, and the utility industry which supplies electricity. Then suppose there are three types of consumers: first, the general public; second, the U. S. government; and third, the export firms. Both the industries and the consumers exercise certain demands on the industries. For instance, suppose the crude oil industry needs 4 units of gasoline to run its pumps and 2 units of electricity. The demand vector, then, for the crude oil industry, will be expressed as $\alpha_c = (0, 4, 2)$. Likewise, we will specify the other demand vectors.

$\alpha_r = (8, 0, 6)$ for the refining industry,
$\alpha_u = (1, 6, 0)$ for the utility industry,
$\alpha_1 = (1, 9, 5)$ for the public,
$\alpha_2 = (8, 8, 8)$ for the U. S. government,
$\alpha_3 = (7, 2, 0)$ for the export firms.

The total demand on the industries is then

$$\alpha_{\text{total}} = \alpha_c + \alpha_r + \alpha_u + \alpha_1 + \alpha_2 + \alpha_3,$$

which turns out to be $\alpha_{\text{total}} = (25, 29, 21)$.

Now suppose the price of crude oil is \$4 per unit, the price of gasoline is \$3 per unit, and the price of electricity is \$2 per unit. This can be expressed as a vector $\beta = (4, 3, 2)$. Assuming that the industries produce what is demanded of them, the income of the crude oil industry is \$4 times 25 units = \$100. Remember that the crude oil industry had to have gasoline and electricity to operate, therefore, its costs were

$$\alpha_c \cdot \beta = (0, 4, 2) \cdot (4, 3, 2) = \$16.$$

Hence, the profit in the crude oil industry is

$$\$100 - \$16 = \$84.$$

Finding the profits (or losses) of the other industries will be left as an exercise.

We have also considered vectors of two and three dimensions from a geometric viewpoint. What has been done here is essentially the first few lessons in a study of that part of mathematics known as vector analysis. The student may wish to pursue this subject on his own. It is quite applicable to such fields as mechanics and electricity, and indeed most modern textbooks are integrating vector analysis with the calculus. The development of vectors has been more evolutionary than many branches of mathematics. There were many fingers in the pie. One of the greatest American contributors to vector analysis was the mathematical physicist, J. W. Gibbs (1839-1903). The German, Herman Grassman (1809-1877), and the Irishman, W. R. Hamilton (1805-1865), probably initiated endeavors in about the middle 1800's. Grassman published a very profound work in 1844 which, although ignored at first, proved to be influential later. Hamilton greatly influenced the development of vectors with his "Quaternions." These men were to some extent contemporaries of the originator of matrices, Cayley (1821-1895).

EXERCISES

1. Find the profits (or losses) of the refining industry and the utility industry in Example 1 of this section.

2. How is Example 1 of this section an oversimplification of an actual economy?

NEW VOCABULARY

vector   2.1   magnitude   2.2
components   2.1   direction angles   2.2
dimension of a vector   2.1   unit vector   2.2
real vector   2.1   scalar (or dot) product   2.3
zero vector or null vector   2.1   row vector   2.3
resultant   2.1   column vector   2.3

3

Mathematical Systems

3.1 DEFINITIONS

We now attempt to organize some of our existing notions of algebraic manipulations. Such organization is important because it helps us to assimilate new knowledge and frequently points the way to new frontiers. We begin by constructing a very general framework called a *mathematical system*. The terms used in the following definition will be discussed in this section.

Definition. *A **mathematical system** consists of a set of elements, at least one equivalence relation among these elements, at least one operation over these elements, and postulates concerning the elements, operations, and relations.*

Example 1. The algebra of real numbers usually taught in high school is a mathematical system where the elements are the real numbers; some of the relations are $=$, $<$, and $>$; two of the operations are $(+)$ and $(\cdot)$; the postulates are the rules of the game, that is, $y \cdot x = x \cdot y$, $a \cdot (x + y) = a \cdot x + a \cdot y$, and others.

Example 2. One of the objects of this text is to construct a mathematical system where the elements are square matrices, the relations are $(=)$ and $(\sim)$ and the operations are addition and multiplication which are of necessity different from the $(+)$ and $(\cdot)$ of Example 1.

In connection with Example 2, we raise the question: What if the matrices are not square? What if we introduce the elements known as scalars and then make use of the operation of multiplying a scalar and a matrix? The answer is that new systems are thus constructed. It is easy to invent a mathematical system. The problem is to develop one that is significant.

In a mathematical discussion it is necessary to begin with a minimum of undefined terms and use them to define new terms which arise in the process of construction. For example, the student probably has an intuitive idea of a "natural number." Likewise we will assume that he has an intuitive idea of a *"set"* as a collection of *"elements,"* where both *"set" and "element"* are undefined terms. We will now discuss *sets, relations, operations,* and *postulates.*

Sets

The concept of a *set* is very important in modern mathematics. It is fundamental and simple. In fact, the notion is now being taught very early in many elementary schools. The collection of all books in your first grade room is an example of a set. Each book in the set is called an element of the set. All the students in your graduating class form a set; all the boys of this set form what we call a *subset.* The examples listed above are *finite sets;* they possess a finite number of elements. The set of all positive integers is an example of an *infinite set.* The collection of all 2 by 2 matrices is also an infinite set.

Relations

What is meant by a relation can be explained by a few illustrations.

Example 3.

(*a*) John is the cousin of Bob; we are expressing a relation between John and Bob. This relation is "is the cousin of."

(*b*) $3 = \frac{6}{2}$; we are expressing a relation between 3 and $\frac{6}{2}$. This relation is $=$.

(*c*) Triangle ABC is congruent to triangle DEF; we are expressing a relation between the two triangles. This relation is "is congruent to."

(*d*) 21 is a multiple of 3; we are expressing a relation between 21 and 3. This relation is "is a multiple of."

In each of the preceding examples we expressed a relation between *two* entities (or elements). Such a relation is known as a **binary relation** and will be designated with R. In general $a \, R \, b$ means "a in the relation R to b" but we may or may not specify R. This is somewhat analogous to what we do in elementary algebra when we let x represent some number although we may not specify what number. The definition of a special kind of relation which is especially important follows.

Definition. *A relation R over a set A is an* **equivalence relation** *over set A if and only if the following properties are valid for all elements a, b, c of A:*

(1) $a R a$ (*reflexive property*);

(2) *if* $a R b$, *then* $b R a$ (*symmetric property*);

(3) *if* $a R b$ *and* $b R c$, *then* $a R c$ (*transitive property*).

Example 4. "Equality" is an example of an equivalence relation over any set because

(1) $a = a$,

(2) if $a = b$, then $b = a$,

(3) if $a = b$ and $b = c$, then $a = c$.

Another example of an equivalence relation is "similarity of triangles" over the set of all triangles in a plane.

"Greater than" is an example of a relation that is not an equivalence relation over, say, the set of integers, because of the reflexive property, that is, $a \ngtr a$ (a is greater than a is not true). This is enough to show that ">" is not an equivalence relation. There is still another property of an equivalence relation which is not valid for ">." Which is it?

In the definition of a mathematical system, remember that at least one equivalence relation is required.

Operations

For a long time the student has made use of four operations in combining two numbers; for example, $4 + 3 = 7$, $6 - 2 = 4$, $3 \cdot 2 = 6$, and $8 \div 2 = 4$. Now we have introduced new types of elements (vectors and matrices) and consequently new operations. It should be obvious that there may possibly exist other sets of elements and operations over them. Thus there is a need for us to be general when discussing operations. We will use the small letter "o" to designate an operation used to combine two elements of a specified set.

Definition. *A **binary operation** "o" over a set S is a rule or procedure by which any two elements of S are combined to produce a unique third element which may or may not belong to S. If the third element always belongs to S, then we say S is **closed** under the operation "o."*

The result of combining two elements a and b by performing the operation o is written $a o b$, which is read "a operation b."

Example 5. $4 + 3 = 7$.

Here the operation is the procedure called addition and the elements are from the set of integers. Moreover the set of integers is closed under this operation.

Example 6.

$$\begin{bmatrix} 2 & 0 \\ 0 & 2 \end{bmatrix} \begin{bmatrix} 2 & 1 \\ 4 & 3 \end{bmatrix} = \begin{bmatrix} 4 & 2 \\ 8 & 6 \end{bmatrix}.$$

Here the operation is matrix multiplication. This example illustrates the idea of closure, because both elements are 2 by 2 matrices with entries that are integers and the result also is a 2 by 2 matrix with integral entries.

In fact, we could show that under the operation of matrix multiplication, the set of all n by n matrices with scalar entries is closed.

Example 7. $(3, 2, 1) \cdot (5, -4, 0) = 7.$

Here the elements are vectors and the operation is the scalar product. The resulting element is a scalar rather than a vector. Thus the set of vectors is an example of a set that is not closed under the operation of scalar multiplication.

Postulates

The postulates are statements concerning the elements, relations, and operations of the system, which are assumed to be valid. From these postulates, theorems are proved which in turn may be used to prove other theorems. Thus the postulates serve as a foundation of a possible mathematical structure.

By now the reader probably has noticed that a study of mathematical systems involves a considerable extension of our previous notions of mathematical structures. Their inclusion requires an extension and generalization of our ideas of elements, relations, and operations, and moreover introduces a new class of mathematical entities, the mathematical systems themselves. What we have said so far in this chapter probably seems very theoretical. To show that the gap between the theoretical and the practical is sometimes very small, we will construct what appears at first to be a rather weird mathematical system, and then show that this simple abstract structure has practical applications.

Example 8.   Remember that a mathematical system must have a set of elements, an equivalence relation among these elements, and at least one operation over these elements, and postulates or rules of behavior. Let the set of elements consist of only two elements designated as 1 and 0. Let the equivalence relation be equality and let there be two operations designated "$\oplus$" and "$\cdot$". Let the postulates be

(1) $0 \cdot 0 = 0$,   (2) $1 \oplus 1 = 1$,

(3) $1 \cdot 1 = 1$,   (4) $0 \oplus 0 = 0$,

(5) $1 \cdot 0 = 0 \cdot 1 = 0$,   (6) $0 \oplus 1 = 1 \oplus 0 = 1$.

Notice that the operations behave differently from those of addition and multiplication with which we are familiar in that $1 \oplus 1 = 1$. This is why we chose to write $\oplus$ instead of $+$. Now we could prove various theorems which probably you would think are of very little use to anyone. We try one as an illustration.

Theorem: $x \cdot (x \oplus y) = x.$

Proof. Since we have only two elements, we can justify this theorem by listing all cases in tabular form.

x	y	$x \oplus y$	$x \cdot (x \oplus y)$
0	0	0	0
0	1	1	0
1	0	1	1
1	1	1	1

Notice that the first and last columns are the same and therefore

$$x \cdot (x \oplus y) = x.$$

The mathematical system that we have constructed is known as a *binary Boolean algebra*. It becomes applicable when we think of the element 0 as an open switch in an electrical circuit and the element 1 as a closed switch; the operation ($\cdot$) can be interpreted as combining two switches in series and the operation $\oplus$ as combining two switches in parallel.

Two open switches in parallel. Current will flow if one switch is closed.

Two open switches in series. Current will flow only if both switches are closed.

The first postulate says that current will not flow if two open switches are connected in series. The second postulate says that current will flow if two closed switches are connected in parallel. The student should interpret the other postulates. The theorem that we proved states that the following arrangement of switches accomplishes the same thing.

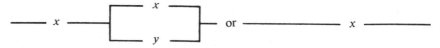

Such theorems (often vastly more complicated) are of great benefit to the circuit designer in simplifying his circuits. Circuit network theory is not the only application of this particular mathematical system. The interested student will find a more comprehensive discussion of Boolean algebra to be both interesting and enlightening.

EXERCISES

1. (*a*) Is the set of all real numbers by itself an example of a mathematical system?
(*b*) Is any set by itself an example of a mathematical system?

2. Why is it necessary to begin with certain undefined terms?   In other words, why can we not define every term we ever use?

3. Referring to Example 8 of this section, express the following equivalent switching arrangements using the terminology of "binary Boolean algebra."

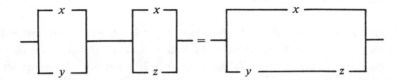

4. (*a*) Referring to Example 8 of this section, prove the following theorems of binary Boolean algebra.

$$x \oplus (x \cdot y) = x \quad \text{and} \quad x \oplus y = y \oplus x.$$

(*b*) Express each of these theorems as an arrangement of switches.   Sketch.

5. Let S be the set of all people in the world.
(*a*) Is "younger than" an equivalence relation among the elements of S?   Why?
(*b*) Is "same age as" an equivalence relation among the elements of S?   Why?
(*c*) Is "resident of same nation as" an equivalence relation among the elements of S?   Why?

6. We have defined a binary operation over a set S.   What would be the natural way to define a *unary operation* over a set S?   Give an example.   How would one define a *ternary operation* over a set S?

7. Let S be the set of all integers.
(*a*) Is $<$ an equivalence relation among the elements of S?   Why?
(*b*) Is "is a multiple of" an equivalence relation among the elements of S?   Why?
(*c*) Is S closed under $+$?   Why?
(*d*) Is S closed under $(\cdot)$?   Why?
(*e*) Give an example of a binary relation over S which satisfies the reflexive and transitive properties but not the symmetric property.

8. Let S be the set of all 2 by 2 matrices with scalar entries.
(*a*) Is $=$ an equivalence relation among the elements of S?   Why?
(*b*) Is $\leq$ an equivalence relation among the elements of S?   Why?
(*c*) Is S closed under matrix addition?   Why?
(*d*) Is S closed under matrix multiplication?   Why?

9. Let S be the set of all 2 by 2 matrices with entries which are odd integers.
(*a*) Is S closed under $+$?   Why?
(*b*) Is matrix multiplication a closed binary operation over S?

(c) If the entries were required to be negative integers instead of odd integers, what would be the answers to (a) and (b)?

10. Let S be the set of all 4-dimensional vectors.
(a) Is = an equivalence relation among the elements of S?   Why?
(b) Is $\geq$ an equivalence relation among the elements of S?   Why?
(c) Is S closed under $+$?   Why?
(d) Is S closed under $(\cdot)$?   Why?

3.2 LAWS OF OPERATIONS

When a certain operation has been defined, it is helpful to understand its behavior.   For instance, in elementary school it was helpful to know that 20 times 2 or twenty 2's was the same as two 20's because it was easier to add 20 and 20 than to add twenty 2's.   In particular we shall be interested now in four so-called "laws of operations."   When a new operation is defined, we shall want to know which of the laws are valid.   It will be found that some of the laws that we have always taken for granted will not be valid for certain new operations.   Notice that the distributive law involves two operations while the others involve only one operation.

Definition. *Commutative Law: An operation "o" is commutative over a set A if $a \, o \, b = b \, o \, a$ for all elements a and b in A.*

Example 1. $2 + 5 = 5 + 2$ where the operation is addition and A is the set of all integers; or $2 \cdot 5 = 5 \cdot 2$ where the operation is multiplication.

Definition. *Associative Law: An operation "o" is associative over a set A if $a \, o \, (b \, o \, c) = (a \, o \, b) \, o \, c$ for every a, b, and c in A.*

Example 2. $\begin{cases} 2 + (3 + 4) = (2 + 3) + 4, \\ \text{or} \quad 2 + 7 = 5 + 4. \end{cases}$ $\begin{cases} 2 \cdot (3 \cdot 4) = (2 \cdot 3) \cdot 4, \\ \text{or } 2 \cdot 12 = 6 \cdot 4. \end{cases}$

We say that $+$ and $(\cdot)$ are *associative* over the set of integers.

Definition. *Distributive Law: For elements a, b, and c in set A and two operations $\oplus$ and $\odot$, if*

$$(a \oplus b) \odot c = (a \odot c) \oplus (b \odot c),$$

*then $\odot$ is **right distributive** with respect to $\oplus$ over A.   And if*

$$a \odot (b \oplus c) = (a \odot b) \oplus (a \odot c),$$

*then $\odot$ is **left distributive** with respect to $\oplus$ over A.   If both the right and left distributive laws are valid, we simply say that $\odot$ is **distributive** with respect to $\oplus$ over A.*

Example 3. $(2 + 3) \cdot 4 = (2 \cdot 4) + (3 \cdot 4) = 8 + 12.$

$4 \cdot (2 + 3) = (4 \cdot 2) + (4 \cdot 3) = 8 + 12.$

Here $\oplus$ is $+$ and $\odot$ is $(\cdot)$. We see that multiplication is right distributive and left distributive (hence distributive) with respect to addition over the set of integers. What about the set of complex numbers?

Example 4.   Show that $+$ is *not* distributive with respect to $(\cdot)$ over the set of integers.

$$4 + (2 \cdot 3) \neq (4 + 2) \cdot (4 + 3).$$
$$(2 \cdot 3) + 4 \neq (2 + 4) \cdot (3 + 4).$$

Definition. *The Cancellation Law: For elements a, b, and c in a set A the operation "o," defined over A, is said to obey the law of cancellation if $a \, o \, b = a \, o \, c$ implies that $b = c$ (if "o" represents multiplication over the set of scalars, then we require that $a \neq 0$).*

Example 5.   If the elements are scalars and the operation is multiplication and if $ax = ab$, then $x = b$ provided $a \neq 0$.

Example 6.   If the elements are scalars and the operation is addition and if $a + x = a + b$, then $x = b$.

EXERCISES

1. If we are given the set of all rational numbers and the operations of $+$ and $(\cdot)$ over this set, determine which of the laws mentioned in this section hold for these operations.

2. If we are given the set of all positive integers and the operation subtraction $(-)$ over this set, determine which of the laws mentioned in this section hold for this operation. Why is it impossible to discuss the distributive law in this problem?

3. If we are given the set of all positive integers and the operation division $(\div)$ over this set, determine which of the laws mentioned in this section hold for this operation.

4. Suppose we are given the set of all positive integers and an operation $(*)$ defined in the following way:

$a * b = a + 2b$ (for example: $4 * 3 = 4 + (2)(3) = 10$).

Determine which of the laws mentioned in this section hold for this operation.

3.3 MATRIX OPERATIONS AND THEIR LAWS

It is now appropriate to determine which of these laws hold when the elements are certain matrices, and the operations are matrix addition and matrix multiplication. In what follows, A, B, and C denote matrices.

Theorem 1. *If A, B, and C are conformable for addition, the commutative and associative laws for matrix addition are valid; that is,*

$$A + B = B + A, \quad and \quad A + (B + C) = (A + B) + C.$$

Proof of 2nd part.

STATEMENT	REASON
(1) $[a_{ij}]_{(m,n)} + ([b_{ij}]_{(m,n)} + [c_{ij}]_{(m,n)})$ $= [a_{ij}]_{(m,n)} + [b_{ij} + c_{ij}]_{(m,n)}$	(1) By definition of matrix addition.
(2) $= [a_{ij} + (b_{ij} + c_{ij})]_{(m,n)}$	(2) By matrix addition.
(3) $= [(a_{ij} + b_{ij}) + c_{ij}]_{(m,n)}$	(3) Addition of scalars is associative.
(4) $= [a_{ij} + b_{ij}]_{(m,n)} + [c_{ij}]_{(m,n)}$	(4) By matrix addition.
(5) $= ([a_{ij}]_{(m,n)} + [b_{ij}]_{(m,n)}) + [c_{ij}]_{(m,n)}.$	(5) By matrix addition.

The proof of the first part of Theorem 1 is left as an exercise.

We have already observed in Example 2 of Section 1.6 that $AB \neq BA$; thus the commutative law for multiplication of matrices does not hold. Although $AB \neq BA$ in general, there are certain matrices where $AB = BA$.

Theorem 2. *If $A = [a_{ij}]_{(m,p)}$, $B = [b_{ij}]_{(p,n)}$, $C = [c_{ij}]_{(n,q)}$, the associative law for matrix multiplication is valid, that is,*

$$A(BC) = (AB)C.$$

Proof (Optional).

STATEMENT	REASON
(1) $BC = \left[\sum_{k=1}^{n} b_{hk}c_{kj} \right]_{(p,q)}.$	(1) $\sum$ notation for a product. See Section 1.7.
(2) $A(BC) = \left[\sum_{h=1}^{p} (a_{ih}) \left(\sum_{k=1}^{n} b_{hk}c_{kj} \right) \right]_{(m,q)}.$	(2) Same.
(3) $AB = \left[\sum_{h=1}^{p} a_{ih}b_{hk} \right]_{(m,n)}.$	(3) Same.
(4) $(AB)C = \left[\sum_{k=1}^{n} \left(\sum_{h=1}^{p} a_{ih}b_{hk} \right) (c_{kj}) \right]_{(m,q)}.$	(4) Same.
(5) $A(BC) = (AB)C.$	(5) The expansions of the right sides of statements (2) and (4) are the same. (See explanation of double summation notation in Section 1.7.)

Example 1.

Let $A = [-2 \;\; 1]$, $\qquad B = \begin{bmatrix} 2 & 0 \\ -1 & 1 \end{bmatrix}$, $\qquad C = \begin{bmatrix} 2 & 1 \\ 4 & 0 \end{bmatrix}$.

Then $BC = \begin{bmatrix} 4 & 2 \\ 2 & -1 \end{bmatrix}$, $\qquad A(BC) = [-2 \;\; 1]\begin{bmatrix} 4 & 2 \\ 2 & -1 \end{bmatrix} = [-6 \;\; -5]$.

$$AB = [-5 \;\; 1], \qquad (AB)C = [-5 \;\; 1]\begin{bmatrix} 2 & 1 \\ 4 & 0 \end{bmatrix} = [-6 \;\; -5].$$

$$A(BC) = (AB)C.$$

It is interesting to note that some types of matrix multiplication can be defined so that the associative law does not hold for that operation. (See Exercise 18.)

Theorem 3. *If $A = [a_{ij}]_{(m,p)}$, $B = [b_{ij}]_{(p,n)}$, $C = [c_{ij}]_{(p,n)}$, then the left distributive law for matrix multiplication with respect to addition is valid, that is,*

$$A(B + C) = AB + AC.$$

Proof.

STATEMENT		REASON
(1) $A(B + C) = [a_{ij}]_{(m,p)}[b_{ij} + c_{ij}]_{(p,n)}$	(1)	Definition of matrix addition.
(2) $\qquad = \left[\sum\limits_{k=1}^{p} a_{ik}(b_{kj} + c_{kj})\right]_{(m,n)}$	(2)	Σ notation for matrix multiplication.
(3) $\qquad = \left[\sum\limits_{k=1}^{p} a_{ik}b_{kj} + \sum\limits_{k=1}^{p} a_{ik}c_{kj}\right]_{(m,n)}$	(3)	Left distributive law for multiplication with respect to addition is valid for scalars. Also rule of Σ notation.
(4) $\qquad = AB + AC.$	(4)	Definition of addition of matrices and notation for product.

Theorem 4. *If $A = [a_{ij}]_{(m,p)}$, $B = [b_{ij}]_{(m,p)}$, $C = [c_{ij}]_{(p,n)}$, then the right distributive law for multiplication with respect to addition is valid, that is,*

$$(A + B)C = AC + BC.$$

Example 2. Let A and B be square matrices of the same order. Show that in general $(A + B)^2 \neq A^2 + 2AB + B^2$.

$(A + B)^2 = (A + B)(A + B) = (A + B)A + (A + B)B$ by the left distributive law,

$$= A^2 + BA + AB + B^2 \text{ by the right distributive law.}$$

But BA does not in general equal AB so that $BA + AB \neq 2AB$.

The cancellation law does hold for matrix addition over the set of m by n matrices, but does not hold in general for multiplication of matrices. The latter statement can be justified by the following counterexample.

Example 3. Consider

$$AB = \begin{bmatrix} 2 & 0 \\ 0 & 0 \end{bmatrix} \begin{bmatrix} 4 & 0 \\ 2 & 1 \end{bmatrix} = \begin{bmatrix} 8 & 0 \\ 0 & 0 \end{bmatrix},$$

$$AC = \begin{bmatrix} 2 & 0 \\ 0 & 0 \end{bmatrix} \begin{bmatrix} 4 & 0 \\ 6 & 7 \end{bmatrix} = \begin{bmatrix} 8 & 0 \\ 0 & 0 \end{bmatrix},$$

$$AB = AC \text{ but } B \neq C.$$

There is another rule of scalar algebra that does not hold for matrix algebra. $AB = 0$ *does not imply that* $A = 0$ *or* $B = 0$.

Example 4. Consider

$$AB = \begin{bmatrix} -1 & 2 \\ -2 & 4 \end{bmatrix} \begin{bmatrix} 2 & 2 \\ 1 & 1 \end{bmatrix} = \begin{bmatrix} 0 & 0 \\ 0 & 0 \end{bmatrix}, \quad \text{and yet } A \neq 0 \text{ and } B \neq 0.$$

Suppose we consider the set of scalars along with our set of matrices. We then have the following theorems. The proofs are left to the student.

Theorem 5. *Multiplication of a matrix and a scalar is commutative; that is,* $cA = Ac$. *(For a definition of Ac, see Exercise 6 of Section 1.5.)*

Theorem 6. *If A and B are conformable for addition, the following distributive laws are valid.*

$$c(A + B) = cA + cB, \quad \text{and} \quad (c + d)A = cA + dA.$$

Theorem 7. *If A and B are conformable for multiplication, the following associative laws are valid.*

$$c(AB) = (cA)B, \quad \text{and} \quad c(dA) = (cd)A, \quad \text{and} \quad (Ac)B = A(cB).$$

In summary, the laws of operations (addition and multiplication) for matrices differ from the laws of operations for scalars in that:

$$AB \text{ does } not \text{ always equal } BA;$$
$$AB = AC \text{ does } not \text{ imply } B = C;$$
$$AB = 0 \text{ does } not \text{ imply that } A = 0 \text{ or } B = 0.$$

EXERCISES

1. Prove the first part of Theorem 1 (commutative law for matrix addition).

2. Show that the associative law for matrix multiplication is valid if

$$A = \begin{bmatrix} 2 \\ 3 \\ 4 \end{bmatrix}, \quad B = [2 \quad -5], \quad C = \begin{bmatrix} -2 & 3 & 3 \\ 1 & -4 & -2 \end{bmatrix}.$$

3. Prove Theorem 4.   **4.** Prove Theorem 5.

5. Prove Theorem 6.   **6.** Prove Theorem 7.

7. Suppose that $A = \begin{bmatrix} 2 & -3 \\ 0 & 1 \end{bmatrix}$, $B = \begin{bmatrix} 4 & 7 \\ 3 & -5 \end{bmatrix}$, and $C = \begin{bmatrix} 2 & 8 \\ -1 & -1 \end{bmatrix}$.

(*a*) Verify the associative law for addition.
(*b*) Verify the associative law for multiplication.
(*c*) Verify the left distributive law for matrix multiplication with respect to addition.
(*d*) Verify the first part of Theorem 7, using $c = 3$.
(*e*) Verify that $AB \neq BA$.
(*f*) Calculate $(A + B)^2$ and then calculate $A^2 + 2AB + B^2$.
(*g*) Calculate $(AC)^2$ and then calculate A^2C^2. How can you account for the difference of answers?

8. We have seen that AB does not always equal BA. In a case when AB does equal BA, we say that A and B are *commutative matrices* and that A and B *commute*.

(*a*) Show that $A = \begin{bmatrix} 2 & 0 \\ 0 & 2 \end{bmatrix}$ and $B = \begin{bmatrix} 3 & 4 \\ 5 & 6 \end{bmatrix}$ are commutative matrices.

(*b*) Does every square matrix commute with itself?

9. Example 3, page 46, illustrates that what is called the **left cancellation law** for matrix multiplication does not hold. Make up an example for which $BA = CA$ but $B \neq C$, thus showing that the **right cancellation law** for matrix multiplication does not hold either.

10. Make up an example (different from Example 4, page 46) which illustrates that $AB = 0$ does not imply that $A = 0$ or $B = 0$.

11. (*a*) Which theorem in this section makes it permissible to write $A + B + C$ without using parentheses?
(*b*) Which theorem in this section makes it permissible to write ABC without using parentheses?

12. (*a*) Prove the following generalization of Theorem 3: $A(B + C + D) = AB + AC + AD$. (*Hint:* Use Theorems 1 and 3.)
(*b*) How can Theorem 3 be generalized further?
(*c*) How can Theorem 6 be generalized?

13. Show that in general $A^2 - B^2 \neq (A - B)(A + B)$ where A and B are square matrices of the same order.

14. Expand $(A + B)^3$, where A and B are square matrices of the same order.

15. Expand $((A + B) + C)^2$ by repeated use of distributive laws (assume conformability).   Simplify if possible.

16. Determine which of the following are true and which are false.   Explain fully.   Assume conformability.

(a) If $C^2 = 0$, then $C = 0$.   (b) $A^2 + B^2 = B^2 + A^2$.

(c) $(AB)C^2 = A(BC^2)$.   (d) If $BA + CA = 0$, then

$$B = -C \text{ or } A = 0.$$

(e) $BA + CA = A(B + C)$.   (f) $A + (B + C) = B + (C + A)$.

17. Can we say that matrix addition is right distributive with respect to matrix multiplication?   Give an example.

18. Let A and B be 2 by 2 matrices.   Define the operation called "*op*" as follows: $A \text{ } op \text{ } B = AB - BA$.   Make up an example to show that "*op*" is nonassociative. Operations that are not associative are becoming increasingly important in such fields as genetics and quantum mechanics.

3.4 VECTOR OPERATIONS AND THEIR LAWS

If we plan to make use of matrix and vector algebra to solve applied problems, we certainly must know what we can and cannot do when performing the various operations.   We therefore consider now the laws for the vector operations $(+)$ and $(\cdot)$.

The proof of the following theorem is left to the student.

Theorem 8.   *For n-dimensional vectors, the commutative and associative laws are valid for addition.*

Theorem 9.   *The scalar product of two n-dimensional vectors is commutative.*

The proof of Theorem 9 is left as an exercise.

The associative law for the scalar product is *not* valid because $(\alpha \cdot \beta) \cdot \gamma$ is not defined. $\alpha \cdot \beta$ is a scalar and the dot product of a vector and a scalar has not been defined.

Theorem 10.   *For n-dimensional vectors, the distributive laws for the scalar product with respect to addition are valid; that is,*

$$\alpha \cdot (\beta + \gamma) = (\alpha \cdot \beta) + (\alpha \cdot \gamma),$$

and
$$(\alpha + \beta) \cdot \gamma = (\alpha \cdot \gamma) + (\beta \cdot \gamma).$$

Proof.

STATEMENT	REASON
(1) $\alpha \cdot (\beta + \gamma)$ $= a_1(b_1 + c_1) + a_2(b_2 + c_2)$ $+ \cdots + a_n(b_n + c_n)$	(1) Definition of scalar product and vector addition.
(2) $= a_1b_1 + a_2b_2 + \cdots + a_nb_n$ $+ a_1c_1 + a_2c_2 + \cdots + a_nc_n$	(2) Scalar multiplication is distributive with respect to addition (generalized distributive law), and scalar addition is commutative.
(3) $= (\alpha \cdot \beta) + (\alpha \cdot \gamma).$	(3) Definition of scalar product.

(4) Similarly it can be proved
that $(\alpha + \beta) \cdot \gamma = \alpha \cdot \gamma + \beta \cdot \gamma.$

The Cancellation Law for the scalar product of two vectors is not valid, as is shown by the following counterexample.

Example 1.   Consider
$$\alpha \cdot \beta = (2, 0, 1) \cdot (0, 1, 2) = 2,$$
$$\alpha \cdot \gamma = (2, 0, 1) \cdot (1, 3, 0) = 2.$$
Obviously $\alpha \cdot \beta = \alpha \cdot \gamma$ but $\beta \neq \gamma.$

Also $\alpha \cdot \beta = 0$ does *not* imply $\alpha = 0$ or $\beta = 0$.

Example 2.   Consider
$$\alpha \cdot \beta = (2, 1, -2) \cdot (3, 2, 4) = 0, \quad \text{but} \quad \alpha \neq 0 \quad \text{and} \quad \beta \neq 0.$$

If we also introduce the set of scalars and the operation of multiplying a vector by a scalar, we have the following properties summed up in one theorem.

Theorem 11.   *Let α, β, γ be n-dimensional vectors and let c and d be scalars. Then*
$$c\alpha = \alpha c,$$
$$c(\alpha + \beta) = c\alpha + c\beta,$$
$$(c + d)\alpha = c\alpha + d\alpha,$$
$$c(\alpha \cdot \beta) = (c\alpha) \cdot \beta,$$
$$c(d\alpha) = (cd)\alpha.$$

The following chart is given to summarize the material in the previous three sections.   Assume conformability.

	Matrices		Vectors	
	Addition	Multiplication	Addition	Multiplication
Commutative Law	$A + B = B + A$	No	$\alpha + \beta = \beta + \alpha$	$\alpha \cdot \beta = \beta \cdot \alpha$
Associative Law	$(A + B) + C$ $= A + (B + C)$	$(AB)C = A(BC)$	$(\alpha + \beta) + \gamma$ $= \alpha + (\beta + \gamma)$	Operation not defined
Distributive Laws	$A(B + C) = AB + AC$ $(A + B)C = AC + BC$		$\alpha \cdot (\beta + \gamma) = \alpha \cdot \beta + \alpha \cdot \gamma$ $(\alpha + \beta) \cdot \gamma = \alpha \cdot \gamma + \beta \cdot \gamma$	
Cancellation Law	$A + B = A + C$ implies $B = C$	No	$\alpha + \beta = \alpha + \gamma$ implies $\beta = \gamma$	No
If $ab = 0$ then $a = 0$ or $b = 0$		No		No

EXERCISES

1. Determine which of the following statements are true and which are false. Assume that all vectors have the same dimension, and are real.

(a) If $\alpha \cdot \beta = 0$, then $\alpha = \mathbf{0}$ or $\beta = \mathbf{0}$.
(b) If $\alpha \cdot \beta + \gamma \cdot \beta = 0$, then $\alpha = -\gamma$ or $\beta = \mathbf{0}$.
(c) $\alpha \cdot \beta - \beta \cdot \alpha = 0$.
(d) If $\alpha^2 = 0$, then $\alpha = \mathbf{0}$.
(e) $\alpha^2 - \beta^z = (\alpha - \beta) \cdot (\alpha + \beta)$.
(f) $(\alpha + \beta)^2 = \alpha^2 + 2\alpha \cdot \beta + \beta^2$.
(g) $(\alpha \cdot \beta) \cdot \gamma^2 = \alpha \cdot (\beta \cdot \gamma^2)$.
(h) $\alpha + (\beta + \gamma) = \gamma + (\beta + \alpha)$.

2. Prove Theorem 8.

3. Prove Theorem 9.

4. (a) Prove the fourth part of Theorem 11.
(b) Explain why the other four parts of Theorem 11 have already essentially been proved.   (*Hint:* See Theorems 5, 6, and 7.)

5. Let $\alpha = (2, -1, 3)$, $\beta = (3, 4, -2)$, and $\gamma = (5, 0, 6)$.
(a) Verify that $(\alpha + \beta) + \gamma = \alpha + (\beta + \gamma)$.
(b) Verify that $\alpha \cdot \beta = \beta \cdot \alpha$.
(c) Verify the two conclusions of Theorem 10.

(d) Does $(\alpha \cdot \gamma) \cdot \beta$ have meaning?

(e) If $c = 4$, verify that $c(\alpha + \beta) = c\alpha + c\beta$.

6. Let $\alpha = (a_1, a_2, a_3)$, $\beta = (b_1, b_2, b_3)$, and $\gamma = (c_1, c_2, c_3)$.

(a) Prove that if $\alpha + \beta = \alpha + \gamma$, then $\beta = \gamma$.

(b) What is the name of the law proved in (a)?

7. Using two-dimensional vectors, make up examples to illustrate the same principles brought out by Examples 1 and 2 of this section.

8. Using the chart given in this section, state the two differences we have discovered between which laws hold for matrices and which laws hold for vectors.

9. Let $\alpha = (5, 0)$, $\beta = (0, 3)$, and $\gamma = (2, 4)$. From a geometric point of view, what is the significance of the equality $(\alpha + \beta) + \gamma = \alpha + (\beta + \gamma)$?

10. Show that $\alpha \cdot (\beta + \gamma + \delta) = \alpha \cdot \beta + \alpha \cdot \gamma + \alpha \cdot \delta$, where all of these vectors have the same dimension. This result is a generalization of what law?

3.5 THE IDENTITY AND THE INVERSE ELEMENTS

In this section we introduce two terms which will be used throughout the remainder of this text. Again you will notice that we generalize; for instance, in the first definition we let ϵ represent any identity element.

Definition. *An element ϵ in a set A, such that $a \circ \epsilon = a$ and $\epsilon \circ a = a$ for every a in A, is called an **identity element** for the operation "o."*

Example 1.

(a) For the set of real numbers and the operation $+$, zero is the identity because $a + 0 = 0 + a = a$.

(b) For the same set and the operation $(\cdot)$, the number 1 is the identity because $a \cdot 1 = 1 \cdot a = a$.

Example 2.

(a) For the set of 3 by 3 matrices with scalar entries and the operation of matrix addition, an identity is the null matrix,

$$0 = \begin{bmatrix} 0 & 0 & 0 \\ 0 & 0 & 0 \\ 0 & 0 & 0 \end{bmatrix}, \quad \text{because} \quad A + 0 = 0 + A = A.$$

(b) For the same set and the operation matrix multiplication, an identity is the matrix,

$$I_3 = \begin{bmatrix} 1 & 0 & 0 \\ 0 & 1 & 0 \\ 0 & 0 & 1 \end{bmatrix}, \quad \text{because} \quad AI_3 = I_3A = A.$$

The matrix I_n (of which I_3 is a special case) is very important. It can be defined formally as a square matrix of order n in which every entry on the main diagonal is 1 and all other entries are 0. I_n is called the **identity matrix of order n.**

Example 3.
(a) For the set of 3-dimensional vectors and the operation vector addition, the null vector $0 = (0, 0, 0)$ is the identity because $\alpha + 0 = 0 + \alpha = \alpha$.

(b) For the same set and the operation scalar multiplication, there is no identity. This is because the scalar product of two vectors is always a scalar and never a vector.

Definition. *Let ϵ be an identity element for the operation o over the set A. If there exists an element q such that $a \, o \, q = q \, o \, a = \epsilon$, where ϵ, a, and q belong to A, then q is called an* **inverse** *of a with respect to the operation o.*

Example 4. For the set of real numbers:
(a) When $+$ is the operation, $(-a)$ is an inverse of a because

$$a + (-a) = -a + a = 0,$$

and 0 is the identity for $+$ over the real numbers.

(b) When $(\cdot)$ is the operation, $1/a$ is an inverse of a because

$$a \cdot \frac{1}{a} = \frac{1}{a} \cdot a = 1, \quad \text{where} \quad a \neq 0,$$

and 1 is the identity for $(\cdot)$ over the real numbers; that is, for the set of all real numbers, excluding 0, $1/a$ is the inverse of a with respect to $(\cdot)$.

Example 5. For a set of m by n matrices:
(a) *When matrix addition is the operation, $(-A)$ is an inverse of A because $A + (-A) = -A + A = 0$, and the null matrix is the identity for matrix addition.*

(b) *When matrix multiplication is the operation and when the matrices are square of a given order, then there sometimes exists a matrix, designated A^{-1}, (and called an inverse of A) such that*

$$AA^{-1} = A^{-1}A = I.$$

For instance if $A = \begin{bmatrix} 3 & 1 \\ 2 & 1 \end{bmatrix}$, there exists a matrix $\begin{bmatrix} 1 & -1 \\ -2 & 3 \end{bmatrix}$, designated A^{-1},

which is a multiplicative inverse of A, because

$$\begin{bmatrix} 3 & 1 \\ 2 & 1 \end{bmatrix}\begin{bmatrix} 1 & -1 \\ -2 & 3 \end{bmatrix} = \begin{bmatrix} 1 & -1 \\ -2 & 3 \end{bmatrix}\begin{bmatrix} 3 & 1 \\ 2 & 1 \end{bmatrix} = \begin{bmatrix} 1 & 0 \\ 0 & 1 \end{bmatrix}.$$

Later we shall devote a whole chapter to a study of the multiplicative inverses of square matrices.

Example 6. For the set of all n-dimensional vectors:

(a) When the operation is vector addition, $(-\alpha)$ is an inverse of α because $\alpha + (-\alpha) = -\alpha + \alpha = 0$.

(b) There is no inverse for the scalar product. Why?

EXERCISES

1. Given the operations $+$ and $(\cdot)$ over the set of all complex numbers.

(a) Why is zero the identity for $+$?

(b) What is the inverse for addition of each of the following: $2, \frac{3}{4}, 0, 2 - 3i$?

(c) Why is 1 the identity element for $(\cdot)$?

(d) Give, if possible, the inverse for multiplication of each of the following: $3, -\frac{1}{2}, 0, \sqrt{2}, 1 + 2i$.

2. Verify that $\begin{bmatrix} 2 & 1 \\ 5 & 3 \end{bmatrix}$ is the inverse of $\begin{bmatrix} 3 & -1 \\ -5 & 2 \end{bmatrix}$ under matrix multiplication over the set of all 2 by 2 matrices.

3. Given the operations of $+$ and $(\cdot)$ over the set of all even integers.

(a) What is the identity for $+$, if any? Why?

(b) What is the identity for $(\cdot)$, if any? Why?

(c) What is the inverse of an even integer a for $+$, if any? Why?

(d) What is the inverse of an even integer a for $(\cdot)$, if any? Why?

4. Given the operation of $(-)$ over the set of all integers. Is there an identity or an inverse for the operation over the set?

5. Given the set of all 2 by 3 matrices and the operations matrix multiplication and addition.

(a) What is the identity element for $+$?

(b) Why is there no identity element for multiplication over this set?

(c) What is the inverse of a 2 by 3 matrix A for addition?

(d) Why is there no inverse for multiplication over this set?

6. Given the set of all 4 by 4 matrices and the operations of matrix addition and multiplication.

(a) What is the identity element for addition? Why?

(b) What is the inverse for addition of a 4 by 4 matrix A? Why?

(c) What is the identity for multiplication?

7. Given the set of all four-dimensional vectors and the operations $+$ and $(\cdot)$. Find, if possible, the identity and inverse elements for $+$ and $(\cdot)$. If that is not possible, state why.

8. Assuming conformability, simplify $AI + AA^{-1} - I^2A$. (A is a square matrix with inverse A^{-1} and I is identity matrix of same order as A.)

9. What is the inverse of I_3 with respect to matrix multiplication?

10. Verify if possible that $\begin{bmatrix} -\frac{1}{11} & \frac{3}{11} & -\frac{1}{11} \\ \frac{2}{11} & \frac{5}{11} & \frac{2}{11} \\ \frac{5}{11} & -\frac{15}{11} & -\frac{6}{11} \end{bmatrix}$ is the inverse of $\begin{bmatrix} 0 & 3 & 1 \\ 2 & 1 & 0 \\ -5 & 0 & -1 \end{bmatrix}$

under matrix multiplication over the set of all 3 by 3 matrices.

11. Let an operation "o" over the set of integers be defined as follows:
$a \, o \, b = a + b - 2$.
(*a*) Which integer is the identity element for "o"?
(*b*) Which integer is the inverse of 3 with respect to "o"?

3.6 FIELD — A MATHEMATICAL SYSTEM (Optional)

We now have the vocabulary necessary to define a specific mathematical system in a formal manner. We will call it a *"system of scalars"* or a *field.* An element of this system is called a *scalar.*

> **Definition.** *A system of scalars (or field) consists of:*
> **A.** *A set S with at least two elements.*
> **B.** *The binary relation, equality, over S.*
> **C.** *Two binary operations $\oplus$ and $\odot$, under which S is closed.*
> **D.** *The nine postulates:*
>
> (1*a*) $\oplus$ *is commutative.*   (1*b*) $\odot$ *is commutative.*
> (2*a*) $\oplus$ *is associative.*   (2*b*) $\odot$ *is associative.*
> (3*a*) *The set S contains*   (3*b*) *The set S contains an*
>   *an identity element*   *identity element ϵ_1*
>   *ϵ_0 for $\oplus$.*   *for $\odot$ ($\epsilon_1 \neq \epsilon_0$).*
> (4*a*) *Each element in S*   (4*b*) *Each element in S except*
>   *has an inverse in S*   *ϵ_0 has an inverse in S*
>   *with respect to $\oplus$.*   *with respect to $\odot$.*
> (5) $\odot$ *is distributive with respect to $\oplus$.*

If the elements are real numbers or complex numbers and the operations are $+$ and $(\cdot)$, we have two familiar examples of a field. It should now be evident why, in the first chapter, the student was allowed to interpret the word "scalar" as a complex number. Under matrix addition and multiplication, the set of all 1 by 1 matrices with scalar entries is another example of a field.

If we omit postulate (4*b*) and add the cancellation law for the operation $\odot$, we have a system that is called an *integral domain.* Note that for the operations of $+$ and $(\cdot)$ the set of all integers forms such a system, whereas it cannot form a field.

It should be emphasized that the concepts of field and integral domain are far more general than the examples mentioned might imply.

Exercise 4 of this section shows that the cancellation law follows as a theorem from the field postulates, and hence a field is actually a special integral domain where postulate (4*b*) holds.

EXERCISES

1. Determine which of the following are examples of fields. If they are not examples of fields, state which of the postulates do not hold. Let operation $\oplus$ be $+$ and $\odot$ be $(\cdot)$ for the first three sets.

(a) the set of all integers;

(b) the set of all rational numbers;

(c) the set of all pure imaginary numbers;

(d) the set of all four-dimensional vectors where $\oplus$ is vector addition and $\odot$ is the dot product;

(e) the set of all 1 by 1 matrices with rational entries where $\oplus$ is matrix addition and $\odot$ is matrix multiplication;

(f) the set of all 2 by 2 matrices (with scalar entries) which have an inverse for multiplication, that is, assume A^{-1} exists. $\oplus$ is matrix addition and $\odot$ is matrix multiplication.

2. Which parts of Exercise 1 above are examples of an integral domain?

3. Suppose we did not require a field to have at least two elements (see part A of definition of field). Verify that in this case the single number zero where $\oplus$ is $+$ and $\odot$ is $(\cdot)$ would form a field. Notice that zero would be both the identity element for addition and the identity element for multiplication. It can be shown that if a field is required to have more than one element then the identity elements for $\oplus$ and $\odot$ must be different. It seems desirable to have different identity elements for $\oplus$ and $\odot$, which explains why we require a field to have at least two elements.

4. (a) Prove that if a and b are elements of a field and $a \odot b = \epsilon_0$ then either $a = \epsilon_0$ or $b = \epsilon_0$.

(b) Prove that if a and b are elements of a field and $a \odot b = \epsilon_0$ implies that either $a = \epsilon_0$ or $b = \epsilon_0$, then the cancellation law for $\odot$ holds.

As a consequence of these two results, we see that the extra postulate for an integral domain actually holds true for a field. Therefore, a field is an integral domain. In fact, a field is an integral domain in which postulate (4b) holds. The result of this problem is the basis for showing a field as a special case of an integral domain in the chart which appears in the next section.

5. Prove that any integral domain with only a finite number of elements is a field. (*Hint*: Show that postulate (4b) must hold.)

3.7 RING — A MATHEMATICAL SYSTEM (Optional)

Another important mathematical system is called a *ring*.

Definition. *A ring is a system consisting of:*

A. *A set of elements S.*

B. *The binary relation of equality over S.*

C. *Two binary operations $\oplus$ and $\odot$, under which S is closed.*

D. *The six postulates:*
  (1a) ⊕ *is commutative.*
  (2a) ⊕ *is associative.*   (2b) ⊙ *is associative.*
  (3a) *The set S contains an*
        identity element ϵ_0 *for* ⊕.
  (4a) *Each element in S has an*
        inverse in S with respect to ⊕.
  (5) ⊙ *is right and left distributive with respect to* ⊕.

The set of n by n matrices, with scalar entries, where ⊕ and ⊙ are matrix addition and matrix multiplication respectively, is an example of a ring. Actually this set has a multiplicative identity also and thus is called a *"ring with unity."* Other examples of a ring, where the operations are ordinary addition and multiplication are:

(1) all integers,   (2) all even integers,

(3) all real numbers,   (4) all complex numbers.

The set of n-dimensional vectors under the operations $(+)$ and $(\cdot)$ is not a ring because the set is not closed with respect to $(\cdot)$ (Example 7, Section 3.1). The student should also ponder this question: Why does the set of odd integers under $(+)$ and $(\cdot)$ not form a ring?

In the past two sections we have considered three mathematical systems involving a set of elements, the relation of equality among these elements, and two binary operations. The diagram (Fig. 3.1) may be helpful in showing how these systems are related.

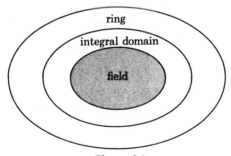

ring

integral domain

field

Figure 3.1

For example, the set of real numbers under $+$ and $(\cdot)$ constitutes a field and thereby also is an integral domain and a ring.

If we consider the set of integers under $+$ and $(\cdot)$, we find we have an integral domain and therefore a ring but not a field. (Not all nonzero elements have multiplicative inverses in the set.)

Consider the set of all 2 by 2 matrices with scalar entries. Let the operations be matrix addition and multiplication. Such a system is a ring. However, it is not an integral domain or a field. Why?

EXERCISES

1. Determine which of the following are examples of a ring. If they do not form a ring, state which of the postulates do not hold:

(a) The set of odd integers where $\oplus$ is $+$ and $\odot$ is $(\cdot)$.
(b) The set of rational numbers where $\oplus$ is $+$ and $\odot$ is $(\cdot)$.
(c) The set of all pure imaginary numbers where $\oplus$ is $+$ and $\odot$ is $(\cdot)$.
(d) All integers which are integral multiples of 3, where $\oplus$ is $+$ and $\odot$ is $(\cdot)$.
(e) All 2 by 2 matrices (with scalar entries). $\oplus$ is matrix addition and $\odot$ is matrix multiplication.
(f) All 1 by 1 matrices with integral entries. $\oplus$ is matrix addition and $\odot$ is matrix multiplication.

2. A ring for which $\odot$ is commutative is called a *commutative ring*. Are any of the parts of Exercise 1 examples of commutative rings?

3. Explain why every integral domain is a ring as the figure in this section indicates.

4. Suppose a set S of elements together with operations $\oplus$ and $\odot$ forms a ring. It may happen that a certain subset of S together with the same operations $\oplus$ and $\odot$ also meets all the requirements for a ring. When this is true, we have what is called a *subring* of the original ring. Determine which of the following subsets of the set of real numbers form a subring of the ring of real numbers. ($\oplus$ is $+$ and $\odot$ is $(\cdot)$.)

(a) The set of all integers.
(b) The set of all positive integers.
(c) The set of all even integers.
(d) The set of numbers of the form $a \oplus b \odot \sqrt{2}$, where a and b are integers.
(e) The set of numbers of the form $a \oplus b \odot \sqrt[3]{2}$, where a and b are integers.

5. Given that the elements w, u, v, and x with operations $\oplus$ and $\odot$ form a ring when the elements combine as shown in the following tables:

$\oplus$	w	u	v	x
w	u	w	x	v
u	w	u	v	x
v	x	v	u	w
x	v	x	w	u

$\odot$	w	u	v	x
w	w	u	w	u
u	u	u	u	u
v	w	u	v	x
x	u	u	x	x

The idea of these tables is analogous to the idea of addition and multiplication tables in arithmetic. Here $x \oplus v = w$, $x \odot v = x$, etc.

(*a*) Why is it clear from the tables that the set of elements is closed under the binary operations $\oplus$ and $\odot$?

(*b*) Verify that $u \oplus v = v \oplus u$. What significance is there in the fact that the table for $\oplus$ is symmetric about its main diagonal?

(*c*) Verify each of the following by using the tables:

$$u \oplus (w \oplus v) = (u \oplus w) \oplus v,$$

$$x \odot (v \odot u) = (x \odot v) \odot u,$$

$$x \odot (w \oplus x) = (x \odot w) \oplus (x \odot x).$$

Why would it be very tedious to verify completely postulates (2*a*), (2*b*), and (5)?

(*d*) Why does $\epsilon_o = u$?

(*e*) What is the inverse of x with respect to $\oplus$?

(*f*) Does this ring satisfy postulate (1*b*) for fields?

(*g*) Does this ring have an identity element for $\odot$?

(*h*) Show that the cancellation law for $\odot$ does not hold, thus proving that this ring is not an integral domain.

(*i*) Do the elements u and x with operations $\oplus$ and $\odot$ form a subring (see Exercise 4) of the given ring?

3.8 GROUP — A MATHEMATICAL SYSTEM (Optional)

In the two preceding sections we considered systems with two operations. We now discuss a system with only one operation.   Naturally since the postulates are less restrictive, we will be able to find more examples.

Definition. *A group is a system consisting of:*

A. *A set of elements S.*

B. *The binary relation of equality over S.*

C. *A binary operation o under which S is closed.*

D. *The three postulates:*

(1) *o is associative.*

(2) *The set S contains an identity element for o.*

(3) *Each element in S has an inverse in S with respect to o.*

Definition. *A group that also has the postulate that o is commutative is called a* **commutative group** *or* **Abelian group.**

Some examples of groups are:

(1) Those previously mentioned as examples of a ring where *o* is $\oplus$.

(2) The set of nonzero real numbers where *o* is ordinary multiplication. This system is an Abelian group.

(3) The set of m by n matrices with scalar entries is an Abelian group under addition.

(4) The set of 3-dimensional vectors under addition.

The set of elements is not necessarily infinite in number. Some examples of *finite groups* are:

(1) The set of numbers on a clock face where $\oplus$ is the addition of hours obtained by the movement of the hour hand. In this group we have the strange sum $9 \oplus 5 = 2$.

(2) The numbers 1, -1, i, $-i$, (where $i^2 = -1$) and o is ordinary multiplication.

(3) The three cube roots of 1 under multiplication. Here S consists of

$$1, \frac{-1 + i\sqrt{3}}{2}, \frac{-1 - i\sqrt{3}}{2}.$$

A Frenchman, Evariste Galois (1811–1832), had a great influence on the early development of group theory. His contributions to mathematics undoubtedly would have been much greater, if he had not been killed in a duel when he was only twenty.

EXERCISES

1. Determine which of the following are examples of groups. If they do not form a group, then state which postulates do not hold.
   (a) All odd integers under addition.
   (b) All odd integers under multiplication.
   (c) All n-dimensional vectors under addition.
   (d) All even integers under addition.
   (e) All even integers under multiplication.
   (f) All integers under subtraction.
   (g) 1, w, w^2, under multiplication ($w^3 = 1$).
   (h) All 2 by 2 matrices (with scalar entries). o is matrix multiplication.
   (i) All 2 by 3 matrices (with scalar entries). o is matrix addition.
   (j) All rational numbers under multiplication.
   (k) All nonzero complex numbers under multiplication.
   (l) The elements a and b under o where o is defined by the following table:

o	a	b
a	a	b
b	b	a

2. Which of the groups in Exercise 1 are commutative groups?

3. Which of the groups of Exercise 1 are finite groups?

4. Is it possible for a group to contain only one element? Answer the same question for fields, integral domains, and rings.

5. Explain why all elements of a field except ϵ_0 form a group, where the group operation is the same as operation $\odot$ of the field.

6. Prove that a group can have only one identity element with respect to the group operation o.

7. Prove that if a, b, and c are elements of a group and $a \, o \, b = a \, o \, c$, then $b = c$.

3.9 SUMMARY

In this chapter we began by studying elements, relations, operations, and the various laws of operations. Making use of these concepts, we formulated certain postulates which yielded a framework called a "Mathematical System." Several of these systems were studied with a particular interest in how the new elements (vectors, matrices) and the old elements fit into the over-all structures that were constructed (fields, rings, groups). There are, of course, many other mathematical systems that can be built. In the next several chapters we study some topics which will enable us to put our new elements to work.

NEW VOCABULARY

mathematical system	3.1	right distributive	3.2	
set	3.1	left distributive	3.2	
relation	3.1	cancellation law	3.2	
operation	3.1	identity element	3.5	
postulate	3.1	inverse element	3.5	
binary relation	3.1	identity matrix	3.5	
binary operation	3.1	field	3.6	
closed set under o	3.1	system of scalars	3.6	
equivalence relation	3.1	integral domain	3.6	
reflexive property	3.1	ring	3.7	
symmetric property	3.1	ring with unity	3.7	
transitive property	3.1	group	3.8	
commutative	3.2	commutative group	3.8	
associative	3.2	Abelian group	3.8	
distributive	3.2	finite group	3.8	

Special Matrices

4.1 TRANSPOSE OF A MATRIX

In the first two chapters, vectors and matrices were introduced, and a few of the areas in which they are useful in solving applied problems were pointed out. In the last chapter, we tried to add to your concepts of the structure of mathematics with particular emphasis placed on vectors and matrices. In this chapter we emphasize important special types of matrices. Again we extend our vocabulary considerably, thus enabling us to speak the language of matrix algebra more fluently. We begin by considering a very important *unary* operation, that is, an operation which is performed on a single element.

Definition. *The **transpose** of a matrix A is a matrix which is formed by interchanging the rows and columns of A. The ith row of A becomes the ith column of the transpose of A.*

The transpose of A will be denoted by A^T in this book, and it should be observed that

$$\text{if } A = [a_{ij}]_{(m,n)}, \quad \text{then} \quad A^T = [a_{ji}]_{(n,m)}.$$

Example 1.

$$A = \begin{bmatrix} 2 & 1 \\ 4 & 3 \\ 6 & 1 \end{bmatrix}, \quad A^T = \begin{bmatrix} 2 & 4 & 6 \\ 1 & 3 & 1 \end{bmatrix}.$$

Now that the transpose of a matrix has been defined it is essential to learn something about its behavior if we plan to use it. The important properties are stated as theorems for future reference. The proofs of all but the third theorem are left as exercises for the student.

Theorem 1. $\qquad\qquad (A^T)^T = A.$

Theorem 2. *If A is conformable to B for addition, then*

$$(A + B)^T = A^T + B^T.$$

Theorem 3. *If A is conformable to B for multiplication, then*

$$(AB)^T = B^T A^T.$$

Proof. We will prove that the two matrices are equal by showing that corresponding entries are equal. Let $C = AB$ where A has order m by k and B has order k by n.

STATEMENT	REASON
(1) The (ij)th entry of C^T (that is, $(AB)^T$) $= (ji)$th entry of C	(1) Definition of transpose.
(2) $= [j$th row of $A] \cdot [i$th column of $B]$	(2) Matrix multiplication.
(3) $= [a_{j1}, a_{j2}, \ldots, a_{jk}] \cdot [b_{1i}, b_{2i}, \ldots, b_{ki}]$	(3) Scalar product of two vectors.
(4) $= [b_{1i}, b_{2i}, \ldots, b_{ki}] \cdot [a_{j1}, a_{j2}, \ldots, a_{jk}]$	(4) Scalar product of two vectors is commutative.
(5) $= [i$th row of $B^T] \cdot [j$th column of $A^T]$	(5) Definition of transpose.
(6) $= (ij)$th entry of $B^T A^T$.	(6) Matrix multiplication.
(7) $(AB)^T$ and $B^T A^T$ have same order.	(7) Why?
(8) $(AB)^T = B^T A^T$.	(8) Definition of equality of matrices.

Example 2.

Let
$$A = \begin{bmatrix} 1 & 0 \\ 2 & 1 \end{bmatrix} \quad \text{and} \quad B = \begin{bmatrix} 0 & 2 \\ 1 & 3 \end{bmatrix}.$$

Then
$$(AB)^T = \begin{bmatrix} 0 & 2 \\ 1 & 7 \end{bmatrix}^T = \begin{bmatrix} 0 & 1 \\ 2 & 7 \end{bmatrix}.$$

$$B^T A^T = \begin{bmatrix} 0 & 1 \\ 2 & 3 \end{bmatrix} \begin{bmatrix} 1 & 2 \\ 0 & 1 \end{bmatrix} = \begin{bmatrix} 0 & 1 \\ 2 & 7 \end{bmatrix}.$$

Theorem 4. $(cA)^T = cA^T$, *where c is a scalar.*

EXERCISES

1. Find the transpose of each of the following matrices:

(a) $\begin{bmatrix} 3 & -3 \\ 5 & 6 \end{bmatrix}$;   (b) $[3 \quad 4 \quad -2]$;   (c) $\begin{bmatrix} 2 & -1 & 0 \\ 3 & 4 & 4 \end{bmatrix}$.

2. The transpose of a column matrix is what kind of a matrix?

3. When does the order of a matrix F equal the order of F^T?

4. When is A conformable to A^T for addition? For multiplication?

5. Let $A = \begin{bmatrix} 3 & 2 \\ 4 & 0 \end{bmatrix}$ and $B = \begin{bmatrix} 0 & 1 & 2 \\ 1 & 2 & 0 \end{bmatrix}$. Verify:

(a) Theorem 1;   (b) Theorem 3.

6. Prove Theorem 1.   7. Prove Theorem 2.

8. Prove Theorem 4.

9. If matrix A is the transpose of matrix B and matrix B is the transpose of matrix C, is matrix A the transpose of matrix C? Explain.

10. Does $(AB)^T = A^T B^T$? Why?

11. Using Theorem 3, show that $(ABC)^T = C^T B^T A^T$.

12. Generalize Theorem 3 as suggested in the preceding exercise.

13. Does $(A - B)^T = A^T - B^T$? If not, give a counterexample. If the relation is true, prove it using Theorems 2 and 4.

14. Simplify: $(A^T B^T + 3C)^T$. Give the reason for each step.

15. Simplify: $(A^T + 2B^T + C)^T$. Give the reason for each step.

4.2 SYMMETRIC MATRIX

Definition. *A matrix A is said to be **symmetric** when $A = A^T$.*

Example 1.

$$A = \begin{bmatrix} 3 & 2 & 1 \\ 2 & 0 & -6 \\ 1 & -6 & 1 \end{bmatrix}, \qquad A^T = \begin{bmatrix} 3 & 2 & 1 \\ 2 & 0 & -6 \\ 1 & -6 & 1 \end{bmatrix}.$$

A is symmetric because $A = A^T$. In the example one should note that the entries of A are symmetric with respect to the main diagonal, thus indicating the reason for the choice of the label "symmetric matrix."

Note that a matrix must be square to be symmetric and that $a_{ij} = a_{ji}$. There are several theorems of interest. One of them will be stated here and others in the exercises.

Theorem 5. *The product of a matrix and its transpose is symmetric.*

Proof. Let $C = AA^T$ (the argument is similar for $C = A^TA$).

STATEMENT	REASON
(1) $C^T = (AA^T)^T = (A^T)^TA^T$	(1) Theorem 3.
(2) $= AA^T$	(2) Theorem 1.
(3) $= C.$	(3) Given.
(4) C is symmetric.	(4) By definition of symmetric matrix.

EXERCISES

1. Determine which of the following are symmetric. If any one is not, state why it is not.

(a) $\begin{bmatrix} 1 & 2 & 5 \\ 2 & 2 & -1 \\ 5 & -1 & 3 \end{bmatrix}$;   (b) $\begin{bmatrix} 2 & 3 \\ 3 & 4 \\ 0 & 0 \end{bmatrix}$;   (c) $\begin{bmatrix} 2 & -1 & -2 \\ 1 & 22 & -1 \\ 2 & 1 & 2 \end{bmatrix}$.

2. Suppose a 3 by 3 matrix A has $a_{12} = a_{21}$, $a_{23} = a_{32}$, and $a_{13} = a_{31}$. Is A symmetric and why?

3. Find, if possible, values of a and b for which the matrix $\begin{bmatrix} a & 3 \\ 3 & b \end{bmatrix}$ will not be symmetric.

4. Prove that if A is a square matrix, then $A + A^T$ is symmetric.

5. Prove that if A is symmetric, then A^2 is symmetric.

6. Prove that if A and B are symmetric and if $AB = BA$, then AB is symmetric.

7. Show that the product of two symmetric matrices of the same order need not be symmetric. (*Hint:* Use an example.)

8. In the proof of Theorem 5 it was justified that AA^T is symmetric. Show that A^TA is also symmetric.

9. Prove that if A is symmetric and c is a scalar, then cA is symmetric.

10. Prove or disprove the following: If $A + B$ is symmetric, then both A and B are symmetric.

11. Does the set of all 2 by 2 symmetric matrices with scalar entries form a group, if matrix addition is the operation? Explain.

4.3 SKEW-SYMMETRIC MATRIX

Definition. *A matrix A is said to be **skew-symmetric** if $A = -A^T$.*

Example 1.

$$\text{If} \quad A = \begin{bmatrix} 0 & -3 & -1 \\ 3 & 0 & 2 \\ 1 & -2 & 0 \end{bmatrix}, \quad A^T = \begin{bmatrix} 0 & 3 & 1 \\ -3 & 0 & -2 \\ -1 & 2 & 0 \end{bmatrix}, \quad -A^T = \begin{bmatrix} 0 & -3 & -1 \\ 3 & 0 & 2 \\ 1 & -2 & 0 \end{bmatrix}.$$

$A = -A^T$ and therefore A is called skew-symmetric.

Note that for A to be skew-symmetric, it must be square and $a_{ij} = -a_{ji}$. Also, each entry on the main diagonal must be zero.

An interesting observation can be made here. Any square matrix A can be expressed as the sum of a skew-symmetric matrix and a symmetric matrix. If A is any square matrix, construct a symmetric matrix S and a skew-symmetric matrix K as follows:

$$S = \frac{A + A^T}{2}, \quad K = \frac{A - A^T}{2}. \quad \text{Then} \quad A = S + K.$$

Example 2.

$$\text{Let} \quad A = \begin{bmatrix} 2 & 2 \\ 1 & 4 \end{bmatrix}; \quad \text{then} \quad A^T = \begin{bmatrix} 2 & 1 \\ 2 & 4 \end{bmatrix}.$$

$$S = \frac{A + A^T}{2} = \frac{1}{2}\begin{bmatrix} 4 & 3 \\ 3 & 8 \end{bmatrix}. \quad\quad K = \frac{A - A^T}{2} = \frac{1}{2}\begin{bmatrix} 0 & 1 \\ -1 & 0 \end{bmatrix}.$$

$$A = S + K = \begin{bmatrix} 2 & \frac{3}{2} \\ \frac{3}{2} & 4 \end{bmatrix} + \begin{bmatrix} 0 & \frac{1}{2} \\ -\frac{1}{2} & 0 \end{bmatrix}.$$

EXERCISES

1. Determine which of the following are skew-symmetric. For those that are not, state why they are not.

$$(a) \quad \begin{bmatrix} 1 & -2 & 3 \\ 2 & 1 & 4 \\ -3 & -4 & 1 \end{bmatrix}; \quad\quad (b) \quad \begin{bmatrix} 0 & 0 & 2 \\ 0 & 0 & -1 \\ -2 & 1 & 0 \end{bmatrix};$$

$$(c) \quad \begin{bmatrix} 0 & 3 \\ -3 & 0 \\ -1 & 1 \end{bmatrix}; \quad\quad (d) \quad \begin{bmatrix} 0 & 0 & 0 \\ 0 & 0 & 0 \\ 0 & 0 & 0 \end{bmatrix}.$$

2. Prove that each entry on the main diagonal of a skew-symmetric matrix must be zero.

3. Make up, if possible, an example of a matrix of order two which is both symmetric and skew-symmetric.

4. Prove: If A is a skew-symmetric matrix, then $AA^T = A^T A$.

5. Prove: If A is skew-symmetric, then A^2 is symmetric.

6. Prove:
(a) If A is square, then $A - A^T$ is skew-symmetric.
(b) If A is skew-symmetric and c is a scalar, then cA is skew-symmetric.
(c) How does it follow from (a) and (b) that $K = (A - A^T)/2$ is skew-symmetric?

7. Express each of the following matrices as the sum of a skew-symmetric matrix and a symmetric matrix:

(a) $\begin{bmatrix} 9 & 7 \\ 6 & -2 \end{bmatrix}$;
(b) $\begin{bmatrix} 3 & 3 & -1 \\ 0 & 3 & -2 \\ -1 & 2 & 2 \end{bmatrix}$.

8. Prove that there is only one method of expressing a square matrix as the sum of a symmetric matrix and a skew-symmetric matrix.

9. Find the main diagonal entries of AA^T when A is a real skew-symmetric matrix.

10. In the preceding exercise what can be said about the main diagonal of A^2?

11. Does the set of all 2 by 2 skew-symmetric matrices with real numbers as entries form a group with matrix addition as the operation? Explain your answer.

4.4 HERMITIAN MATRIX (Optional)

Hermitian matrices are especially important to atomic physicists and others who deal with matrices whose entries are complex numbers. We recall that, if x and y are real numbers, the *conjugate* of the complex number $a = x + yi$ is $\bar{a} = x - yi$.

Definition. *If the entries of a matrix A are complex numbers, the conjugate of A is the matrix $\bar{A}$ whose entries are the conjugates of the corresponding entries of A.*

Example 1.

If $\quad A = [a_{ij}]_{(2.2)} = \begin{bmatrix} i & 2 \\ 2+i & 0 \end{bmatrix}$, then $\bar{A} = [\bar{a}_{ij}]_{(2.2)} = \begin{bmatrix} -i & 2 \\ 2-i & 0 \end{bmatrix}$.

$(\bar{A})^T$ is called the **transposed conjugate** or **tranjugate matrix** of A and is denoted by A^*.

Example 2. Using A of the previous example

$$A^* = (\bar{A})^T = [\bar{a}_{ji}]_{(n.m)} = \begin{bmatrix} -i & 2-i \\ 2 & 0 \end{bmatrix}.$$

Definition. *A matrix A is said to be **Hermitian** if $A = A^*$.*

The name comes from the French mathematician, Charles Hermite (1822–1901).

Example 3.

(a) A in the previous two examples is not Hermitian because $A \neq A^*$.

(b) Let $B = \begin{bmatrix} 3 & 2+i \\ 2-i & \sqrt{2} \end{bmatrix}$; then $\bar{B} = \begin{bmatrix} 3 & 2-i \\ 2+i & \sqrt{2} \end{bmatrix}$, and

$$B^* = (\bar{B})^T = \begin{bmatrix} 3 & 2+i \\ 2-i & \sqrt{2} \end{bmatrix}.$$

Since $B = B^*$, B is a Hermitian matrix.

Note that a Hermitian matrix must be square and that the main diagonal must consist of real numbers. Also, if the entries of a symmetric matrix are real numbers then the matrix is Hermitian, for a real complex number is its own conjugate.

A matrix A is said to be **skew-Hermitian** if $A = -A^*$.

EXERCISES

1. Find the conjugate matrix and the tranjugate matrix of each of the following:

(a) $\begin{bmatrix} i & 2-i & 2 \\ 0 & 3i & 4 \end{bmatrix}$;   (b) $\begin{bmatrix} 2 & 2+i \\ i & 2i \end{bmatrix}$;   (c) $\begin{bmatrix} 0 & 3+i \\ 3-i & 2 \end{bmatrix}$;

(d) $\begin{bmatrix} 2 & 3 \\ 3 & 1 \end{bmatrix}$;   (e) $\begin{bmatrix} 0 & i & 2i \\ i & 0 & -4 \\ 2i & 4 & 0 \end{bmatrix}$.

Note that $\bar{A}$ and A^* have meaning even if A is not square.

2. Which of the matrices in Exercise 1 (if any) are Hermitian matrices? Which are skew-Hermitian?

3. Justify all of the assertions in the paragraph which follows Example 3.

4. Prove or disprove that $(\bar{A})^T = \overline{(A^T)}$, where A is any matrix whose entries are complex numbers.

5. Show that each entry on the main diagonal of a skew-Hermitian matrix must be either zero or a pure imaginary number.

6. Prove that $A = \bar{\bar{A}}$, where $\bar{\bar{A}} = \overline{(\bar{A})}$.

7. Let x and y be complex numbers:
(a) Prove that $\overline{x+y} = \bar{x} + \bar{y}$.   (b) Prove that $\overline{xy} = \bar{x}\,\bar{y}$.

8. Assuming conformability, prove that:
(a) $\overline{A+B} = \bar{A} + \bar{B}$;   (b) $\overline{AB} = \bar{A}\,\bar{B}$;
(c) $\overline{cA} = \bar{c}\,\bar{A}$, where c is a scalar.

9. The following theorems are analogous to those in Section 4.1.

1 $(A^*)^* = A$.

II. $(A + B)^* = A^* + B^*$.

III. $(AB)^* = B^* A^*$.

IV. $(cA)^* = \bar{c} A^*$.

V. AA^* and A^*A are Hermitian.

Illustrate these theorems with the matrices

$$A = \begin{bmatrix} i & 2 + i \\ 2 & -2i \end{bmatrix} \quad \text{and} \quad B = \begin{bmatrix} 0 & i \\ 1 + i & 2 \end{bmatrix} \quad \text{and the scalar } c = 1 + i.$$

10. Prove the theorems of the previous exercise (assume conformability).

11. Does the set of all 2 by 2 Hermitian matrices form a group with matrix addition as the operation? Explain your answer.

12. (a) Prove: If A and B are Hermitian matrices of the same order, then $A + B$ is Hermitian.

(b) Disprove the following statement by finding a counterexample: If A and B are Hermitian matrices of the same order, then AB is Hermitian.

4.5 TRIANGULAR AND ECHELON MATRICES

Definition. *A square matrix is said to be* **triangular** *if all the entries either above or below the main diagonal are zeros.*

Example 1.

$$\begin{bmatrix} 1 & 0 \\ 2 & 1 \end{bmatrix}, \quad \begin{bmatrix} 1 & 4 & 1 \\ 0 & 2 & 2 \\ 0 & 0 & 3 \end{bmatrix}, \quad \begin{bmatrix} 0 & 4 & 2 \\ 0 & 0 & 1 \\ 0 & 0 & 0 \end{bmatrix}, \quad \text{and} \quad \begin{bmatrix} 0 & 0 & 0 \\ 0 & 0 & 0 \\ 0 & 0 & 0 \end{bmatrix} \text{ are triangular matrices.}$$

As was stated earlier in the book, many applications of matrices arise from consideration of systems of equations. The echelon matrix defined below will play a big part in our use of matrices to solve systems of equations in Chapter 8.

Definition. *An* **echelon matrix** *is an m by n matrix constructed in the following manner:*

(a) *Each of the first k rows has some nonzero entries. The entries are all zeros in the remaining m–k rows $(1 \leq k \leq m)$.*

(b) *The first nonzero entry in each of the first k rows is 1.*

(c) *In any one of the first k rows, the number of zeros preceding the first nonzero entry is smaller than it is in the next following row.*

Example 2.

$$\begin{bmatrix} 0 & 1 & 3 & 0 & 2 \\ 0 & 0 & 0 & 1 & 2 \\ 0 & 0 & 0 & 0 & 0 \end{bmatrix} \quad \text{and} \quad \begin{bmatrix} 1 & 3 & 3 & 4 \\ 0 & 1 & 6 & 2 \\ 0 & 0 & 1 & 0 \end{bmatrix} \quad \text{are echelon matrices.}$$

Part (a) of the definition says that if there are any rows containing all zeros, then they must be last. This is not the case in the matrix $\begin{bmatrix} 1 & 2 & 3 & 4 \\ 0 & 0 & 0 & 0 \\ 0 & 0 & 1 & 2 \end{bmatrix}$; therefore it is not an echelon matrix.

Part (b) of the definition requires that the first nonzero entry in every row is 1. This is not the case in the matrix $\begin{bmatrix} 0 & 1 & 2 & 0 \\ 0 & 0 & 3 & 1 \\ 0 & 0 & 0 & 0 \end{bmatrix}$; therefore it is not an echelon matrix.

Part (c) requires that the number of zeros preceding the first nonzero entry increase with every row. This is not so in $\begin{bmatrix} 1 & 2 & 4 & 2 \\ 0 & 0 & 1 & 2 \\ 0 & 0 & 1 & 3 \end{bmatrix}$; therefore it is not an echelon matrix. Note that the number of zeros must increase; they cannot remain the same. It can be seen that a square echelon matrix is a triangular matrix.

EXERCISES

1. Which of the following are triangular matrices and which are echelon matrices?

(a) $\begin{bmatrix} 0 & 1 & 1 & 3 & 4 \\ 0 & 0 & 1 & 2 & 6 \\ 0 & 0 & 1 & 1 & 3 \\ 0 & 0 & 0 & 1 & 2 \end{bmatrix}$;

(b) $\begin{bmatrix} 0 & 1 & 0 \\ 0 & 0 & 1 \\ 0 & 0 & 0 \end{bmatrix}$;

(c) $\begin{bmatrix} 1 & 4 & 0 & 0 \\ 0 & 1 & 1 & 0 \\ 0 & 0 & 1 & 2 \end{bmatrix}$;

(d) 0_3;

(e) I_4;

(f) $\begin{bmatrix} 1 & 2 \\ 0 & 1 \\ 0 & 0 \end{bmatrix}$;

(g) $\begin{bmatrix} 1 & 0 & 0 \\ 3 & 1 & 0 \\ 2 & 4 & 1 \end{bmatrix}$;

(h) $\begin{bmatrix} 2 & 0 \\ 4 & 3 \end{bmatrix}$;

(i) $\begin{bmatrix} 1 & 0 & 0 \\ 0 & 1 & 2 \\ 0 & 0 & 2 \end{bmatrix}$;

(j) $\begin{bmatrix} 0 & 0 & 0 \\ 0 & 1 & 3 \\ 0 & 0 & 0 \end{bmatrix}$;

(k) $\begin{bmatrix} 0 & 1 \\ 0 & 0 \\ 0 & 0 \end{bmatrix}$.

2. Is every echelon matrix a triangular matrix? Explain.

3. Is the transpose of a triangular matrix also a triangular matrix? Explain.

4. Give, if possible, an example of a symmetric echelon matrix.

5. Does the set of all third-order triangular matrices form a group under the operation of matrix addition? Explain your answer.

4.6 DIAGONAL AND SCALAR MATRICES

Other special matrices of interest are diagonal and scalar matrices.

Definition. *If all the entries which are not on the main diagonal of a square matrix are zero, then the matrix is said to be a **diagonal matrix**. The entries on the main diagonal may or may not be zero.*

Example 1.

$$\begin{bmatrix} 2 & 0 & 0 \\ 0 & 1 & 0 \\ 0 & 0 & 4 \end{bmatrix} \text{ and } \begin{bmatrix} 1 & 0 & 0 & 0 \\ 0 & 0 & 0 & 0 \\ 0 & 0 & 2 & 0 \\ 0 & 0 & 0 & 0 \end{bmatrix} \text{ are examples of diagonal matrices.}$$

Definition. *If all the entries on the main diagonal of a diagonal matrix are equal scalars, the matrix is said to be a **scalar matrix**.*

Example 2.

$$\begin{bmatrix} 2 & 0 & 0 \\ 0 & 2 & 0 \\ 0 & 0 & 2 \end{bmatrix} \text{ and } \begin{bmatrix} -6 & 0 & 0 & 0 \\ 0 & -6 & 0 & 0 \\ 0 & 0 & -6 & 0 \\ 0 & 0 & 0 & -6 \end{bmatrix} \text{ are examples of scalar matrices.}$$

The identity matrices I_n and all square null matrices are other examples of scalar matrices. Notice that any scalar matrix is a diagonal matrix. Not every diagonal matrix is a scalar matrix, however; this is illustrated by Example 1 of this section.

If the student will examine the behavior of scalar matrices under the various operations, he will note a striking correspondence to the behavior of scalars. For example, to every scalar c there corresponds a third-order

scalar matrix $\begin{bmatrix} c & 0 & 0 \\ 0 & c & 0 \\ 0 & 0 & c \end{bmatrix}$, and conversely. This one-to-one correspondence is preserved under the operations of addition and multiplication. That is, for every sum of scalars $c + d$ there corresponds a matrix

$$\begin{bmatrix} c+d & 0 & 0 \\ 0 & c+d & 0 \\ 0 & 0 & c+d \end{bmatrix}$$

which is the sum of $\begin{bmatrix} c & 0 & 0 \\ 0 & c & 0 \\ 0 & 0 & c \end{bmatrix}$ and $\begin{bmatrix} d & 0 & 0 \\ 0 & d & 0 \\ 0 & 0 & d \end{bmatrix}$, and conversely. Similarly

we could illustrate the fact that the one-to-one correspondence is preserved under multiplication. Such a one-to-one correspondence between two sets of elements which preserve the sums and products is an example of what is called an *isomorphism* ("*iso*" meaning "the same" and "*morphos*" meaning "form"). The general concept of isomorphism is a powerful tool of modern algebra.

EXERCISES

1. Tell whether each of the following is true or false. If false, give a counter-example.
   (a) The transpose of a diagonal matrix is a diagonal matrix.
   (b) Every diagonal matrix is also a scalar matrix.
   (c) Every scalar matrix is a square matrix.
   (d) Every scalar matrix is Hermitian.
   (e) Every diagonal matrix is a triangular matrix.
   (f) Every scalar matrix is an echelon matrix.
   (g) The product of two diagonal matrices of the same order is a diagonal matrix.

2. Under what conditions, if any, is a scalar matrix skew-symmetric?

3. Prove that matrix addition and matrix multiplication are commutative for scalar matrices of order n.

4. If $a \neq 0$, what is the multiplicative inverse of the scalar matrix $\begin{bmatrix} a & 0 & 0 \\ 0 & a & 0 \\ 0 & 0 & a \end{bmatrix}$?

5. Does the set of all scalar matrices of order n form a field if $\oplus$ is matrix addition and $\odot$ is matrix multiplication? Why?

6. Does the set of all diagonal matrices of order n form a field if $\oplus$ is matrix addition and $\odot$ is matrix multiplication? Why?

7. In each of the following find a third-order scalar matrix A which satisfies the given matrix equation.
   (a) $A^2 + 3A + 2I = 0$;   (b) $A^2 - 4I = 0$;
   (c) $A^3 + A^2 + 2A + 2I = 0$.

4.7 SUBMATRICES AND PARTITIONING

Definition. *A submatrix of a matrix A is the rectangular array that remains if certain rows or columns (or both) of A are deleted.*

Example 1.

Let
$$A = \begin{bmatrix} 2 & 3 & 5 \\ 2 & 2 & 2 \\ 4 & 6 & 6 \end{bmatrix}.$$

(a) $B = \begin{bmatrix} 2 & 3 & 5 \\ 2 & 2 & 2 \\ 4 & 6 & 6 \end{bmatrix} = \begin{bmatrix} 2 & 5 \\ 4 & 6 \end{bmatrix}$ is a submatrix of A.

(b) $C_1 = \begin{bmatrix} 2 & 3 & 5 \\ 2 & 2 & 2 \\ 4 & 6 & 6 \end{bmatrix} = \begin{bmatrix} 2 \\ 2 \\ 4 \end{bmatrix}$, $C_2 = \begin{bmatrix} 3 \\ 2 \\ 6 \end{bmatrix}$, $C_3 = \begin{bmatrix} 5 \\ 2 \\ 6 \end{bmatrix}$

are submatrices of A. Also, it is customary to consider A as a submatrix of itself.

Frequently it is helpful to express matrices in which the entries are submatrices. For instance, in the example above we can use the submatrices C_1, C_2, C_3 and write

$$A = [C_1 \mid C_2 \mid C_3] = \begin{bmatrix} 2 & 3 & 5 \\ 2 & 2 & 2 \\ 4 & 6 & 6 \end{bmatrix}.$$

We say that A has been **partitioned.**

We can partition another matrix D as follows:

$$D = \begin{bmatrix} D_{11} & D_{12} \\ D_{21} & D_{22} \end{bmatrix} = \begin{bmatrix} 2 & 3 & 2 & 1 \\ 3 & 2 & 4 & 6 \\ 2 & 0 & 0 & 2 \\ 1 & 1 & 1 & 1 \end{bmatrix}.$$

Using this notation it can be justified that we can then postmultiply D by

$$E = \begin{bmatrix} E_{11} & E_{12} \\ E_{21} & E_{22} \end{bmatrix}$$ in the following manner.

$$DE = \begin{bmatrix} D_{11}E_{11} + D_{12}E_{21} & D_{11}E_{12} + D_{12}E_{22} \\ D_{21}E_{11} + D_{22}E_{21} & D_{21}E_{12} + D_{22}E_{22} \end{bmatrix}$$

provided the various submatrices are conformable. Because D is partitioned in such a manner that D_{11} is a 2 by 2 submatrix, then E must be partitioned so that E_{11} is a 2 by p submatrix. It will be enlightening for the student to figure out the necessary orders of the other submatrices E_{12}, E_{21}, and E_{22} in order for DE to be calculated as shown above. Note that E_{11} does not have to be of the same order as D_{11}.

Example 2.

Let
$$A = \begin{bmatrix} 2 & 1 & 0 \\ 0 & 2 & 1 \\ \hline 3 & 1 & 1 \end{bmatrix} \quad \text{and} \quad B = \begin{bmatrix} 2 & 1 \\ 1 & 0 \\ \hline 1 & 2 \end{bmatrix}.$$

Then
$$AB = \begin{bmatrix} \begin{bmatrix} 2 & 1 \\ 0 & 2 \end{bmatrix}\begin{bmatrix} 2 \\ 1 \end{bmatrix} + \begin{bmatrix} 0 \\ 1 \end{bmatrix}[1] & \begin{bmatrix} 2 & 1 \\ 0 & 2 \end{bmatrix}\begin{bmatrix} 1 \\ 0 \end{bmatrix} + \begin{bmatrix} 0 \\ 1 \end{bmatrix}[2] \\ \hline [3 \ 1]\begin{bmatrix} 2 \\ 1 \end{bmatrix} + [1][1] & [3 \ 1]\begin{bmatrix} 1 \\ 0 \end{bmatrix} + [1][2] \end{bmatrix}$$

$$= \begin{bmatrix} \begin{bmatrix} 5 \\ 2 \end{bmatrix} + \begin{bmatrix} 0 \\ 1 \end{bmatrix} & \begin{bmatrix} 2 \\ 0 \end{bmatrix} + \begin{bmatrix} 0 \\ 2 \end{bmatrix} \\ \hline [7] + [1] & [3] + [2] \end{bmatrix} = \begin{bmatrix} 5 & 2 \\ 3 & 2 \\ \hline 8 & 5 \end{bmatrix}.$$

Partitioning can be useful in working with very large matrices. For example the product of two 100 by 100 matrices can be found by considering eight products of 50 by 50 matrices. Space considerations on computers frequently require this approach. Partitioning also is useful sometimes in finding the inverse of a matrix; that is, given A, find a matrix B such that $AB = BA = I$. As we said once before, this inverse is usually denoted by A^{-1}.

EXERCISES

1. Find AB using the indicated partitioning if possible. If it is not possible, state why.

(a) $A = \begin{bmatrix} 0 & 2 \\ \hline 4 & 3 \\ 2 & 1 \end{bmatrix}$, $B = \begin{bmatrix} 1 & 2 \\ 0 & 4 \end{bmatrix}$;

(b) $A = \begin{bmatrix} 0 & 2 \\ 4 & 1 \end{bmatrix}$, $B = \begin{bmatrix} 3 & 2 & 1 \\ \hline 4 & 0 & 2 \end{bmatrix}$;

(c) $A = \begin{bmatrix} 2 & 1 & 4 \\ \hline 3 & 2 & 1 \\ 0 & 6 & 2 \end{bmatrix}$, $B = \begin{bmatrix} 2 & 1 \\ 3 & 2 \\ \hline 4 & 0 \end{bmatrix}$.

2. Write the three 2 by 2 submatrices of $\begin{bmatrix} 1 & 0 & -2 \\ 4 & 5 & 3 \end{bmatrix}$.

3. Write all the submatrices of the matrix in the previous exercise.

4. Write the nine 2 by 2 submatrices of $\begin{bmatrix} a_{11} & a_{12} & a_{13} \\ a_{21} & a_{22} & a_{23} \\ a_{31} & a_{32} & a_{33} \end{bmatrix}$.

5. Given $B = \begin{bmatrix} 2 & 3 & 2 \\ 1 & 4 & 6 \\ 2 & 1 & 0 \end{bmatrix}$, $C = [2 \ 0 \ 1]$, $R = \begin{bmatrix} 3 \\ 2 \\ 1 \end{bmatrix}$, and f is a scalar,

(a) construct the matrix $[B \ \vdots \ I_3]$;

(b) construct the matrix $\begin{bmatrix} B & \vdots & I_3 & \vdots & C^T \\ -- & \vdots & -- & \vdots & -- \\ R^T & \vdots & 0 & \vdots & f \end{bmatrix}$.

4.8 COEFFICIENT AND AUGMENTED MATRICES

In Section 1.8 we learned that matrices can be used to represent a system of linear equations. That is,

$$\begin{cases} a_{11}x_1 + \cdots + a_{1n}x_n = b_1, \\ \qquad \cdot \qquad \cdot \qquad \cdot \\ a_{m1}x_1 + \cdots + a_{mn}x_n = b_m, \end{cases}$$

can be written as

$$AX = B.$$

Definition. *For a system of linear equations*

$$AX = B,$$

A is called the **coefficient matrix***, and* $[A \ \vdots \ B]$ *is the* **augmented matrix***.*

Example 1. Given the system

$$\begin{cases} 2x_1 + 3x_2 - x_3 = 4, \\ x_1 \qquad - x_3 = 2, \\ x_1 + x_2 - x_3 = 0. \end{cases}$$

The coefficient matrix is $\begin{bmatrix} 2 & 3 & -1 \\ 1 & 0 & -1 \\ 1 & 1 & -1 \end{bmatrix}$.

The augmented matrix is $\begin{bmatrix} 2 & 3 & -1 & 4 \\ 1 & 0 & -1 & 2 \\ 1 & 1 & -1 & 0 \end{bmatrix}$.

EXERCISES

1. Write the augmented and coefficient matrices for:

(a) $\begin{cases} x_1 - x_2 + x_3 = 4, \\ 2x_1 \quad\; + \; x_3 = 2, \\ \quad\; x_2 + 2x_3 = 1. \end{cases}$

(b) $\begin{cases} x_1 + x_2 + x_3 - \; x_4 = 2, \\ x_1 \qquad\; + x_3 + 2x_4 = 1. \end{cases}$

(c) $\begin{cases} x_1 + \; x_2 - 2 = 0, \\ x_1 + 2x_2 - 4 = 0, \\ 2x_1 - \; x_2 + 2 = 0. \end{cases}$

(d) $\begin{cases} x_1 + x_2 + 1 = 0, \\ x_2 - x_1 \quad\;\; = 0. \end{cases}$

2. The augmented matrix of a certain system of linear equations is $\begin{bmatrix} 1 & 3 & 1 \\ 4 & 2 & 5 \\ 2 & 6 & 4 \end{bmatrix}$. Write the system.

3. If the coefficient matrix of a system of linear equations is a diagonal matrix, how should one proceed to find a solution?

4. If the augmented matrix of a system of linear equations is a 4 by 5 echelon matrix, how should one proceed to find a solution?

NEW VOCABULARY

transpose   4.1
symmetric matrix   4.2
skew-symmetric matrix   4.3
Hermitian matrix   4.4
conjugate matrix   4.4
tranjugate matrix   4.4
skew-Hermitian   4.4
triangular matrix   4.5

echelon matrix   4.5
diagonal matrix   4.6
scalar matrix   4.6
submatrix   4.7
partitioned matrix   4.7
coefficient matrix   4.8
augmented matrix   4.8

5

Determinants

5.1 DEFINITION OF A DETERMINANT

It has been observed that the definition of a matrix A does *not* assign a value to A. *The first purpose of this chapter is to define a function of the entries of a square matrix in such a way that to every square matrix of scalars there corresponds a single scalar. This function is called the **determinant** of the matrix.* It is denoted by det A or $|A|$ (where A must be a square matrix).

The origin of determinants was closely associated with techniques for solving systems of linear equations. There is evidence that the Chinese, before the time of Christ, made use of bamboo rods to develop methods of solving simultaneous equations. Their methods indicate that they had an idea similar to what we now call the expansion of a determinant. The idea of determinants did not begin to take definite form, however, until about 1683 in Japan and about 1693 in Germany. Seki Kowa, the great Japanese mathematician, and G. W. Leibniz, the famous German, were responsible. The works of these men were amplified by G. Cramer of Switzerland in 1750. The gist of these early developments for a simple special case was essentially this: A system of equations

$$\begin{cases} ax + by = c, \\ a'x + b'y = c', \end{cases}$$

can be solved for x by the formula

$$x = \frac{cb' - bc'}{ab' - ba'}, \qquad \text{when the denominator is not 0.}$$

Using present-day terminology, we say that the numerator and denominator in this formula are expansions of second-order determinants written

$$x = \frac{\begin{vmatrix} c & b \\ c' & b' \end{vmatrix}}{\begin{vmatrix} a & b \\ a' & b' \end{vmatrix}}.$$

Thus, $\begin{vmatrix} c & b \\ c' & b' \end{vmatrix}$ means $(cb' - bc')$ and $\begin{vmatrix} a & b \\ a' & b' \end{vmatrix}$ means $(ab' - ba')$.

For example, $\begin{vmatrix} 2 & 4 \\ 9 & 3 \end{vmatrix} = 2 \cdot 3 - 4 \cdot 9 = 6 - 36 = -30.$

This method of solving for x will be amplified in Section 5.5.

In 1771, the French mathematician Vandermonde recognized determinants as independent functions, and in 1812 Cauchy, also French, gave the function its present name "determinant." After Cauchy had begun what is known as the theory of determinants, the subject attracted widespread attention for about a hundred years. By this time the determinant was considered an established tool of the trade. It is interesting to note that Arthur Cayley, the inventor of the matrix, was one of the greatest contributors to determinant theory. He developed the notation presently in use of a square array between two bars. The historical relationship between a matrix and a determinant may be seen in Cayley's own words. In 1894 in reply to a question about what led him to matrices, he wrote, "I certainly did not get the notion of a matrix in any way through quaternions: it was either directly from that of a determinant or as a convenient mode of expression of the equations

$$\begin{cases} x' = ax + by, \\ y' = cx + dy. \end{cases}"*$$

Before proceeding to the definition of a determinant of an n by n array, we give an example of what is meant by an *interchange*.

Example 1. Determine the number of interchanges necessary to reduce the sequence 2, 4, 3, 1 to natural order, that is, 1, 2, 3, 4.

One interchange changes 2, 4, 3, 1 to 1, 4, 3, 2. A second interchange changes 1, 4, 3, 2 to 1, 2, 3, 4.

If we proceed in a different manner we might require more interchanges but in any event we would need an even number.

A well-known theorem of group theory states that although the number of interchanges used to restore the natural order is not unique, the oddness or evenness of the number of interchanges is not affected.

---

*C. G. Knott, *Life and Scientific Work of Peter Guthrie Tait* (New York, G. P. Putnam's Sons, 1911), p. 164.

Definition. *The determinant of $A = [a_{ij}]_n$ is the sum of all terms of the form $(-1)^t a_{1j_1} a_{2j_2} \ldots a_{nj_n}$, where the second subscripts assume all possible arrangements in which each column is represented exactly once in each term of the sum, and the exponent, t, is the number of interchanges necessary to bring the second subscripts into natural order (that is, $1, 2, 3, \ldots, n$).*

Example 2. By definition,

$$|A_2| = \det \begin{bmatrix} a_{11} & a_{12} \\ a_{21} & a_{22} \end{bmatrix} = (-1)^0 a_{11} a_{22} + (-1)^1 a_{12} a_{21}$$

$$= a_{11} a_{22} - a_{12} a_{21}.$$

The right side is called the *expansion* of the determinant.

Note: The row subscripts maintain natural order, and the column subscripts assume all possible arrangements.

Example 3. By definition,

$$|A_3| = \det \begin{bmatrix} a_{11} & a_{12} & a_{13} \\ a_{21} & a_{22} & a_{23} \\ a_{31} & a_{32} & a_{33} \end{bmatrix} = (-1)^0 a_{11} a_{22} a_{33} + (-1)^1 a_{11} a_{23} a_{32}$$
$$+ (-1)^1 a_{12} a_{21} a_{33} + (-1)^2 a_{12} a_{23} a_{31}$$
$$+ (-1)^2 a_{13} a_{21} a_{32} + (-1)^1 a_{13} a_{22} a_{31}.$$

Example 4. By definition,

$$\det \begin{bmatrix} 2 & 1 & 3 \\ 4 & 8 & 6 \\ 0 & 7 & 5 \end{bmatrix} = (-1)^0 2 \cdot 8 \cdot 5 + (-1)^1 2 \cdot 6 \cdot 7$$
$$+ (-1)^1 1 \cdot 4 \cdot 5 + (-1)^2 1 \cdot 6 \cdot 0$$
$$+ (-1)^2 3 \cdot 4 \cdot 7 + (-1)^1 3 \cdot 8 \cdot 0$$
$$= 80 - 84 - 20 + 0 + 84 - 0$$
$$= 60.$$

The symbol $\sum_{(j)}$ can be used to indicate the particular sum that was used in the definition of a determinant.

Thus,
$$|A| = \det A = \sum_{(j)} (-1)^t a_{1j_1} a_{2j_2} \ldots a_{nj_n},$$

where the index of summation (j) is understood to mean that the second subscripts take on all of the arrangements specified in the definition.

It can be verified that det A is also equal to

$$\sum_{(i)} (-1)^t a_{i_1 1} a_{i_2 2} \ldots a_{i_n n}.$$

When A is of order n, we say that det A is of **order** n.

EXERCISES

1. Evaluate by definition:

(a) $\begin{vmatrix} 2 & 3 \\ -6 & 1 \end{vmatrix};$ (b) $\det \begin{bmatrix} 0 & -2 \\ -1 & 4 \end{bmatrix};$

(c) $\begin{vmatrix} 1 & -i \\ i & 2i \end{vmatrix};$ (d) $\det \begin{bmatrix} 1 & t \\ 4 & t \end{bmatrix}.$

2. Write a second-order determinant which is equal to $cb-ad$.

3. How many terms are there in the expansion of a fourth-order determinant? (*Hint:* A knowledge of permutations will be helpful.) How many terms are there in the expansion of an nth-order determinant?

4. Write any two of the terms of the expansion of a fourth-order determinant.

5. Is t odd or even in the term $(-1)^t a_{14}a_{22}a_{31}a_{45}a_{53}$ of the expansion of a fifth-order determinant? Is t unique?

6. (a) Evaluate by definition: $\det [5]$.
   (b) Evaluate by definition: $\det [a]$.

7. If $A = [a_{ij}]_3$, find $\det A$ using $\det A = \sum_{(i)} (-1)^t a_{i_11}a_{i_22}a_{i_33}$. Verify that your result agrees with that for Example 3 on page 78.

5.2 COFACTOR EXPANSION

In order to establish a general procedure for evaluating a determinant we first make the following definitions.

Definition. *The minor of an entry a_{ij} of a square matrix A is the determinant of the submatrix of A obtained by deleting the ith row and jth column.*

Example 1. The minor of a_{32} in A_3 is

$$\det \begin{bmatrix} a_{11} & a_{12} & a_{13} \\ a_{21} & a_{22} & a_{23} \\ a_{31} & a_{32} & a_{33} \end{bmatrix} = \det \begin{bmatrix} a_{11} & a_{13} \\ a_{21} & a_{23} \end{bmatrix}.$$

Definition. *The cofactor of an entry a_{ij} of a square matrix A is the product of the minor and $(-1)^{i+j}$. This cofactor is denoted by A_{ij}.*

Example 2. For a third-order matrix A:

$$A_{31} = (-1)^{3+1} \det \begin{bmatrix} a_{12} & a_{13} \\ a_{22} & a_{23} \end{bmatrix} = (a_{12}a_{23} - a_{13}a_{22}),$$

$$A_{32} = (-1)^{3+2} \det \begin{bmatrix} a_{11} & a_{13} \\ a_{21} & a_{23} \end{bmatrix} = (-1)(a_{11}a_{23} - a_{13}a_{21}),$$

$$A_{33} = (-1)^{3+3} \det \begin{bmatrix} a_{11} & a_{12} \\ a_{21} & a_{22} \end{bmatrix} = (a_{11}a_{22} - a_{12}a_{21}).$$

Example 3. In Example 3 of Section 5.1, suppose we rearrange the products in such a way that the entries of the 3rd row appear first

$$|A| = a_{33}(a_{11}a_{22}) - a_{32}(a_{11}a_{23}) - a_{33}(a_{12}a_{21}) + a_{31}(a_{12}a_{23}) + a_{32}(a_{13}a_{21}) - a_{31}(a_{13}a_{22}).$$

Then factoring out these entries of the third row, we obtain

$$|A| = a_{31}(a_{12}a_{23} - a_{13}a_{22}) + a_{32}(a_{13}a_{21} - a_{11}a_{23}) + a_{33}(a_{11}a_{22} - a_{12}a_{21}).$$

By the preceding example this can be expressed as

$$|A| = a_{31}A_{31} + a_{32}A_{32} + a_{33}A_{33}.$$

The final expression is called the ***cofactor expansion*** about the 3rd row. A generalization of Example 3 leads us to the following theorem.

Theorem 1.

$$\det A_n = a_{i1}A_{i1} + a_{i2}A_{i2} + \cdots + a_{in}A_{in},$$

or

$$\det A_n = a_{1j}A_{1j} + a_{2j}A_{2j} + \cdots + a_{nj}A_{nj}.$$

If we write the cofactor expansion about the other two rows of A_3 as we did in Example 3, then we obtain a justification of the first part of the theorem when $n = 3$. For the general case, however, matters become considerably more involved. The student is referred to Section 5.4 for a complete proof of Theorem 1. We find that this theorem is extremely useful in the calculation of higher-order determinants as the following examples will illustrate.

Example 4.

To evaluate $|A| = \det A = \det \begin{bmatrix} 1 & 6 & 2 \\ 3 & 2 & 0 \\ 4 & 6 & 4 \end{bmatrix} = \begin{vmatrix} 1 & 6 & 2 \\ 3 & 2 & 0 \\ 4 & 6 & 4 \end{vmatrix}$, expand $|A|$ about the 2nd row. We get

$$|A| = (3)(-1)^{2+1} \begin{vmatrix} 6 & 2 \\ 6 & 4 \end{vmatrix} + 2(-1)^{2+2} \begin{vmatrix} 1 & 2 \\ 4 & 4 \end{vmatrix} + 0$$

$$= (3)(-1)(12) + (2)(+1)(-4) = -36 - 8 = -44.$$

Example 5.

Evaluate

$$|A| = \begin{vmatrix} 3 & 4 & 6 & 1 \\ 0 & 1 & 0 & 3 \\ 0 & 1 & 0 & 4 \\ 1 & -2 & 1 & 3 \end{vmatrix}.$$

If we expand $|A|$ about the 3rd column, we obtain

$$6(-1)^{1+3}\begin{vmatrix} 0 & 1 & 3 \\ 0 & 1 & 4 \\ 1 & -2 & 3 \end{vmatrix} + 0 + 0 + (1)(-1)^{4+3}\begin{vmatrix} 3 & 4 & 1 \\ 0 & 1 & 3 \\ 0 & 1 & 4 \end{vmatrix}$$

$$= 6\begin{vmatrix} 0 & 1 & 3 \\ 0 & 1 & 4 \\ 1 & -2 & 3 \end{vmatrix} - \begin{vmatrix} 3 & 4 & 1 \\ 0 & 1 & 3 \\ 0 & 1 & 4 \end{vmatrix}.$$

Both of these should be expanded about the first column.

$$|A| = 6\left\{0 + 0 + (1)(-1)^{3+1}\begin{vmatrix} 1 & 3 \\ 1 & 4 \end{vmatrix}\right\} - \left\{(3)(-1)^{1+1}\begin{vmatrix} 1 & 3 \\ 1 & 4 \end{vmatrix} + 0 + 0\right\}$$

$$= 6\{1\} - \{3\} = 3.$$

EXERCISES

1. Given $A = \begin{bmatrix} 2 & 3 & 0 \\ 3 & 2 & 2 \\ -1 & 4 & 0 \end{bmatrix}$:

   (a) Expand $|A|$ about the first column;
   (b) Expand $|A|$ about the third row;
   (c) Expand $|A|$ about the third column;
   (d) What is the cofactor of the entry in the third row and second column?
   (e) What is the minor of the entry in the first row and second column?

2. Evaluate $|A|$ by row or column expansion. (*Hint:* Make good use of the zeros.)

$$A = \begin{bmatrix} 3 & 0 & 2 & 0 \\ 3 & 0 & 0 & 2 \\ 0 & 2 & 3 & 0 \\ 2 & 0 & 1 & 3 \end{bmatrix}.$$

3. The value of the minor of the entry in the 13th row and 11th column of a 22nd-order matrix is found to be 4. What is the cofactor of this entry? Why?

4. The cofactor of a_{ij} was defined as the product of the minor of a_{ij} and $(-1)^{i+j}$. The quantity $(-1)^{i+j}$ may be found by the so-called "Checker board rule"

$$\begin{vmatrix} + & - & + & - & + & \cdots \\ - & + & - & + & - & \cdots \\ + & - & + & - & + & \cdots \\ - & + & - & + & - & \cdots \\ & & \cdots & & \end{vmatrix}.$$

The sign in the upper left-hand corner must be positive. If movement is made either horizontally or vertically (but not diagonally) the position signs alternate.

By this rule determine the signs which should precede the minors in evaluating the cofactors of a_{41}, a_{24}, and a_{34} in

$$\begin{vmatrix} a_{11} & a_{12} & a_{13} & a_{14} \\ a_{21} & a_{22} & a_{23} & a_{24} \\ a_{31} & a_{32} & a_{33} & a_{34} \\ a_{41} & a_{42} & a_{43} & a_{44} \end{vmatrix}$$

5. (a) Evaluate $\begin{vmatrix} a_{11} & a_{12} & a_{13} \\ 0 & a_{22} & a_{23} \\ 0 & 0 & a_{33} \end{vmatrix}$.

(b) Evaluate $\begin{vmatrix} a_{11} & 0 & 0 & 0 & \cdots & 0 \\ a_{21} & a_{22} & 0 & 0 & \cdots & 0 \\ a_{31} & a_{32} & a_{33} & 0 & \cdots & 0 \\ \cdot & \cdot & \cdot & \cdot & \cdots & \cdot \\ a_{n1} & a_{n2} & a_{n3} & a_{n4} & \cdots & a_{nn} \end{vmatrix}$ (all zeros above main diagonal).

(c) Evaluate $\begin{vmatrix} 2 & 0 & 0 & 0 & 0 & 0 \\ 9 & 1 & 0 & 0 & 0 & 0 \\ 7 & 6 & 2 & 0 & 0 & 0 \\ 4 & 9 & 6 & 2 & 0 & 0 \\ 3 & 8 & 9 & 6 & 2 & 0 \\ 9 & 7 & 4 & 3 & 0 & 1 \end{vmatrix}$ with a minimum of work.

6. (a) Find the minor of each entry of $A = [a_{ij}]_2$.
   (b) Find the cofactor of each entry of $A = [a_{ij}]_2$.
   (c) Find the cofactors of a_{32} and a_{22} of A_3.

7. Follow the pattern of Example 3, page 80, to show that det A, where $A = [a_{ij}]_3$, equals $a_{12}A_{12} + a_{22}A_{22} + a_{32}A_{32}$.

8.
(a) Evaluate $\begin{vmatrix} 1 & -1 & 2 \\ 4 & 0 & 5 \\ -3 & -3 & 3 \end{vmatrix}$.

(b) Evaluate $\begin{vmatrix} 0 & 2 & 5 & 1 \\ 1 & -1 & 0 & 1 \\ 2 & 0 & 2 & -1 \\ 3 & 2 & 1 & 0 \end{vmatrix}$.

(c) Verify: $\begin{vmatrix} 0 & -1 & 1 & 1 \\ 0 & 2 & -1 & -1 \\ 2 & -3 & 2 & 4 \\ 2 & -2 & 1 & 3 \end{vmatrix} = 0$.

(d) Verify: $\begin{vmatrix} 1 & 0 & 2 & -1 \\ 3 & -2 & 6 & 4 \\ 5 & 4 & 3 & 0 \\ 2 & 2 & -5 & 6 \end{vmatrix} = -132$.

5.3 PROPERTIES OF DETERMINANTS

For future reference some of the properties of determinants will now be stated. Many of these will prove to be very useful in later portions of this book. All matrices mentioned in this section must be considered square. Also, the word "line" is used to signify either row or column. Proofs of the following theorems are given in the next section.

Theorem 2. *If a matrix B is formed from a matrix A by the interchange of two parallel lines (rows or columns), then $|A| = -|B|$.*

Example 1.

Let $A = \begin{bmatrix} 2 & 1 & 3 \\ 1 & 1 & 0 \\ 4 & 1 & 3 \end{bmatrix}$ and let $B = \begin{bmatrix} 3 & 1 & 2 \\ 0 & 1 & 1 \\ 3 & 1 & 4 \end{bmatrix}$ where the first and third columns have been interchanged. By Theorem 2, $|A| = -|B|$.

Theorem 3. *The determinants of a matrix and its transpose are equal; that is, $|A| = |A^T|$.*

Example 2.

Let $A = \begin{bmatrix} 1 & 2 & 3 \\ 0 & 2 & 1 \\ 0 & 0 & 4 \end{bmatrix}$ and hence $A^T = \begin{bmatrix} 1 & 0 & 0 \\ 2 & 2 & 0 \\ 3 & 1 & 4 \end{bmatrix}$.

By Theorem 3, $|A| = |A^T|$.

Theorem 4. *If all of the entries of any line of A are zero, then $|A| = 0$.*

Example 3. Because all of the entries in the third row are zero, we know that

$$|A| = \begin{vmatrix} 0 & 1 & 4 \\ 2 & 1 & 6 \\ 0 & 0 & 0 \end{vmatrix} = 0, \text{ by Theorem 4.}$$

Theorem 5. *The expressions*

$$c_1 A_{i1} + c_2 A_{i2} + \cdots + c_n A_{in},$$

and

$$c_1 A_{1j} + c_2 A_{2j} + \cdots + c_n A_{nj},$$

are equal to the determinants of matrices which are the same as A except that the entries of the ith row and the jth column, respectively, have been replaced by the scalars $c_1, c_2, \ldots, c_n$.

Example 4. Expanding $|A|$ about the first column we obtain

$$\begin{vmatrix} 2 & 6 & 1 \\ 3 & 3 & 2 \\ 4 & 4 & 1 \end{vmatrix} = 2 \begin{vmatrix} 3 & 2 \\ 4 & 1 \end{vmatrix} - 3 \begin{vmatrix} 6 & 1 \\ 4 & 1 \end{vmatrix} + 4 \begin{vmatrix} 6 & 1 \\ 3 & 2 \end{vmatrix}.$$

However, if the entries of the first column are replaced by the scalars c_1, c_2, c_3, there results

$$\begin{vmatrix} c_1 & 6 & 1 \\ c_2 & 3 & 2 \\ c_3 & 4 & 1 \end{vmatrix} = c_1 \begin{vmatrix} 3 & 2 \\ 4 & 1 \end{vmatrix} - c_2 \begin{vmatrix} 6 & 1 \\ 4 & 1 \end{vmatrix} + c_3 \begin{vmatrix} 6 & 1 \\ 3 & 2 \end{vmatrix}.$$

Theorem 6. *The determinant of a matrix with two identical parallel lines is zero.*

Example 5. Because the first two columns are identical, Theorem 6 assures us that $\begin{vmatrix} 2 & 2 & 1 \\ 3 & 3 & 1 \\ 4 & 4 & 0 \end{vmatrix} = 0.$

Theorem 7. *The sum of the products of the entries of one line of A by the cofactors of the corresponding entries of a different parallel line of A is zero; that is,*

$$a_{i1}A_{k1} + a_{i2}A_{k2} + \cdots + a_{in}A_{kn} = 0, \qquad if\ i \neq k,$$

$$a_{1j}A_{1k} + a_{2j}A_{2k} + \cdots + a_{nj}A_{nk} = 0, \qquad if\ j \neq k.$$

Example 6. If $|A|$ is expanded about the first column,

$$\begin{vmatrix} 2 & 4 & 1 \\ 3 & 4 & 6 \\ 4 & 0 & 1 \end{vmatrix} = 2 \begin{vmatrix} 4 & 6 \\ 0 & 1 \end{vmatrix} - 3 \begin{vmatrix} 4 & 1 \\ 0 & 1 \end{vmatrix} + 4 \begin{vmatrix} 4 & 1 \\ 4 & 6 \end{vmatrix}.$$

However, if we replace the elements of the first column in the expansion by the elements of any other column, say the second, the value is zero; that is, ·

$$4 \begin{vmatrix} 4 & 6 \\ 0 & 1 \end{vmatrix} - 4 \begin{vmatrix} 4 & 1 \\ 0 & 1 \end{vmatrix} + 0 \begin{vmatrix} 4 & 1 \\ 4 & 6 \end{vmatrix} = 0.$$

Theorem 8. *The value of a determinant, $|A|$, is multiplied by a scalar c when every entry of a row (or column) of A is multiplied by c.*

Notice that this is different from the multiplication of a matrix by a scalar.

Example 7.

$$(a)\ c|B| = c \begin{vmatrix} b_{11} & b_{12} & b_{13} \\ b_{21} & b_{22} & b_{23} \\ b_{31} & b_{32} & b_{33} \end{vmatrix} = \begin{vmatrix} cb_{11} & cb_{12} & cb_{13} \\ b_{21} & b_{22} & b_{23} \\ b_{31} & b_{32} & b_{33} \end{vmatrix} = \begin{vmatrix} b_{11} & cb_{12} & b_{13} \\ b_{21} & cb_{22} & b_{23} \\ b_{31} & cb_{32} & b_{33} \end{vmatrix}.$$

$$(b)\ If\ |A| = \begin{vmatrix} 2 & 1 \\ 2 & 3 \end{vmatrix}, \quad then\ 2|A| = \begin{vmatrix} 2 & 1 \\ 4 & 6 \end{vmatrix}.$$

Theorem 9. *The determinant of the product of two square matrices of the same order is equal to the product of the determinants of the two matrices; that is,* $|AB| = |A| \, |B|$.

Example 8. Let $A = \begin{bmatrix} 3 & 0 \\ 2 & 1 \end{bmatrix}$ and $B = \begin{bmatrix} 1 & 2 \\ 0 & 1 \end{bmatrix}$. Then $AB = \begin{bmatrix} 3 & 6 \\ 2 & 5 \end{bmatrix}$, and

by Theorem 9, $|AB| = |A| \, |B| = 3 \cdot 1 = 3$.

Theorem 10. *If a matrix B is obtained from a matrix A by adding to each entry of a line of A a constant multiple of the corresponding entry of a parallel line, then* $|B| = |A|$.

Example 9.

Let
$$A = \begin{bmatrix} 1 & 0 & 1 \\ 0 & 4 & 6 \\ -2 & 2 & 1 \end{bmatrix}.$$

If we multiply the first row of A by 2 and add to the third row (abbreviated $2R_1 + R_3$), there results a matrix whose determinant is equal to det A. That is,

$$\begin{vmatrix} 1 & 0 & 1 \\ 0 & 4 & 6 \\ -2 & 2 & 1 \end{vmatrix} \underset{2R_1+R_3}{=} \begin{vmatrix} 1 & 0 & 1 \\ 0 & 4 & 6 \\ 0 & 2 & 3 \end{vmatrix}.$$

Notice that the only row that changed was the third row — the recipient of the operation. The student should also observe that an operation such as $2R_1 + 3R_3$ is not permitted by Theorem 10; the coefficient of the recipient line must be 1.

Theorem 10 will prove to be of great help in the evaluation of higher-order determinants. For instance, in the example above, the original third-order determinant has been reduced essentially to a constant times a second-order determinant. (See Theorem 1.)

Example 10.

$$\text{Evaluate} \quad \begin{vmatrix} 198 & 0 & 99 & 99 \\ 1 & 1 & -2 & 0 \\ 1 & 2 & 1 & 2 \\ 1 & -3 & 6 & 1 \end{vmatrix}.$$

By Theorem 8 we have

$$99 \begin{vmatrix} 2 & 0 & 1 & 1 \\ 1 & 1 & -2 & 0 \\ 1 & 2 & 1 & 2 \\ 1 & -3 & 6 & 1 \end{vmatrix} \underset{-2R_2+R_3}{=} 99 \begin{vmatrix} 2 & 0 & 1 & 1 \\ 1 & 1 & -2 & 0 \\ -1 & 0 & 5 & 2 \\ 1 & -3 & 6 & 1 \end{vmatrix} \underset{3R_2+R_4}{=} 99 \begin{vmatrix} 2 & 0 & 1 & 1 \\ 1 & 1 & -2 & 0 \\ -1 & 0 & 5 & 2 \\ 4 & 0 & 0 & 1 \end{vmatrix}$$

$$\underset{\text{(Expand on } C_2)}{=} (99)(-1)^{2+2}(1)\begin{vmatrix} 2 & 1 & 1 \\ -1 & 5 & 2 \\ 4 & 0 & 1 \end{vmatrix} \underset{-4C_3+C_1}{=} (99)\begin{vmatrix} -2 & 1 & 1 \\ -9 & 5 & 2 \\ 0 & 0 & 1 \end{vmatrix}$$

$$\underset{\text{(Expand on } R_3)}{=} 99(-1)^{3+3}(1)\begin{vmatrix} -2 & 1 \\ -9 & 5 \end{vmatrix} = -99.$$

EXERCISES

1. Tell whether the following statements are true or false. Give your reasons. Do *not* expand.

(a) $\begin{vmatrix} 1 & 2 & 3 & 4 \\ 5 & 6 & 7 & 8 \\ 8 & 7 & 6 & 5 \\ 4 & 3 & 2 & 1 \end{vmatrix} = \begin{vmatrix} 2 & 1 & 4 & 3 \\ 6 & 5 & 8 & 7 \\ 7 & 8 & 5 & 6 \\ 3 & 4 & 1 & 2 \end{vmatrix}$;

(b) $\begin{vmatrix} 1 & 3 & -4 \\ 2 & 8 & 3 \\ 0 & -2 & -5 \end{vmatrix} = \begin{vmatrix} 1 & 2 & 0 \\ 3 & 8 & -2 \\ -4 & 3 & -5 \end{vmatrix}$;

(c) $\begin{vmatrix} 2x & 3x & 4x \\ 5x & 6x & 7x \\ 8x & 9x & 9x \end{vmatrix} = x\begin{vmatrix} 2 & 3 & 4 \\ 5 & 6 & 7 \\ 8 & 9 & 9 \end{vmatrix}$, if $x \neq 0$ and $x \neq 1$.

2. Without expanding, by making use of two theorems,

evaluate $\begin{vmatrix} 2 & 4 & 6 & 4 \\ 0 & 4 & 6 & 9 \\ 2 & 1 & 4 & 0 \\ 1 & 2 & 3 & 2 \end{vmatrix}$.

3. Given that det $A = 8$, and that B is a matrix the same as A except that the first and fourth rows have been interchanged. What is the value of det B? Justify your answer.

4. Does 2 det A = det $(2\,A)$? Why? (Assume that the order of A is greater than one.)

5. If det $[a_{i\,j}]_{(3,3)} = 4$, find det $3[a_{i\,j}]_{(3,3)}$. Give reasons for your answer.

6. Show that $\begin{vmatrix} x+y & -z(x+y) \\ z+x & y(z+x) \end{vmatrix} = (x+y)(z+x)(y+z)$ by using Theorem 8.

7. Without expanding show that

$$\begin{vmatrix} x^2 - y^2 & x+y & x \\ x - y & 1 & 1 \\ x - y & 1 & y \end{vmatrix} = 0.$$

Give reasons for your steps.

8. Change the form but not the value of

$$|A| = \begin{vmatrix} -1 & 1 & 2 & 0 \\ -2 & 1 & 3 & 1 \\ 1 & 0 & 2 & -1 \\ 2 & 1 & -1 & 2 \end{vmatrix}$$

so that zeros occur everywhere in the first column except in the third row.   (*Hint:* Use Theorem 10.)

9. Evaluate $|A|$ in the previous problem.

10. (*a*) What is the difference between the determinant $\begin{vmatrix} 2 & 3 & 4 \\ 5 & 6 & 7 \\ 8 & 9 & 1 \end{vmatrix}$ and the determi-

nant whose expansion is

$$y \begin{vmatrix} 2 & 4 \\ 8 & 1 \end{vmatrix} -x \begin{vmatrix} 3 & 4 \\ 9 & 1 \end{vmatrix} -z \begin{vmatrix} 2 & 3 \\ 8 & 9 \end{vmatrix} ?$$

(*b*) Verify that $5 \begin{vmatrix} 6 & 7 \\ 9 & 1 \end{vmatrix} -6 \begin{vmatrix} 5 & 7 \\ 8 & 1 \end{vmatrix} +7 \begin{vmatrix} 5 & 6 \\ 8 & 9 \end{vmatrix} = 0$.   Is there any connec-

tion between this result and Theorem 7?

11. Verify Theorem 9 for each of the following:

(*a*) $A = \begin{bmatrix} 3 & 5 \\ 2 & -8 \end{bmatrix}$, $B = \begin{bmatrix} -1 & -3 \\ -4 & 6 \end{bmatrix}$;

(*b*) $A = \begin{bmatrix} 0 & 1 & 1 \\ -2 & 2 & 3 \\ 1 & 0 & -1 \end{bmatrix}$, $B = \begin{bmatrix} 1 & 3 & 1 \\ 0 & 0 & 2 \\ -4 & -5 & -6 \end{bmatrix}$.

12. Let $A = [a_{ij}]_n$, $B = [b_{ij}]_n$, and $C = [c_{ij}]_n$. Using Theorem 9, prove that $|ABC| = |A| |B| |C|$.

13. Find an example of second-order matrices A and B such that

$$\det (A + B) = \det A + \det B.$$

14. Let $A = [a_{ij}]_3$. Compare $a_{11}A_{11} + a_{12}A_{12} + a_{13}A_{13}$ with $a_{21}A_{11} + a_{22}A_{12} + a_{23}A_{13}$. (*Hint:* Make use of theorems.)

15. Evaluate each determinant making use of Theorem 10:

(*a*) $\begin{vmatrix} 3 & -1 & 3 \\ 2 & 5 & -3 \\ 5 & 4 & -1 \end{vmatrix}$;

(*b*) $\begin{vmatrix} 1 & 1 & 1 & 1 \\ 1 & 0 & -1 & 0 \\ 0 & 1 & 1 & -1 \\ 2 & 0 & -1 & -3 \end{vmatrix}$;

(c) $\begin{vmatrix} 2 & -2 & 1 & 3 \\ 0 & 2 & -1 & -1 \\ 2 & -3 & 2 & 4 \\ 0 & -1 & 1 & 1 \end{vmatrix}$;

(d) det $\begin{bmatrix} 2 & 1 & 5 & 2 \\ 2 & 2 & 3 & 0 \\ 2 & 0 & 2 & 1 \\ 3 & 2 & 1 & 0 \end{bmatrix}$;

(e) det $\begin{bmatrix} 3 & -3 & 0 & 0 \\ 3 & 2 & 1 & 2 \\ 0 & 2 & 0 & 3 \\ -3 & 0 & -2 & 0 \end{bmatrix}$.

5.4 PROOFS OF DETERMINANT THEOREMS 1–10

Theorem 2 will be proved first because it is needed in the proof of Theorem 1.

Theorem 2. *If a matrix B is formed from a matrix A by the interchange of two parallel lines (rows or columns), then* $|A| = -|B|$.

Proof. Assume that two rows are interchanged, say the kth and pth rows.

STATEMENT	REASON
(1) $|A| = \sum_{(j)} (-1)^{t_1}\, a_{1j_1} \dots a_{kj_k} \dots a_{pj_p} \dots a_{nj_n}.$	(1) By definition of a determinant.
(2) $|B| = \sum_{(j)} (-1)^{t_2}\, a_{1j_1} \dots a_{pj_p} \dots a_{kj_k} \dots a_{nj_n}.$	(2) Given that the kth and pth rows are interchanged.
(3) Except for the exponents t_1 and t_2, the right sides of statements 1 and 2 are the same.	(3) Scalar multiplication is associative and commutative.
(4) $t_2 = t_1 + 1$ and hence $(-1)^{t_2} = -(-1)^{t_1}.$	(4) Only one interchange is necessary to obtain $j_1, \dots, j_p, \dots, j_k, \dots, j_n$ from $j_1, \dots, j_k, \dots, j_p, \dots, j_n.$
(5) $|B| = -|A|.$	(5) By statements 3 and 4.

A similar proof can be made if two columns are interchanged.

Theorem 1.

$$\det A_n = a_{i1}A_{i1} + a_{i2}A_{i2} + \cdots + a_{in}A_{in},$$

or

$$\det A_n = a_{1j}A_{1j} + a_{2j}A_{2j} + \cdots + a_{nj}A_{nj}.$$

Proof of the first part. By definition we know that each term of the expansion of $|A|$ contains precisely one factor from row i. If all of the terms of the expansion of $|A|$ that contain the entry a_{ij} are collected, and if this is done for each j (as we did in Section 5.2 for the justification of this theorem when $n = 3$), then

$$|A| = a_{i1}p_{i1} + a_{i2}p_{i2} + \cdots + a_{in}p_{in}$$

results, where p_{ij} represents what is left after a_{ij} has been factored out. It should be evident that we must now show that

$$p_{ij} = A_{ij} = (-1)^{i+j}M_{ij}$$

where M_{ij} is the minor of a_{ij}. This can be accomplished in three steps.

FIRST: We show that $a_{11}p_{11} = a_{11}M_{11}$. From the definition of a determinant, it is apparent that the corresponding terms of these two quantities are numerically the same. Moreover the signs of the terms of $a_{11}p_{11}$ are the same as the signs of the corresponding terms of $a_{11}M_{11}$ because the number of interchanges required to reduce the column subscripts to natural order in the terms of the expansion of M_{11} is not changed by premultiplying each term by a_{11}.

SECOND: Consider any arbitrary entry $a_{ij} = m$. This entry can be moved to the original position of a_{11} by performing $i - 1$ interchanges of adjacent rows and $j - 1$ interchanges of adjacent columns in such a way that the minor of the entry m remains unchanged. By Theorem 2 the determinant of this new matrix B is

$$|B| = (-1)^{i-1+j-1}|A| = (-1)^{i+j}|A|.$$

THIRD: By the first part of our proof (because m is in the upper left-hand corner), the sum of all the terms involving m in the expansion of $|B|$ is equal to m times its minor in B. But in the second part of our proof, the minor of m in B is the same as the minor of m in A, that is, M_{ij}. Hence, the sum of all the terms involving m in the expansion of $|A|$ is equal to $(-1)^{i+j}mM_{ij}$, that is,

$$a_{ij}p_{ij} = (-1)^{i+j}a_{ij}M_{ij},$$

or

$$p_{ij} = A_{ij} = (-1)^{i+j}M_{ij}$$

as we set out to prove.

Theorem 3. *The determinants of a matrix and its transpose are equal; that is $|A| = |A^T|$.*

Proof. First, we will verify that $|A| = \sum_{(i)} (-1)^t a_{i_1 1} \ldots a_{i_n n}$. Recall that $|A|$ was defined as $\sum_{(j)} (-1)^t a_{1 j_1} \ldots a_{n j_n}$. Because both of these expansions are the sum of terms consisting of exactly one factor from each row and each column, there is a one-to-one correspondence between the terms of the two expansions. These corresponding terms can differ only by a sign. However, when we interchange the factors $a_{1j_1} \ldots a_{nj_n}$ to put the column subscripts in natural order, we are simultaneously interchanging the row subscripts away from natural order. Thus the sign of the term $a_{1j_1} \ldots a_{nj_n}$ is the same as the sign of the corresponding term $a_{i_1 1} \ldots a_{i_n n}$ because the interchanges necessary to reduce $j_1, \ldots, j_n$ to natural order are the same interchanges, in reverse order, necessary to bring $i_1, \ldots, i_n$ back to natural order.

Theorem 3 now follows immediately because by definition,

$$|A| = \sum_{(j)} (-1)^t a_{1j_1} \ldots a_{nj_n} \quad \text{and} \quad |A^T| = \sum_{(i)} (-1)^t a_{i_1 1} \ldots a_{i_n n}; \quad \text{and} \quad \text{we}$$

have just shown that these are equal.

Theorem 4. *If all of the entries of any line of A are zero, then $|A| = 0$.*

Proof. Expansion about the particular line which consists of all zeros yields 0. (Theorem 1)

The proof of Theorem 5 is left for the student with the hint to make use of Theorem 1. (Exercise 1, page 91)

Theorem 6. *The determinant of a matrix with two identical parallel lines is zero.*

Proof. Let the kth and pth lines be identical in a matrix A.

STATEMENT	REASON
(1) $|A| = |B|$, where B is the matrix obtained by interchanging the kth and pth lines of A.	(1) $B = A$.
(2) $|B| = -|A|$.	(2) By Theorem 2.
(3) $|A| = -|A|$.	(3) Substitute (1) into (2).
(4) $2|A| = 0,$ $|A| = 0.$	(4) By rules of scalar algebra.

A proof of Theorem 7 is left for the student with the hint to use Theorem 5 and then Theorem 6. (Exercise 2, page 91)

Theorem 8 is to be proved by the student in Exercise 3 on page 91.

The proof of Theorem 9 is quite cumbersome unless one has studied elementary matrices. This topic will be considered in Chapter 7; then the student is referred to *Theory of Matrices* by Perlis* for a proof of Theorem 9.

Theorem 10. *If a matrix B is obtained from a matrix A by adding to each entry of a line of A a constant multiple of the corresponding entry of a parallel line, then* $|B| = |A|$.

Proof.

Let
$$A = \begin{bmatrix} a_{11} & \cdots & a_{1k} & \cdots & a_{1p} & \cdots & a_{1n} \\ & & & \cdot & \cdot & \cdot & \\ a_{n1} & \cdots & a_{nk} & \cdots & a_{np} & \cdots & a_{nn} \end{bmatrix}.$$

Construct
$$B = \begin{bmatrix} a_{11} & \cdots & a_{1k} & \cdots & (a_{1p} + ca_{1k}) & \cdots & a_{1n} \\ & & & \cdot & \cdot & \cdot & \\ a_{n1} & \cdots & a_{nk} & \cdots & (a_{np} + ca_{nk}) & \cdots & a_{nn} \end{bmatrix}.$$

If we expand $|B|$ about the pth column, there results

$$|B| = (a_{1p} + ca_{1k})A_{1p} + \cdots + (a_{np} + ca_{nk})A_{np}$$
$$= (a_{1p}A_{1p} + \cdots + a_{np}A_{np}) + c(a_{1k}A_{1p} + \cdots + a_{nk}A_{np})$$
$$= \det A + 0 \qquad \text{by Theorem 1 and Theorem 7.}$$

A similar proof could be made if a constant multiple of each entry of some *row* were added to the corresponding entry of another *row*.

EXERCISES

1. Prove Theorem 5. 2. Prove Theorem 7.

3. Prove Theorem 8.

4. Prove the following theorem: If any two parallel lines of a matrix A are proportional, then $\det A = 0$.

5. Prove that the converse of the theorem in the preceding exercise is *not* true.

6. Prove that
$$\begin{vmatrix} a & b & c \\ d & e & f \\ g+h & i+j & k+l \end{vmatrix} = \begin{vmatrix} a & b & c \\ d & e & f \\ g & i & k \end{vmatrix} + \begin{vmatrix} a & b & c \\ d & e & f \\ h & j & l \end{vmatrix}.$$

7. Rewrite the proof of Theorem 3 in statement-reason form.

5.5 APPLICATIONS

Determinants have many applications in both theoretical and applied mathematics. A few of the places where they have proved useful are in the

* Sam Perlis, *Theory of Matrices* (Reading, Massachusetts, Addison-Wesley Publishing Co., 1952), pp. 79–80.

study of: tensor algebra, modern geometry, vector analysis, statistics, and matrix theory.

Determinants are also useful in the study of systems of linear equations. This will be pursued further in three of the next four chapters of this book, but we will consider one use in detail at this time. One way (and probably *not* the best) to solve n linear equations in n unknowns is called Cramer's Rule (Swiss Mathematician G. Cramer, 1704–1752). Consider the system

$$\begin{cases} a_{11}x_1 + a_{12}x_2 + \cdots + a_{1n}x_n = b_1, \\ \quad \cdot \quad \cdot \quad \cdot \\ a_{n1}x_1 + a_{n2}x_2 + \cdots + a_{nn}x_n = b_n, \end{cases}$$

or
$$AX = B.$$

Clearly A is a square matrix. Let (^iA) denote the matrix obtained from A by replacing the jth column of A by the vector B.

Theorem 11 (*Cramer's Rule*). *If* $\det A \neq 0$, *then the system* $AX = B$ *has exactly one solution; this solution is*

$$x_j = \frac{\det (^iA)}{\det A}, \qquad j = 1, 2, \ldots, n.$$

The proof of this theorem will be given in the next chapter after adjoint matrices have been studied.

Example 1. Solve by Cramer's rule

$$\begin{cases} 2x_1 + x_2 + x_3 = 0, \\ x_1 - x_2 + 5x_3 = 0, \\ x_2 - x_3 = 4. \end{cases}$$

$$x_1 = \frac{\begin{vmatrix} 0 & 1 & 1 \\ 0 & -1 & 5 \\ 4 & 1 & -1 \end{vmatrix}}{\begin{vmatrix} 2 & 1 & 1 \\ 1 & -1 & 5 \\ 0 & 1 & -1 \end{vmatrix}} = \frac{4\begin{vmatrix} 1 & 1 \\ -1 & 5 \end{vmatrix}}{-6} = \frac{24}{-6} = -4.$$

$$x_2 = \frac{\begin{vmatrix} 2 & 0 & 1 \\ 1 & 0 & 5 \\ 0 & 4 & -1 \end{vmatrix}}{\det A} = \frac{-4\begin{vmatrix} 2 & 1 \\ 1 & 5 \end{vmatrix}}{-6} = \frac{-36}{-6} = 6.$$

$$x_3 = \frac{\begin{vmatrix} 2 & 1 & 0 \\ 1 & -1 & 0 \\ 0 & 1 & 4 \end{vmatrix}}{\det A} = \frac{4\begin{vmatrix} 2 & 1 \\ 1 & -1 \end{vmatrix}}{-6} = \frac{-12}{-6} = 2.$$

EXERCISES

1. In each of the following systems find y by Cramer's rule and then find the other unknowns by substitution.

(a) $\begin{cases} x + y = 5, \\ 2x - y = 7. \end{cases}$

(b) $\begin{cases} x + y + z = 0, \\ - y + 2z = 4, \\ 2x + 2y = 1. \end{cases}$

(c) $\begin{cases} x - 2y + z + t = 3, \\ x + y = 0, \\ 2x - y - t = 0, \\ x + y + z + t = 0. \end{cases}$

2. In each of the following systems, find each unknown by Cramer's rule.

(a) $\begin{cases} 2x - 2y = 5, \\ x - 4y = 7. \end{cases}$

(b) $\begin{cases} x + y + z = 2, \\ 2x + 3y + 4z = 3, \\ x - 2y - z = 1. \end{cases}$

(c) $\begin{cases} x + y + z - t = 0, \\ 2x + 3y - t = 0, \\ 3x + y + 4z - 3t = 0, \\ x - y + z = 1. \end{cases}$

(d) $\begin{cases} 3x + y + 3z + 6w = 1, \\ 2x + 3y + 2z - w = 9, \\ x - y - z + 3w = -9, \\ x + 2y + z + 2w = 2. \end{cases}$

5.6 RANK OF A MATRIX

Determinants are also used to define the **rank** of a matrix. (The matrix does not have to be square.) The usefulness of rank will be explained in Chapter 8.

Definition. *The rank of a matrix is the order of the largest square submatrix whose determinant is not zero. When all of the entries are zero the rank is zero.*

Example 1.

Given

$$A = \begin{bmatrix} 2 & -1 & 1 \\ 1 & 4 & 5 \\ 3 & 2 & 5 \end{bmatrix}.$$

The rank is *not* 3 because det $A = 0$. The rank is 2 because the determinant of at least one of the 2 by 2 submatrices is not zero.

Example 2.

Given

$$A = \begin{bmatrix} 2 & 1 & 3 & 0 \\ 0 & 0 & 0 & 2 \\ 1 & 0 & 0 & 0 \end{bmatrix}.$$

Since there are no submatrices of order 4, the rank is at most 3. To find whether it is 3, we must start calculating the determinants of the four 3 by 3 submatrices. As soon as we find one (if we do) whose determinant is *not* zero, we can stop with assurance that the rank is 3.

$$\det \begin{bmatrix} 2 & 1 & 3 & 0 \\ 0 & 0 & 0 & 2 \\ 1 & 0 & 0 & 0 \end{bmatrix} = 2 \neq 0, \qquad \therefore \text{ rank} = 3.$$

One of the other third-order submatrices has a nonzero determinant and it could also have been used to reach the same conclusion.

If a matrix has many rows and columns it is difficult to find its rank directly from the definition. A better method will be developed in Chapter 7.

EXERCISES

1. Are the following statements true or false? Give your reasons.

(a) If $[a_{ij}]_{(4, 5)}$ has rank 3, then the determinant of every fourth-order submatrix is 0; and, conversely, if every such fourth-order determinant is zero, the rank of the matrix is 3.
(b) The rank of A is equal to the rank of A^T.
(c) If A_3 is skew-symmetric, its rank is less than 3.

2. What is the largest possible rank of an m by n matrix under the assumption that $m > n$?

3. Find the ranks of:

(a) $\begin{bmatrix} 1 & 2 & -1 \\ 4 & 1 & 5 \\ 3 & -1 & 6 \end{bmatrix}$;
(b) $\begin{bmatrix} 3 & 1 & 4 & 4 \\ 2 & 1 & 3 & 1 \\ 0 & 2 & 2 & 0 \end{bmatrix}$;

(c) $\begin{bmatrix} 2 & 4 \\ -4 & -8 \\ 1 & 2 \end{bmatrix}$;
(d) $\begin{bmatrix} 0 & 0 & 0 \\ 0 & 0 & 0 \end{bmatrix}$;
(e) $\begin{bmatrix} 0 & 0 & 2 \\ 0 & 0 & 0 \end{bmatrix}$.

4. Under what condition is the rank of the following matrix 3? Is it possible for the rank to be 1? Why?

$$\begin{bmatrix} 2 & 4 & 2 \\ 2 & 1 & 2 \\ 1 & 0 & x \end{bmatrix}.$$

5. Find the ranks of the augmented matrix and the coefficient matrix of the system

$$\begin{cases} x + y = 6, \\ x + 3y = 4, \\ 2x - y = 2. \end{cases}$$

6. Make up an example of a 4 by 4 matrix which has rank 2.

7. If the second column of $A = [a_{ij}]_{(4,3)}$ consists entirely of zeros, what can be said about the rank of A?

8. Let $A = [a_{ij}]_{(4,4)}$.
(a) If det $A = 0$, what can be said about the rank of A?
(b) If det $A \neq 0$, what can be said about the rank of A?

9. In 3-dimensional space, show that the cubic space curve with parametric equations $x = t$, $y = t^2$, and $z = t^3$ is the locus of points (x, y, z) where the matrix

$$\begin{bmatrix} x & y & z \\ 1 & x & y \end{bmatrix}$$ has rank 1.

10. (a) Let (x_1, y_1), $(4, 5)$, and $(7, 6)$ be three fixed points in a plane. Show that these three points are collinear if and only if the rank of the matrix $\begin{bmatrix} x_1 & y_1 & 1 \\ 4 & 5 & 1 \\ 7 & 6 & 1 \end{bmatrix}$ is less than 3.
(b) Repeat part (a) for the points (x_1, y_1), (x_2, y_2), (x_3, y_3), and the matrix

$$\begin{bmatrix} x_1 & y_1 & 1 \\ x_2 & y_2 & 1 \\ x_3 & y_3 & 1 \end{bmatrix}.$$

NEW VOCABULARY

determinant	5.1	minor	5.2
interchange	5.1	cofactor	5.2
expansion of a		cofactor expansion	5.2
determinant	5.1	Cramer's rule	5.5
order of a determinant	5.1	rank	5.6

The Inverse Matrix

6.1 INTRODUCTION

The student should review Section 3.5 where the inverse of an element with respect to a given binary operation was defined. It was stated that the inverse of an element for the given operation is another element (in one instance the same) such that when the two are combined by the operation, the identity element results. For example, $\frac{1}{6}$ is the multiplicative inverse of 6 because $6 \cdot \frac{1}{6} = \frac{1}{6} \cdot 6 = 1$. Our purpose in this chapter is to discuss the multiplicative inverse when the elements of a system are square matrices of a given order. Throughout the rest of this book, by inverse we will mean the multiplicative inverse. In addition to the theoretical importance of the inverse matrix, there is practical application in methods of solution of certain types of simultaneous linear equations.

Definition. *An inverse, A^{-1}, of a given square matrix A, if it exists, is a square matrix such that*

$$AA^{-1} = A^{-1}A = I,$$

where I is the identity matrix whose order is the same as that of A.

First we must be concerned with two fundamental questions: (1) When will an inverse of a matrix exist? (2) If it does exist, how can we find it? These questions will be answered by Theorem 1 of Section 6.3.

6.2 THE COFACTOR MATRIX AND ADJOINT MATRIX

The following definitions will be needed in the development of Theorem 1.

Definition. *A square matrix A is said to be **singular** if* det $A = 0$ *and* **nonsingular** *if* det $A \neq 0$.

Definition. *Let* $A = [a_{ij}]_n$ *be a square matrix where* $n \geq 2$. *The* **cofactor matrix** *of A, designated by* cof A, *is the matrix of order n whose entry in row i and column j is* A_{ij}, *the cofactor of* a_{ij} *in A.*

Example 1.

Let
$$A = \begin{bmatrix} 2 & 1 & 0 \\ 0 & 2 & 1 \\ 3 & 0 & 2 \end{bmatrix}.$$

$$\text{cof } A = \begin{bmatrix} +\begin{vmatrix} 2 & 1 \\ 0 & 2 \end{vmatrix} & -\begin{vmatrix} 0 & 1 \\ 3 & 2 \end{vmatrix} & +\begin{vmatrix} 0 & 2 \\ 3 & 0 \end{vmatrix} \\ -\begin{vmatrix} 1 & 0 \\ 0 & 2 \end{vmatrix} & +\begin{vmatrix} 2 & 0 \\ 3 & 2 \end{vmatrix} & -\begin{vmatrix} 2 & 1 \\ 3 & 0 \end{vmatrix} \\ +\begin{vmatrix} 1 & 0 \\ 2 & 1 \end{vmatrix} & -\begin{vmatrix} 2 & 0 \\ 0 & 1 \end{vmatrix} & +\begin{vmatrix} 2 & 1 \\ 0 & 2 \end{vmatrix} \end{bmatrix} = \begin{bmatrix} 4 & 3 & -6 \\ -2 & 4 & 3 \\ 1 & -2 & 4 \end{bmatrix}.$$

Also since det $A = 11 \neq 0$ we can say that A is nonsingular.

Definition. *The **adjoint matrix**, designated* adj A, *of a square matrix A is the transpose of* cof A.

Example 2. Using A of the previous example, we have

$$\text{adj } A = (\text{cof } A)^T = \begin{bmatrix} 4 & 3 & -6 \\ -2 & 4 & 3 \\ 1 & -2 & 4 \end{bmatrix}^T = \begin{bmatrix} 4 & -2 & 1 \\ 3 & 4 & -2 \\ -6 & 3 & 4 \end{bmatrix}.$$

EXERCISES

1. Calculate the adjoint matrices for the following matrices:

$$A = \begin{bmatrix} 2 & 3 \\ -4 & 1 \end{bmatrix}; \quad B = \begin{bmatrix} 0 & 1 & -1 \\ 0 & -2 & 2 \\ -1 & -1 & 0 \end{bmatrix}; \quad C = \begin{bmatrix} 1 & 3 & 0 \\ 2 & 1 & 0 \\ 0 & 1 & -1 \end{bmatrix};$$

$$D = \begin{bmatrix} 1 & 0 & 0 & 1 \\ 0 & 0 & 1 & 0 \\ 0 & 2 & 0 & 0 \\ 0 & 0 & 0 & 2 \end{bmatrix}.$$

2. Determine whether the matrices A, B, C, and D in the problem above are non-singular or singular.

3. Prove that if A and B are nonsingular of order n, then AB is nonsingular. (A similar statement could be made for the product of three or more nonsingular matrices of the same order.)

4. Illustrate Exercise 3 with two 2 by 2 matrices.

5. (a) What can be said about the rank of a nonsingular matrix of order 3?
(b) What can be said about the rank of a singular matrix of order 3?

6. Suppose A is a singular matrix. Can we tell whether A^T will also be singular? Explain.

7. If cof A is symmetric, how do cof A and adj A compare?

8. If $A = \begin{bmatrix} 2 & 1 & 0 \\ 0 & 2 & 1 \\ 3 & 0 & 2 \end{bmatrix}$ (see illustrative Examples 1 and 2), show that

$$\det(\text{adj } A) = (\det A)^2.$$

9. If $G = \begin{bmatrix} a & b \\ c & d \end{bmatrix}$ is a nonsingular matrix with scalar entries, show that

$$\det G = \det(\text{adj } G).$$

6.3 INVERSE MATRIX

When will an inverse of a matrix exist? If it does exist, how can we find it? We are now in a position to answer these questions with the following theorem.

Theorem 1. *For a square matrix A, A^{-1} exists if and only if A is nonsingular. Moreover if A^{-1} exists then*

$$A^{-1} = \frac{1}{|A|} \text{ adj } A.$$

Proof. Since the first assertion is an "if and only if" statement, we must prove two things: (1) The nonsingularity of A implies the existence of A^{-1}, and conversely, (2) the existence of A^{-1} implies that A is nonsingular.

I. Assume A is nonsingular (that is, $|A| \neq 0$): Prove A^{-1} exists.

STATEMENT

REASON

(1) $A(\text{adj } A) =$
$$\begin{bmatrix} a_{11} & a_{12} & \cdots & a_{1n} \\ a_{21} & a_{22} & \cdots & a_{2n} \\ \cdot & \cdot & & \cdot \\ \cdot & \cdot & & \cdot \\ \cdot & \cdot & & \cdot \\ a_{n1} & a_{n2} & \cdots & a_{nn} \end{bmatrix} \begin{bmatrix} A_{11} & A_{21} & \cdots & A_{n1} \\ A_{12} & A_{22} & \cdots & A_{n2} \\ \cdot & \cdot & & \cdot \\ \cdot & \cdot & & \cdot \\ \cdot & \cdot & & \cdot \\ A_{1n} & A_{2n} & \cdots & A_{nn} \end{bmatrix}$$

(1) By definition of the adjoint matrix of Section 6.2, and by Theorem 1 of Section 5.2 and Theorem 7 of Section 5.3 after matrix multiplication. (The student should write out the details of the multiplication.)

$$= \begin{bmatrix} |A| & 0 & 0 & 0 & \cdots & 0 \\ 0 & |A| & 0 & 0 & \cdots & 0 \\ 0 & 0 & |A| & 0 & \cdots & 0 \\ \cdot & \cdot & \cdot & \cdot & & \cdot \\ \cdot & \cdot & \cdot & \cdot & & \cdot \\ \cdot & \cdot & \cdot & \cdot & & \cdot \\ 0 & 0 & 0 & 0 & \cdots & |A| \end{bmatrix}$$

(2) $\qquad = |A|I_n.$

(2) Definition of multiplication of matrix by a scalar.

(3) $|A| \neq 0.$

(3) By assumption.

(4) $A \dfrac{\text{adj } A}{|A|} = I_n.$

(4) Statements (1), (2), and (3).

(5) A^{-1} exists and moreover

$$A^{-1} = \frac{1}{|A|} \text{adj } A.$$

(5) Since by the same argument
$$\frac{(\text{adj } A)}{|A|} A = I_n,$$
and thus
$$\frac{(\text{adj } A)}{|A|} A$$
$$= A \frac{(\text{adj } A)}{|A|} = I_n.$$

Thus the first part of the proof is complete. Moreover we have developed a formula for calculating A^{-1}.

II. Assume A^{-1} exists: Prove A is nonsingular.

STATEMENT	REASON
(1) $AA^{-1} = A^{-1}A = I_n$.	(1) By assumption that A^{-1} exists.
(2) $|A|\,|A^{-1}| = |I_n|$.	(2) By Theorem 9 of Section 5.3, $|AA^{-1}| = |A|\,|A^{-1}|$.
(3) $|A| \neq 0$ (that is, A is nonsingular).	(3) If $|A| = 0$, then by statement (2), $|I_n| = 0$. But $|I_n| \neq 0$, $\therefore |A| \neq 0$.

The following examples illustrate the use of the formula in Theorem 1.

Example 1. In Examples 1 and 2 of the previous section we found that if

$$A = \begin{bmatrix} 2 & 1 & 0 \\ 0 & 2 & 1 \\ 3 & 0 & 2 \end{bmatrix}, \text{ then adj } A = \begin{bmatrix} 4 & -2 & 1 \\ 3 & 4 & -2 \\ -6 & 3 & 4 \end{bmatrix}.$$ We find that $|A| = 11$; there-

fore $A^{-1} = \dfrac{\text{adj } A}{|A|} = \begin{bmatrix} \frac{4}{11} & -\frac{2}{11} & \frac{1}{11} \\ \frac{3}{11} & \frac{4}{11} & -\frac{2}{11} \\ -\frac{6}{11} & \frac{3}{11} & \frac{4}{11} \end{bmatrix}.$ To check our result, show that

$$AA^{-1} = A^{-1}A = I_3.$$

Example 2.

Let $A = \begin{bmatrix} 4 & 1 \\ 3 & 2 \end{bmatrix}.$ Then cof $A = \begin{bmatrix} 2 & -3 \\ -1 & 4 \end{bmatrix}$ and adj $A = \begin{bmatrix} 2 & -1 \\ -3 & 4 \end{bmatrix}.$ Also,

det $A = 5$, hence $A^{-1} = \dfrac{\text{adj } A}{\det A} = \begin{bmatrix} \frac{2}{5} & -\frac{1}{5} \\ -\frac{3}{5} & \frac{4}{5} \end{bmatrix}.$

The formula used above is not the only method of calculating A^{-1} as we shall see later. Neither is it always the most efficient method because of the labor involved in calculating the cofactors when the order is large. It is, however, of theoretical importance.

It should be observed that a nonsquare matrix cannot have an inverse. The reason for this is left as an exercise for the student.

Negative exponents for nonsingular square matrices can now be defined as follows:

$$A^{-2} = (A^{-1})^2 = A^{-1}A^{-1},$$
$$A^{-3} = (A^{-1})^3 = A^{-1}A^{-1}A^{-1}, \text{ etc.}$$

EXERCISES

1. Making use of the answers to Exercise 1 of Section 6.2, calculate the inverse of those matrices, if possible. If it is not possible, state why.

2. Calculate the inverses of the following matrices where possible. Check by $AA^{-1} = A^{-1}A = I$.

$$A = \begin{bmatrix} 2 & -1 \\ 4 & 3 \end{bmatrix}; \quad B = \begin{bmatrix} 2 & 1 \\ 4 & 0 \end{bmatrix}; \quad C = \begin{bmatrix} 4 & 2 \\ 2 & 1 \end{bmatrix}; \quad D = \begin{bmatrix} 2 & 0 & 3 \\ -1 & 0 & 2 \\ 0 & 1 & 1 \end{bmatrix};$$

$$E = \begin{bmatrix} 3 & 2 & 1 \\ 2 & -1 & -1 \\ 1 & 4 & 0 \end{bmatrix}.$$

3. State why it is impossible for a matrix that is not square to have an inverse.

4. If $A = \begin{bmatrix} 3 & 2 \\ 0 & 1 \end{bmatrix}$, find A^{-2} and A^{-3}.

5. If $B = \begin{bmatrix} 2 & 1 & 0 \\ 3 & 0 & 1 \end{bmatrix}$, is B^{-3} defined? Why?

6. If $C = \begin{bmatrix} 2 & x \\ 4 & 2 \end{bmatrix}$, under what condition is C^{-2} defined? Find C^{-2} under that condition.

7. Prove that if $\det A \neq 0$, then $\det (A^{-1}) = (\det A)^{-1}$. (*Hint:* Make use of Theorem 9 of Chapter 5.) Note the different meanings of the exponents in this exercise.

8. If A is a fifth-order matrix and A^{-1} exists, do we know what the rank of A is? Why?

9. An *orthogonal matrix* A is a matrix which satisfies the equality $A^{-1} = A^T$.
(*a*) Why must an orthogonal matrix be square and nonsingular?

(*b*) Show that $A = \begin{bmatrix} \frac{1}{2} & \frac{1}{2}\sqrt{3} \\ -\frac{1}{2}\sqrt{3} & \frac{1}{2} \end{bmatrix}$ is orthogonal.

10. If $G = \begin{bmatrix} a & b \\ c & d \end{bmatrix}$ is a nonsingular matrix with scalar entries, show that

$G^{-1} = \dfrac{1}{ad - bc} \begin{bmatrix} d & -b \\ -c & a \end{bmatrix}$ by using the formula developed in Theorem 1.

11. A *unitary matrix* A is a matrix such that $A^* = A^{-1}$. Verify that

$A = \begin{bmatrix} i & 0 \\ 0 & 1 \end{bmatrix}$ is a unitary matrix.

12. Given $A^{-1} = \begin{bmatrix} 3 & 2 \\ 1 & 6 \end{bmatrix}$. Find A.

6.4 PROPERTIES OF AN INVERSE MATRIX

Now that we have learned how to determine the existence of an inverse of a matrix and then a method of calculation when an inverse does exist we ask the question: Is the inverse unique? That is, is there only one inverse for A?

Theorem 2. *If A has an inverse, then it is unique.*

Proof. We will assume that there are two inverses and then show that they are the same.

Assume: $AB = BA = I$ and $AC = CA = I$.

Statements: $B = BI = B(AC) = (BA)C = IC = C$.

The reasons for the statements are left as an exercise for the student.

There are other properties of the inverse which will now be stated. Most of the proofs will be left for the student.

Theorem 3. *If the product of two square matrices is I_n, then that product is commutative; that is, if $AB = I_n$, then $AB = BA$.*

The significance of Theorem 3 is that if A and B are square, and if $AB = I$, then B is A^{-1} and hence automatically commutes with A; therefore, in proving that B is the inverse of A, if we can show that $AB = I$, we need not worry about showing that $BA = I$.

Theorem 4. *If A and B are of the same order and nonsingular, then*

$$(AB)^{-1} = B^{-1}A^{-1}.$$

Proof. If we can show that $(AB)(B^{-1}A^{-1}) = (B^{-1}A^{-1})(AB) = I$, then by Theorem 2, $B^{-1}A^{-1}$ must be the inverse of (AB).

STATEMENT	REASON
(1) $(AB)(B^{-1}A^{-1}) = A(BB^{-1})A^{-1}$	(1) Follows from the associative law.
(2) $= AIA^{-1}$	(2) Definition of inverse.
(3) $= AA^{-1}$	(3) Property of I.
(4) $= I.$	(4) Definition of inverse.
(5) Also $(B^{-1}A^{-1})(AB) = I.$	(5) By Theorem 3.
(6) Therefore the inverse of AB is $B^{-1}A^{-1}$.	(6) Theorem 2.

Example 1. Verify Theorem 4 for the matrices

$$A = \begin{bmatrix} 1 & 0 \\ 4 & 2 \end{bmatrix}, \quad \text{and} \quad B = \begin{bmatrix} 1 & 1 \\ 2 & 3 \end{bmatrix}. \quad \text{We find}$$

$$A^{-1} = \begin{bmatrix} 1 & 0 \\ -2 & \frac{1}{2} \end{bmatrix}, \quad B^{-1} = \begin{bmatrix} 3 & -1 \\ -2 & 1 \end{bmatrix}, \quad \text{and} \quad B^{-1}A^{-1} = \begin{bmatrix} 5 & -\frac{1}{2} \\ -4 & \frac{1}{2} \end{bmatrix}.$$

Also $AB = \begin{bmatrix} 1 & 1 \\ 8 & 10 \end{bmatrix}, \quad (AB)^{-1} = \begin{bmatrix} 5 & -\frac{1}{2} \\ -4 & \frac{1}{2} \end{bmatrix}.$

Obviously $(AB)^{-1} = B^{-1}A^{-1}$, as we expected.

Theorem 5. *If A is nonsingular, $(A^T)^{-1} = (A^{-1})^T$.*

Theorem 6. *If A is nonsingular, $(A^{-1})^{-1} = A$.*

Proofs of the preceding two theorems are left as exercises. The following theorem can be proved by making use of the inverse.

Theorem 7. *If $AB = 0$, and if A and B are square of order n, then $A = 0$ or $B = 0$ or both A and B are singular.*

Proof. Because A and B are square, two situations can exist: (1) At least one matrix is nonsingular; or (2) both are singular.

STATEMENT	REASON
(1) Assume A is nonsingular and therefore A^{-1} exists.	(1) Theorem 1.
(2) $AB = 0$.	(2) Given.
(3) $A^{-1}(AB) = A^{-1}0$.	(3) Premultiplication by A^{-1}.
(4) $IB = 0$, $B = 0$.	(4) Associative law and definitions of inverse and identity.
(5) Likewise by assuming $|B| \neq 0$ we can show that $A = 0$.	(5) Similar to steps (1) through (4).
(6) The only other alternative is that A and B are singular.	(6) From assumption that A and B are square and by definition of singular matrix.

It should be noted that if A and B are not square it is also possible to have $AB = 0$. For example,

$$\begin{bmatrix} 2 & 0 & 1 \\ 4 & 0 & 2 \end{bmatrix} \begin{bmatrix} 0 & -1 \\ 4 & 1 \\ 0 & 2 \end{bmatrix} = \begin{bmatrix} 0 & 0 \\ 0 & 0 \end{bmatrix}.$$

Some authors define all nonsquare matrices to be singular, as well as square matrices whose determinants are zero.

Remember that in the third chapter we remarked that if $AB = 0$ neither A nor B was necessarily a null matrix. This was *not* analogous with scalar algebra. Theorem 7 simply contributes more information concerning this discussion.

The following theorem can be proved by use of the inverse.

Theorem 8. *If A, B, and C are square and of order n and if A is nonsingular, then $AB = AC$ implies that $B = C$.*

Thus *the cancellation law is valid for matrix multiplication over the set of all nonsingular matrices of order n.* In Chapter 3 we illustrated that this law is not true in general for the set of all matrices under matrix multiplication.

EXERCISES

1. Using $A = \begin{bmatrix} 1 & -3 \\ 2 & 0 \end{bmatrix}$, and $B = \begin{bmatrix} 3 & 2 \\ 1 & 1 \end{bmatrix}$, illustrate:

(a) Theorem 4;   (b) Theorem 5.

2. Let $A = \begin{bmatrix} 4 & 2 \\ 1 & 0 \end{bmatrix}$ and $B = \begin{bmatrix} 2 & 1 \\ 3 & 2 \end{bmatrix}$, and repeat Exercise 1.

3. Give reasons for the statements of the proof of Theorem 2.

4. Prove Theorem 3.   5. Prove Theorem 5.

6. Prove Theorem 6.   7. Prove Theorem 8.

8. Prove that if A, B, ..., M are all nonsingular and of order n, then $(AB \ldots M)^{-1} = M^{-1} \ldots B^{-1}A^{-1}$.

9. Prove that the inverse of a nonsingular symmetric matrix is also symmetric. (*Hint:* Use Theorem 5.)

10. Let B and C be 2 by 2 matrices. If $A = \begin{bmatrix} 5 & 4 \\ 6 & 5 \end{bmatrix}$ and $AB = AC$, does $B = C$? Explain.

11. Let A, B, and C be square matrices of the same order. If A is nonsingular, prove that $BA = CA$ implies that $B = C$.

12. Verify Theorem 7 for $A = \begin{bmatrix} 0 & 1 \\ 0 & 0 \end{bmatrix}$ and $B = \begin{bmatrix} 3 & 0 \\ 0 & 0 \end{bmatrix}$. Do the same for $A = \begin{bmatrix} 0 & 0 \\ 0 & 0 \end{bmatrix}$ and $B = \begin{bmatrix} 2 & 1 \\ -1 & -2 \end{bmatrix}$.

13. Suppose A and B are square matrices of order 2 such that $A \neq 0$, $B \neq 0$, and $AB = 0$. What can be said about the ranks of A and B and why?

14. Suppose A and B are square matrices of order 2 such that A is nonsingular and $AB = 0$. What can be said about B and why?

6.5 SOLUTION OF *n* LINEAR EQUATIONS WITH *n* UNKNOWNS

Our knowledge of the inverse can be applied to the solution of n equations with n unknowns.

Given:
$$\begin{cases} a_{11}x_1 + \cdots + a_{1n}x_n = b_1, \\ \qquad \cdots \\ a_{n1}x_1 + \cdots + a_{nn}x_n = b_n, \end{cases}$$

which can be written in matrix notation as $AX = B$ (Section 1.8). Assuming that a unique solution exists, it can be found as follows. Premultiply both sides by A^{-1}. (The student should observe why it is necessary to *premultiply*.)

$$A^{-1}(AX) = A^{-1}B$$
$$(A^{-1}A)X = A^{-1}B$$
$$IX = A^{-1}B,$$
$$X = A^{-1}B.$$

Thus $A^{-1}B$ is a column vector which gives us the values of all the x_i's, and we have proved the following theorem.

Theorem 9. *If the system $AX = B$, where A is nonsingular, has a unique solution, the solution is $X = A^{-1}B$.*

Example 1.

$$\text{To solve} \begin{cases} x_1 + x_2 + x_3 = 2, \\ x_1 \qquad + x_3 = 0, \\ 2x_1 - x_2 \qquad = 2, \end{cases} \text{ or } AX = B \text{ where } A = \begin{bmatrix} 1 & 1 & 1 \\ 1 & 0 & 1 \\ 2 & -1 & 0 \end{bmatrix}$$

and $B = \begin{bmatrix} 2 \\ 0 \\ 2 \end{bmatrix}$, first use the formula of Theorem 1 to obtain A^{-1}. We find

$$A^{-1} = \begin{bmatrix} \frac{1}{2} & -\frac{1}{2} & \frac{1}{2} \\ 1 & -1 & 0 \\ -\frac{1}{2} & \frac{3}{2} & -\frac{1}{2} \end{bmatrix}.$$

$$X = A^{-1}B = \begin{bmatrix} \frac{1}{2} & -\frac{1}{2} & \frac{1}{2} \\ 1 & -1 & 0 \\ -\frac{1}{2} & \frac{3}{2} & -\frac{1}{2} \end{bmatrix} \begin{bmatrix} 2 \\ 0 \\ 2 \end{bmatrix} = \begin{bmatrix} 2 \\ 2 \\ -2 \end{bmatrix}.$$

This method of solving a system of linear equations is valid only when the number of equations equals the number of unknowns and when A is nonsingular. With high-speed computers to do the labor of finding A^{-1}, this method of solving n equations with n unknowns is important. The method is especially adapted to problems involving sets of systems of equations, $AX = B$, in which all systems have the same coefficient matrix, A, but different matrices, B.

Example 2. The management of a certain company is confronted with a decision. One of its factories makes use of two different machines, M and N, to manufacture two different products, P and Q. Machine M can operate 12 hours and Machine N can operate 16 hours per day. For each unit of Product P that the factory produces, it requires 2 hours work by Machine M and 1 hour of work by Machine N. For each unit of Product Q that it produces, the factory must use Machine M for 2 hours and Machine N for 3 hours. Find the number of units of each product that the factory should make in a day in order to keep the machines working to capacity. Also, what will be the effect on production if we buy more of each type of machine?

Solution. Let x_1 = number of units of product P which are produced. Let x_2 = number of units of product Q which are produced. Machine M then spends $2x_1$ hours on product P and $2x_2$ hours on product Q. If machine M operates full time we have the equation

$$2x_1 + 2x_2 = 12.$$

Similarly if machine N operates full time we get the equation

$$x_1 + 3x_2 = 16.$$

The two simultaneous equations can be expressed as the matrix equation

$$AX = B \quad \text{where} \quad A = \begin{bmatrix} 2 & 2 \\ 1 & 3 \end{bmatrix}, \quad \text{and} \quad B = \begin{bmatrix} 12 \\ 16 \end{bmatrix}.$$

Therefore, $$X = A^{-1}B = A^{-1}\begin{bmatrix} 12 \\ 16 \end{bmatrix}.$$

By the adjoint method we can easily find A^{-1} to be

$$\begin{bmatrix} \frac{3}{4} & -\frac{1}{2} \\ -\frac{1}{4} & \frac{1}{2} \end{bmatrix}, \quad \text{hence,} \quad X = \begin{bmatrix} \frac{3}{4} & -\frac{1}{2} \\ -\frac{1}{4} & \frac{1}{2} \end{bmatrix}\begin{bmatrix} 12 \\ 16 \end{bmatrix} = \begin{bmatrix} 1 \\ 5 \end{bmatrix}.$$

One unit of product P should be produced, and five units of product Q should be produced.

Now if we buy more machines we can determine the change in production by simply changing B and recalculating $A^{-1}B$. Notice that A^{-1} does not change, and it is in the calculation of the inverse matrix that most of the work lies. Suppose we buy an extra machine M. This increases the capacity of machines M to 24 hours, thus

$$X = A^{-1}B = A^{-1}\begin{bmatrix} 24 \\ 16 \end{bmatrix} = \begin{bmatrix} \frac{3}{4} & -\frac{1}{2} \\ -\frac{1}{4} & \frac{1}{2} \end{bmatrix}\begin{bmatrix} 24 \\ 16 \end{bmatrix} = \begin{bmatrix} 10 \\ 2 \end{bmatrix}.$$

EXERCISES

1. Using the procedure taught in this section, solve the following systems of equations.

(a) $\begin{cases} x_1 + 3x_2 = 4, \\ 2x_1 - 2x_2 = 6. \end{cases}$ (b) $\begin{cases} x_1 - 4x_2 = 2, \\ 2x_1 + x_2 = 1. \end{cases}$ (c) $\begin{cases} x_1 + 2x_2 + x_3 = 0, \\ x_1 \qquad\;\; + x_3 = 1, \\ \qquad x_2 - x_3 = 3. \end{cases}$

(d) $\begin{cases} 2x_1 + 5x_2 + 3x_3 = 1, \\ 3x_1 + x_2 + 2x_3 = 1, \text{ or } AX = B, \text{ where cof } A = \begin{bmatrix} -3 & -1 & 5 \\ 1 & -1 & 1 \\ 7 & 5 & -13 \end{bmatrix}, \\ x_1 + 2x_2 + x_3 = 0, \end{cases}$

and $|A| = 4$.

2. Solve $\begin{bmatrix} 6 & -5 \\ 3 & -3 \end{bmatrix}\begin{bmatrix} x & -5 \\ y & -6 \end{bmatrix} - 3I_2 = 0$ for x and y by finding the inverse of

$\begin{bmatrix} 6 & -5 \\ 3 & -3 \end{bmatrix}$.

3. Let A, B, C, X, be square matrices of the same order. Under what conditions is the equation $B \, X \, C = A$ solvable for X. Solve for X assuming these conditions are satisfied.

6.6 PROOF OF CRAMER'S RULE

Recall in Section 5.5 that a procedure using determinants called Cramer's rule was used to solve n linear equations with n unknowns, provided A was nonsingular. Now we wish to justify that procedure and at the same time show that it is only a variation of the method of solution shown in the previous section.

Given a system $AX = B$, if $|A| \neq 0$, the solution of the system is

$X = A^{-1}B$ (Theorem 9)

$$= \frac{\text{adj } A}{|A|} B \qquad \text{(Theorem 1)}$$

$$= \frac{1}{|A|} (\text{cof } A)^T B \qquad \text{(definition of adj } A)$$

$$= \frac{1}{|A|} \begin{bmatrix} A_{11} & A_{21} & \cdots & A_{n1} \\ A_{12} & A_{22} & \cdots & A_{n2} \\ \cdot & \cdot & \cdot & \cdot \\ \cdot & \cdot & \cdot & \cdot \\ \cdot & \cdot & \cdot & \cdot \\ A_{1n} & A_{2n} & \cdots & A_{nn} \end{bmatrix} \begin{bmatrix} b_1 \\ b_2 \\ \cdot \\ \cdot \\ \cdot \\ b_n \end{bmatrix}$$

$$= \frac{1}{|A|} \begin{bmatrix} (b_1 A_{11} + b_2 A_{21} + \cdots + b_n A_{n1}) \\ (b_1 A_{12} + b_2 A_{22} + \cdots + b_n A_{n2}) \\ \cdot \\ \cdot \\ \cdot \\ (b_1 A_{1n} + b_2 A_{2n} + \cdots + b_n A_{nn}) \end{bmatrix} = \begin{bmatrix} \dfrac{\det (^1A)}{\det A} \\ \dfrac{\det (^2A)}{\det A} \\ \cdot \\ \cdot \\ \cdot \\ \dfrac{\det (^nA)}{\det A} \end{bmatrix}$$

by Theorem 5 of Chapter 5 [notation (^iA) was explained in Section 5.5].

$$\therefore \; x_i = \frac{\det (^iA)}{\det A} \qquad \text{for} \qquad i = 1, 2, \ldots, n.$$

6.7 SUMMARY

In this chapter we proved that an inverse does exist for any square, non-singular matrix, and moreover, that it is unique. Thus, for matrices, we can speak of "the" inverse. We discovered a method for calculating this inverse, and we learned that the inverse can be useful in solving certain systems of linear equations.

NEW VOCABULARY

nonsingular matrix	6.2	inverse matrix	6.1, 6.3
singular matrix	6.2	orthogonal matrix	6.3
cofactor matrix	6.2	unitary matrix	6.3
adjoint matrix	6.2	unique inverse	6.4

Elementary Matrix Transformations

7.1 ELEMENTARY ROW OPERATIONS

There are, of course, many ways of transforming a given matrix into another matrix. Three ways that are important enough to give them a special name are now defined.

Definition. *The three operations:*

(1) *interchange any two rows,*

(2) *multiply any row by a nonzero scalar,*

(3) *add to any row a scalar multiple of another row,*

are called **elementary row operations**.

Elementary column operations are defined by replacing the word "row" by "column" throughout the preceding definition. An **elementary operation** is any operation that is either an elementary row operation or an elementary column operation. If a matrix A can be transformed into a matrix B by means of one or more elementary operations, we write $A \sim B$ and say that A is **equivalent** to B. In particular we may say that A is **row equivalent** (or **column equivalent**) to B if only elementary row (or column) operations are involved in the transformation. In this section, as in most of the book, we are primarily concerned with row operations.

Example 1.

The matrix $\begin{bmatrix} 1 & 3 & 4 \\ -2 & 3 & 1 \end{bmatrix}$ can be transformed to $\begin{bmatrix} 1 & 3 & 4 \\ 0 & 9 & 9 \end{bmatrix}$ by elementary row operation (3) (multiply the first row by 2 and add to the second row). This then can be transformed to $\begin{bmatrix} 1 & 3 & 4 \\ 0 & 1 & 1 \end{bmatrix}$ by elementary row operation (2) (multiply the second row by $\frac{1}{9}$). Note that we have transformed the original matrix to an echelon matrix.

These elementary row operations correspond to the operations that are used to obtain a solution of a system of linear equations by the so-called "addition-subtraction" method. Consider the system for which the first matrix in Example 1 was the augmented matrix,

$$\begin{cases} x + 3y = 4, \\ -2x + 3y = 1. \end{cases}$$

Multiply the members of the first equation by 2 and add to those of the second.

$$\begin{cases} x + 3y = 4, \\ 9y = 9. \end{cases}$$

Multiply the members of the second equation by $\frac{1}{9}$.

$$\begin{cases} x + 3y = 4, \\ y = 1. \end{cases}$$

Note that the operations performed here and in Example 1 are really the same. The three systems of equations stated above are said to be *equivalent* because they have the same solution.

In Example 1, $\begin{bmatrix} 1 & 3 & 4 \\ -2 & 3 & 1 \end{bmatrix}$ is row equivalent to $\begin{bmatrix} 1 & 3 & 4 \\ 0 & 9 & 9 \end{bmatrix}$ and also is row equivalent to $\begin{bmatrix} 1 & 3 & 4 \\ 0 & 1 & 1 \end{bmatrix}$ because only elementary row operations were used to transform one matrix to another.

It can be shown that if A is row equivalent to B then B is row equivalent to A. Row equivalence is a binary relation over the set of all m by n matrices.

Example 2. Given the system $\begin{cases} 2x + y = 4, \\ x - 2y = 1. \end{cases}$

The augmented matrix is $\begin{bmatrix} 2 & 1 & 4 \\ 1 & -2 & 1 \end{bmatrix}$, which can be transformed as follows:

$$\begin{bmatrix} 2 & 1 & 4 \\ 1 & -2 & 1 \end{bmatrix} \sim \begin{bmatrix} 1 & -2 & 1 \\ 2 & 1 & 4 \end{bmatrix} \quad \text{(by interchange of 2 rows which we will denote by } R_1 \leftrightarrow R_2\text{),}$$

$$\underset{-2R_1 + R_2}{\sim} \begin{bmatrix} 1 & -2 & 1 \\ 0 & 5 & 2 \end{bmatrix} \quad \text{(−2 times first row plus the second row),}$$

$$\underset{\frac{1}{5} R_2}{\sim} \begin{bmatrix} 1 & -2 & 1 \\ 0 & 1 & \frac{2}{5} \end{bmatrix} \quad (\frac{1}{5} \text{ times the second row).}$$

This last matrix is an echelon matrix. It represents the augmented matrix of a system which is equivalent to the original system.

We will find several applications for the elementary row operations. They can be used to transform any matrix to an echelon matrix. This procedure will be used to solve m equations with n unknowns. Elementary row operations can also be used to invert a matrix; and they are needed in the simplex method of linear programming. All of these applications will be considered later in this text.

As we shall learn in the next section, it is sometimes useful to apply elementary operations to columns as well as rows; at the beginning of this section we stated that a matrix thus obtained is *equivalent* to the original matrix. *Equivalence of matrices* is an example of an *equivalence relation* as defined in Chapter 3.

EXERCISES

1. Which elementary row operation (if any) transforms the first matrix into the second?

(a) $\begin{bmatrix} 2 & 1 \\ 4 & 6 \end{bmatrix}, \begin{bmatrix} 2 & 1 \\ 0 & 4 \end{bmatrix}$;

(b) $\begin{bmatrix} 2 & 4 & 6 \\ 1 & 2 & 4 \end{bmatrix}, \begin{bmatrix} 1 & 2 & 3 \\ 1 & 2 & 4 \end{bmatrix}$;

(c) $\begin{bmatrix} 2 & 4 & 3 & 1 \\ 1 & 2 & 3 & 4 \\ 0 & 1 & 4 & 6 \end{bmatrix}, \begin{bmatrix} 1 & 2 & 3 & 4 \\ 0 & 1 & 4 & 6 \\ 2 & 4 & 3 & 1 \end{bmatrix}$.

2. In each exercise, using elementary row operations, write an echelon matrix which is row equivalent to the given matrix. Describe what you did in each step using the abbreviated notation shown in Example 2 of this section.

(a) $\begin{bmatrix} -2 & 2 & 1 \\ 4 & 6 & 0 \end{bmatrix}$;

(b) $\begin{bmatrix} 1 & 4 & 3 & 2 \\ 1 & 8 & 0 & 2 \\ 2 & 0 & 4 & 2 \end{bmatrix}$;

(c) $\begin{bmatrix} 3 & 1 & 4 & 6 \\ 2 & 1 & 0 & 4 \end{bmatrix}$;

(d) $\begin{bmatrix} 2 & 1 & 3 \\ 1 & 0 & -3 \\ 3 & 1 & 0 \end{bmatrix}$.

3. Write the augmented matrix for each of the following systems. Transform this augmented matrix into a row equivalent echelon matrix. Then write the system for which this echelon matrix is the augmented matrix. What is the solution of the resulting system? What is the solution of the original system?

(a) $\begin{cases} 2x + y = 6, \\ 2x + 4y = 9. \end{cases}$

(b) $\begin{cases} x + y + z = 4, \\ y + z = 6, \\ 3x - y - 2z = 9. \end{cases}$

4. Solve the system $\begin{cases} 4x + 3y = 2, \\ x + 2y = 3, \end{cases}$ by the old addition-subtraction method.

(Keep two equations at all times). Then use the corresponding elementary row operations on the augmented matrix to achieve the same solution.

5. In each of the following pairs of systems of equations, are the two systems equivalent? Why?

(a) $\begin{cases} x + y = 2, \\ x - y = 4, \end{cases}$ and $\begin{cases} x + y = 2, \\ -x + y = 2. \end{cases}$

(b) $\begin{cases} x + y = 2, \\ x - y = 4, \end{cases}$ and $\begin{cases} x - y = 4, \\ 2x + 2y = 4. \end{cases}$

6. (a) Show that if matrix B can be obtained from matrix A by one elementary row operation, then matrix A can be obtained from matrix B by one elementary row operation of the same type.

(b) How does it follow from (a) that if a matrix A is row equivalent to matrix B, then matrix B is row equivalent to matrix A?

7. If matrix A is row equivalent to matrix B, how does the order of A compare with the order of B?

8. Without interchanging rows, change $\begin{bmatrix} 1 & 2 \\ 3 & 4 \end{bmatrix}$ to $\begin{bmatrix} 3 & 4 \\ 1 & 2 \end{bmatrix}$ in four steps using elementary row operations [that is, using only elementary row operations of types (2) and (3)]. [As this example suggests, it is possible to show that we can do the same things with elementary row operations (2) and (3) as we can with (1), (2), and (3).]

7.2 NORMAL FORM AND RANK

Elementary operations can be used to reduce a matrix to what is called **normal form**.

Definition. *When a matrix has been reduced by elementary operations to one of the forms*

$$\begin{bmatrix} I_r \\ \hline 0 \end{bmatrix}, \qquad [I_r \mid 0], \qquad \begin{bmatrix} I_r & 0 \\ \hline 0 & 0 \end{bmatrix}, \qquad \text{or} \quad I_r \ (r = rank),$$

*we say that it has been reduced to **normal form**.*

Example 1.

Reduce $A = \begin{bmatrix} 2 & 1 & 4 \\ 1 & 0 & 4 \\ -2 & 0 & 2 \end{bmatrix}$ to normal form.

$$A \underset{C_1 \leftrightarrow C_2}{\sim} \begin{bmatrix} 1 & 2 & 4 \\ 0 & 1 & 4 \\ 0 & -2 & 2 \end{bmatrix}$$

The purpose of this step is to obtain a 1 in the a_{11} position and we are lucky enough to get zeros elsewhere in the first column.

$$\underset{\substack{-2C_1+C_2 \\ -4C_1+C_3}}{\sim} \begin{bmatrix} 1 & 0 & 0 \\ 0 & 1 & 4 \\ 0 & -2 & 2 \end{bmatrix}$$

Here we obtain zeros in the first row, except the first column, without disturbing the rest of the matrix.

$$\underset{2R_2+R_3}{\sim} \begin{bmatrix} 1 & 0 & 0 \\ 0 & 1 & 4 \\ 0 & 0 & 10 \end{bmatrix}$$

We begin repeating the process for the lower right 2 by 2 submatrix.

$$\underset{-4C_2+C_3}{\sim} \begin{bmatrix} 1 & 0 & 0 \\ 0 & 1 & 0 \\ 0 & 0 & 10 \end{bmatrix} \underset{(\frac{1}{10})R_3}{\sim} \begin{bmatrix} 1 & 0 & 0 \\ 0 & 1 & 0 \\ 0 & 0 & 1 \end{bmatrix}.$$

Since $|A| \neq 0$, what we did in Example 1 could have been done with row operations only, but not as easily. There are many paths by which one may travel to attain the normal form. We suggest that the student establish some suitable, systematic procedure and stick to it. We will use the normal form of a matrix as a possible shortcut for finding the rank of a matrix. We justify the procedure by the following theorem.

Theorem 1. *Equivalent matrices have the same rank.*

Outline of proof. (optional) The details are left as an exercise. The proof is split into 2 parts.

FIRST: Show that elementary operations (1) and (2) will not change a nonzero minor to zero, nor change a zero minor to one that is nonzero and therefore will not alter the rank of a matrix.

SECOND: Show that elementary operation (3) will not increase the rank of a matrix A. If the rank r of A is as large as the order of A will permit, then by Theorem 10 of Chapter 5 our job is accomplished. If the rank r of A is not as large as the order permits, then consider all submatrices of order $r + 1$ after elementary operation (3) has been applied. By a generalization of Exercise 6 of Section 5.4 and Theorem 8 of Section 5.3, the determinants of these submatrices can be expressed as $|S| + k |R|$ where S is a submatrix of A of order $r + 1$. Either R is a submatrix of A of order $r + 1$ with perhaps one line out of place or it has two identical lines. In any event $|R| = 0$; also $|S| = 0$ because the rank of A was r. Therefore all submatrices of order $r + 1$ of the transformed matrix have a rank no greater than r, and thus the rank of A is no greater than r. Neither is the rank less than r because the inverse transformation (of the same type) would cause an increase in rank, which we have just shown is impossible.

Example 2.

Find the rank of

$$A = \begin{bmatrix} 2 & 1 & 3 & 1 \\ 1 & 0 & 1 & 1 \\ 2 & 1 & 3 & 1 \\ -1 & 0 & -1 & -1 \end{bmatrix}.$$

$$A \underset{C_1 \leftrightarrow C_2}{\sim} \begin{bmatrix} 1 & 2 & 3 & 1 \\ 0 & 1 & 1 & 1 \\ 1 & 2 & 3 & 1 \\ 0 & -1 & -1 & -1 \end{bmatrix} \underset{-R_1 + R_3}{\sim} \begin{bmatrix} 1 & 2 & 3 & 1 \\ 0 & 1 & 1 & 1 \\ 0 & 0 & 0 & 0 \\ 0 & -1 & -1 & -1 \end{bmatrix}$$

$$\underset{\substack{-2C_1 + C_2 \\ -3C_1 + C_3 \\ -C_1 + C_4}}{\sim} \begin{bmatrix} 1 & 0 & 0 & 0 \\ 0 & 1 & 1 & 1 \\ 0 & 0 & 0 & 0 \\ 0 & -1 & -1 & -1 \end{bmatrix} \underset{R_2 + R_4}{\sim} \begin{bmatrix} 1 & 0 & 0 & 0 \\ 0 & 1 & 1 & 1 \\ 0 & 0 & 0 & 0 \\ 0 & 0 & 0 & 0 \end{bmatrix}$$

$$\underset{\substack{-C_2 + C_3 \\ -C_2 + C_4}}{\sim} \begin{bmatrix} 1 & 0 & 0 & 0 \\ 0 & 1 & 0 & 0 \\ 0 & 0 & 0 & 0 \\ 0 & 0 & 0 & 0 \end{bmatrix} = \begin{bmatrix} I_2 & \vdots & 0 \\ \cdots & \vdots & \cdots \\ 0 & \vdots & 0 \end{bmatrix}.$$

Thus the rank of the normal form is obviously 2. Therefore, by Theorem 1, the rank of A is also 2.

EXERCISES

In each of the Exercises 1 through 6 find the rank of the given matrix by reducing it to normal form:

1. $\begin{bmatrix} 3 & 2 & -1 \\ 7 & 8 & 0 \\ 4 & 6 & 1 \end{bmatrix}.$

2. $\begin{bmatrix} 0 & 1 & 3 & 0 \\ 0 & 4 & 0 & 2 \\ 1 & 0 & 3 & 0 \\ -1 & 1 & 0 & 0 \end{bmatrix}.$

3. $\begin{bmatrix} 3 & 1 & 4 & 6 & 2 \\ 4 & 1 & 3 & 9 & 6 \end{bmatrix}.$

4. $\begin{bmatrix} 3 & 2 & 7 \\ 4 & -3 & -2 \\ 0 & 1 & 2 \\ 6 & 1 & 8 \end{bmatrix}.$

5. $\begin{bmatrix} 4 & 9 & -3 & 1 \\ 6 & 9 & -4 & 0 \\ 2 & 9 & -2 & 2 \\ -2 & 0 & 1 & 1 \end{bmatrix}.$

6. $\begin{bmatrix} -1 & 0 & -1 & 3 & 2 \\ -1 & 4 & 0 & 0 & 1 \\ 0 & 0 & 0 & 4 & 2 \\ 1 & 0 & 1 & 1 & 0 \\ 0 & 4 & 1 & 1 & 1 \end{bmatrix}.$

7. What is the normal form of a 4 by 6 matrix of rank 2? Express the answer using submatrices.

8. Is $\begin{bmatrix} 2 & 1 & 4 \\ 0 & 1 & 3 \\ 2 & 0 & 1 \end{bmatrix}$ equivalent to I_3? Why?

9. Which of the following matrices are equivalent?

$$A = \begin{bmatrix} 2 & 1 \\ 4 & 3 \end{bmatrix}; \quad B = \begin{bmatrix} 2 & 1 & 1 \\ 4 & 0 & 1 \end{bmatrix}; \quad C = \begin{bmatrix} -2 & 1 & 0 \\ 4 & 3 & 2 \\ 0 & 5 & 2 \end{bmatrix};$$

$$D = \begin{bmatrix} 1 & 0 & 0 \\ 0 & 4 & 0 \\ 2 & 0 & 1 \end{bmatrix}; \quad E = \begin{bmatrix} 1 & 3 & 0 \\ 2 & 1 & 4 \end{bmatrix}; \quad F = \begin{bmatrix} 4 & 1 \\ 3 & 2 \\ 0 & 1 \end{bmatrix}; \quad G = \begin{bmatrix} 0 & 1 \\ 4 & 3 \end{bmatrix}.$$

10. Give a complete proof of Theorem 1.

11. State a necessary and sufficient condition for two matrices to be equivalent.

12. What is the normal form of a fourth-order nonsingular matrix?

7.3 ELEMENTARY MATRICES

Definition. *An elementary matrix is a matrix that can be obtained from the identity matrix I by an elementary operation.*

Elementary matrices are of three types of which $\begin{bmatrix} 1 & 0 & 0 \\ 0 & 0 & 1 \\ 0 & 1 & 0 \end{bmatrix}$, $\begin{bmatrix} 1 & 0 & 0 \\ 0 & c & 0 \\ 0 & 0 & 1 \end{bmatrix}$,

and $\begin{bmatrix} 1 & 0 & 0 \\ 0 & 1 & 0 \\ 0 & c & 1 \end{bmatrix}$ are examples. Any single elementary operation on a matrix can be accomplished by multiplying the matrix by a suitably chosen *elementary matrix*.

Example 1. The first and second *rows* of a matrix $A = [a_{ij}]_{(3,2)}$ may be interchanged by *premultiplying* A by

$$E = \begin{bmatrix} 0 & 1 & 0 \\ 1 & 0 & 0 \\ 0 & 0 & 1 \end{bmatrix}.$$

Note that the desired elementary matrix E is found by simply performing *the specified elementary operation* on an identity matrix of the appropriate order.

$$EA = \begin{bmatrix} 0 & 1 & 0 \\ 1 & 0 & 0 \\ 0 & 0 & 1 \end{bmatrix} \begin{bmatrix} a_{11} & a_{12} \\ a_{21} & a_{22} \\ a_{31} & a_{32} \end{bmatrix} = \begin{bmatrix} a_{21} & a_{22} \\ a_{11} & a_{12} \\ a_{31} & a_{32} \end{bmatrix}.$$

The first and second *columns* are interchanged by *postmultiplying A* by

$$E = \begin{bmatrix} 0 & 1 \\ 1 & 0 \end{bmatrix}.$$

$$AE = \begin{bmatrix} a_{11} & a_{12} \\ a_{21} & a_{22} \\ a_{31} & a_{32} \end{bmatrix} \begin{bmatrix} 0 & 1 \\ 1 & 0 \end{bmatrix} = \begin{bmatrix} a_{12} & a_{11} \\ a_{22} & a_{21} \\ a_{32} & a_{31} \end{bmatrix}.$$

Example 2. To multiply the second *row* of $A = [a_{ij}]_{(3,2)}$ by a nonzero scalar c,

premultiply by $E = \begin{bmatrix} 1 & 0 & 0 \\ 0 & c & 0 \\ 0 & 0 & 1 \end{bmatrix}$.

$$EA = \begin{bmatrix} 1 & 0 & 0 \\ 0 & c & 0 \\ 0 & 0 & 1 \end{bmatrix} \begin{bmatrix} a_{11} & a_{12} \\ a_{21} & a_{22} \\ a_{31} & a_{32} \end{bmatrix} = \begin{bmatrix} a_{11} & a_{12} \\ ca_{21} & ca_{22} \\ a_{31} & a_{32} \end{bmatrix}.$$

To multiply the second *column* by c, postmultiply A by $E = \begin{bmatrix} 1 & 0 \\ 0 & c \end{bmatrix}$.

Example 3. To add k times the second *row* to the first *row* of A, we premultiply

by $E = \begin{bmatrix} 1 & k & 0 \\ 0 & 1 & 0 \\ 0 & 0 & 1 \end{bmatrix}$.

$$\begin{bmatrix} 1 & k & 0 \\ 0 & 1 & 0 \\ 0 & 0 & 1 \end{bmatrix} \begin{bmatrix} a_{11} & a_{12} \\ a_{21} & a_{22} \\ a_{31} & a_{32} \end{bmatrix} = \begin{bmatrix} (a_{11} + ka_{21}) & (a_{12} + ka_{22}) \\ a_{21} & a_{22} \\ a_{31} & a_{32} \end{bmatrix}.$$

To add k times the second *column* to the first *column* of A we postmultiply by

$$E = \begin{bmatrix} 1 & 0 \\ k & 1 \end{bmatrix}.$$

By definition, elementary matrices are obtained by performing a single elementary operation on an identity matrix. We can therefore conclude that any elementary matrix E is nonsingular and thus has an inverse. (Why? See Exercise 15 of this Section.) This inverse, E^{-1}, when applied to a matrix will undo whatever E did. That is, if $EA = B$, then premultiplication of both sides by E^{-1} will yield

$$E^{-1}EA = E^{-1}B,$$

$$IA = E^{-1}B,$$

$$A = E^{-1}B.$$

Theorem 2. *If two matrices A and B are equivalent, then there exist two nonsingular matrices P and Q, such that A = PBQ.*

Outline of proof. Since A and B are equivalent, there exist elementary matrices $P_1, P_2, \ldots, P_p$ and $Q_1, Q_2, \ldots, Q_q$ such that, by repeated use of the associative law, we obtain

$$A = (P_p \ldots P_2 P_1) B (Q_1 Q_2 \ldots Q_q).$$

Also, because the elementary matrices are nonsingular, their products are nonsingular (see Theorem 9, Section 5.3).

EXERCISES

In each of the Exercises 1–6, write the elementary matrix E which performs the indicated elementary transformation on $A = \begin{bmatrix} -3 & 2 & -1 \\ 4 & 0 & 1 \end{bmatrix}$. Then multiply the matrices to obtain the desired transformation.

1. Interchange the first and second rows.

2. Interchange the first and third columns.

3. Multiply the second row by 9.

4. Multiply the third column by 7.

5. Add 4 times the first row to the second row.

6. Add 5 times the third column to the first column.

In each of the Exercises 7–10, illustrate Theorem 2 by finding matrices P and Q. Is P unique?

7. $B = \begin{bmatrix} 1 & 2 \\ 3 & 4 \end{bmatrix}, \quad A = \begin{bmatrix} 1 & 0 \\ 0 & 1 \end{bmatrix}.$

8. $B = \begin{bmatrix} 1 & 1 & 0 \\ 0 & 1 & 0 \\ 0 & 0 & 4 \end{bmatrix}, \quad A = \begin{bmatrix} 1 & 0 & 0 \\ 0 & 1 & 0 \\ 0 & 0 & 1 \end{bmatrix}.$

9. $B = \begin{bmatrix} 1 & 0 & 0 \\ 0 & 1 & 0 \\ 1 & 0 & 1 \end{bmatrix}, \quad A = \begin{bmatrix} 1 & 0 & 0 \\ 0 & 1 & 0 \\ 0 & 0 & 1 \end{bmatrix}.$

10. $B = \begin{bmatrix} 1 & 2 \\ 3 & 0 \\ 0 & 1 \end{bmatrix}, \quad A = \begin{bmatrix} 1 & 0 \\ 0 & 1 \\ 0 & 0 \end{bmatrix}.$

11. Assume $B = \begin{bmatrix} 3 & 2 \\ 1 & 4 \\ 6 & 0 \end{bmatrix}$ is obtained from a matrix A by adding 2 times the second column of A to the first column of A. This elementary operation can be expressed as

$$AE = B, \quad \text{or} \quad AEE^{-1} = BE^{-1}, \quad \text{or} \quad A = BE^{-1}.$$

Find A by first finding E, then E^{-1}, and then multiply as shown above.

12. Repeat Exercise 11 using $B = \begin{bmatrix} 3 & 2 \\ 4 & 1 \end{bmatrix}$.

13. Repeat Exercise 11 if $B = \begin{bmatrix} 1 & 0 \\ 0 & 1 \end{bmatrix}$. Can we conclude that $E = A^{-1}$ in this exercise?

14. Give a detailed proof of Theorem 2.

15. Prove: Any elementary matrix has an inverse. (*Hint:* Use certain Theorems of Chapter 5.)

7.4 CALCULATION OF THE INVERSE BY ELEMENTARY OPERATIONS

Theorem 3. *If A is nonsingular and if the matrix $[A \mid I]$ is transformed to the equivalent matrix $[I \mid P]$ by elementary row operations, then P is the inverse of A.*

Proof. Since a nonsingular matrix A can be reduced to normal form I_r by a sequence of elementary row operations, we say that there exists a matrix P (which is the product of elementary matrices) such that $PA = I$. By Theorem 3 and Theorem 2 of Chapter 6, P must be the inverse of A. Hence

$$[A \mid I] \sim P[A \mid I] = [PA \mid PI] = [I \mid P] = [I \mid A^{-1}].$$

The justification for saying $P[A \mid I] = [PA \mid PI]$ is explained in Section 4.7.

Example 1. Find A^{-1} if $A = \begin{bmatrix} 1 & 2 & 1 \\ -1 & -1 & 1 \\ 0 & 1 & 3 \end{bmatrix}$.

$$[A \mid I] = \begin{bmatrix} 1 & 2 & 1 & \vdots & 1 & 0 & 0 \\ -1 & -1 & 1 & \vdots & 0 & 1 & 0 \\ 0 & 1 & 3 & \vdots & 0 & 0 & 1 \end{bmatrix} \underset{R_1+R_2}{\sim} \begin{bmatrix} 1 & 2 & 1 & \vdots & 1 & 0 & 0 \\ 0 & 1 & 2 & \vdots & 1 & 1 & 0 \\ 0 & 1 & 3 & \vdots & 0 & 0 & 1 \end{bmatrix}$$

$$\underset{\substack{-R_2+R_3 \\ -2R_2+R_1}}{\sim} \begin{bmatrix} 1 & 0 & -3 & \vdots & -1 & -2 & 0 \\ 0 & 1 & 2 & \vdots & 1 & 1 & 0 \\ 0 & 0 & 1 & \vdots & -1 & -1 & 1 \end{bmatrix} \underset{\substack{-2R_3+R_2 \\ 3R_3+R_1}}{\sim} \begin{bmatrix} 1 & 0 & 0 & \vdots & -4 & -5 & 3 \\ 0 & 1 & 0 & \vdots & 3 & 3 & -2 \\ 0 & 0 & 1 & \vdots & -1 & -1 & 1 \end{bmatrix}.$$

$$\therefore A^{-1} = \begin{bmatrix} -4 & -5 & 3 \\ 3 & 3 & -2 \\ -1 & -1 & 1 \end{bmatrix}. \quad \text{Check: } AA^{-1} = I.$$

EXERCISES

In each of the Exercises 1–6, find A^{-1} by the method taught in this section. Check by showing that $AA^{-1} = I$.

1. $A = \begin{bmatrix} 1 & 3 \\ 4 & 0 \end{bmatrix}.$
2. $A = \begin{bmatrix} 4 & -1 \\ 7 & 2 \end{bmatrix}.$
3. $A = \begin{bmatrix} 1 & 0 & 1 \\ 3 & 1 & 0 \\ 1 & 0 & 0 \end{bmatrix}.$

4. $A = \begin{bmatrix} 0 & 4 & 1 \\ 0 & 3 & 1 \\ 1 & 2 & -3 \end{bmatrix}.$
5. $A = \begin{bmatrix} 1 & 3 & 1 \\ 1 & 4 & 0 \\ 2 & -2 & 1 \end{bmatrix}.$
6. $A = \begin{bmatrix} 4 & 1 & 4 \\ 0 & 1 & 0 \\ 2 & 0 & 3 \end{bmatrix}.$

7. Suppose that the same elementary row transformations were performed on two matrices $A = [a_{ij}]_{(3,3)}$ and $K = \begin{bmatrix} k & 0 & 0 \\ 0 & k & 0 \\ 0 & 0 & k \end{bmatrix}$ in such a way that they became

$I = \begin{bmatrix} 1 & 0 & 0 \\ 0 & 1 & 0 \\ 0 & 0 & 1 \end{bmatrix}$ and $B = [b_{ij}]_{(3,3)}$ respectively. What is the relationship between A and B?

8. Find A^{-1} in Exercise 5 by the method learned in Chapter 6.

9. Explain what would happen if one tried to apply the method of finding A^{-1} taught in this section to a *singular matrix A.*

10. Why is it necessary to use only elementary *row* operations in Theorem 3?

NEW VOCABULARY

8

Systems of Linear Equations

8.1 INTRODUCTION

At the beginning of this book it was stated that one of our objectives was to study matrices sufficiently for them to be used to solve systems of linear equations. So far we have been studying background material, much of which will be used now to accomplish this objective. Along the way we did learn two methods of attacking certain systems in which the number of equations equaled the number of unknowns and in which A^{-1} existed. In this chapter no such restrictions are placed.

The student may wonder how a system may arise in which there are more unknowns than equations, or more equations than unknowns. Consider the following two problems.

A certain company produces three different products (R, S, and T). This production requires the services of two groups of workers; the members of one group are highly trained technicians and the other group consists of the unskilled laborers. Product R requires a day's work from each of 5 technicians and 5 laborers for each unit produced. Product S needs 10 technicians and 10 laborers for each unit produced. Product T requires 2 technicians and 4 laborers for each unit produced. The company wants to know how many units of each product should be produced each day to keep all of its 100 technicians and 150 laborers employed. Let x_1, x_2, and x_3 stand for the number of units of R, S, and T respectively which are manufactured each day. Mathematically the problem becomes: Solve the system

$$\begin{cases} 5x_1 + 10x_2 + 2x_3 = 100, \\ 5x_1 + 10x_2 + 4x_3 = 150. \end{cases}$$

There is not a unique answer. Subtracting the members of the first equation from those of the second we find $x_3 = 25$. If this is substituted in either equation, after reduction the equation becomes $x_1 = 10 - 2x_2$. The possible integral values of x_2 are 0, 1, 2, 3, 4, 5. With $x_3 = 25$ we have the following solutions for x_1 and x_2:

x_1	10	8	6	4	2	0
x_2	0	1	2	3	4	5

To choose among these possibilities the company will have to use other considerations.

A system of linear equations in which there are more equations than unknowns can be obtained from an electrical circuit shown in Fig. 8.1. I_1, I_2, and I_3 are the currents, measured in amperes, in the respective parts of the circuit.

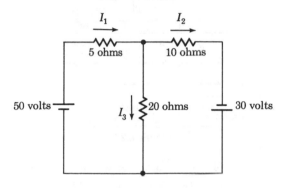

Figure 8.1

$$\begin{cases} I_1 - I_2 - I_3 = 0, \\ 5I_1 \quad\quad + 20I_3 = 50, \\ \quad\quad 10I_2 - 20I_3 = 30, \\ 5I_1 + 10I_2 \quad\quad = 80. \end{cases}$$

This system has only one answer that will satisfy all equations simultaneously; that is, $I_1 = 6$, $I_2 = 5$, $I_3 = 1$. Of course, as was stated in the first chapter, there are many other instances in applied work where there occur m linear equations in n unknowns. It is our job now to learn how to use matrices to attack such problems.

Consider the system:

$$\begin{cases} a_{11}x_1 + \cdots + a_{1n}x_n = b_1, \\ \quad\quad \cdots \\ a_{m1}x_1 + \cdots + a_{mn}x_n = b_m. \end{cases}$$

As we have seen, such a system of equations can be expressed as a matrix equation

$$AX = D.$$

In the following, the entries of A, B, and X are elements of a field (scalars). Any vector X which satisfies the above matrix equation is called a **solution** of the system. When $B = 0$, we call the system **homogeneous,** and when $B \neq 0$, we say that the system is **nonhomogeneous.**

We will show in this chapter that a system of m linear equations in n unknowns may: (1) have no solution, in which case it is called an **inconsistent** system, or (2) have exactly one solution (called a unique solution), or (3) have an infinite number of solutions. In the latter two cases the system is said to be **consistent.** (See Fig. 8.2.)

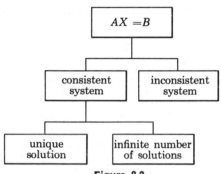

Figure 8.2

Theorems 1 and 2 enable one to discover which of the previous situations exists for a given system by finding the ranks of the coefficient and augmented matrices.

Theorem 1. *A system of linear equations $AX = B$ is consistent if and only if the rank of the augmented matrix is equal to the rank of the coefficient matrix. (This common value, if it exists, will be denoted by r and is often called the rank of the system.)*

The proofs of this theorem and the next will be outlined at the end of this section.

Theorem 2. *A consistent system of linear equations $AX = B$ has a unique solution if and only if $r = n$. (n represents the number of unknowns of the system.)*

Example 1.

The system $AX = B$, or $\begin{cases} x_1 + 3x_2 + x_3 = 2, \\ x_1 - 2x_2 - 2x_3 = 3, \\ 2x_1 + x_2 - x_3 = 6, \end{cases}$ in which $n = m = 3$,

is inconsistent because the rank of $[A \mid B]$ is 3 and the rank of A is 2.

Example 2.

The system $AX = B$, or
$$\begin{cases} x_1 + x_2 - 4x_3 = 2, \\ x_1 - 2x_2 + x_3 = 1, \\ x_1 + x_2 + x_3 = 0, \\ 2x_1 - x_2 + 2x_3 = 1, \end{cases}$$
in which $m = 4, n = 3$,

is consistent because the rank of $[A \mathbin{\vdots} B]$ is 3, and the rank of A is 3. Therefore $r = 3$. The system has only one solution because the rank of the system equals the number of unknowns.

Example 3.

The system $AX = B$, or
$$\begin{cases} 3x_1 - x_2 - 2x_3 = 8, \\ 2x_1 - 2x_2 - x_3 = 2, \\ x_1 + x_2 - x_3 = 6, \end{cases}$$
where $m = n = 3$,

is consistent because the rank of $[A \mathbin{\vdots} B]$ is 2, and the rank of A is 2. The solution is not unique (that is, there are an infinite number of solutions) because $r = 2$ and $n = 3$.

Complete formal proofs of the two theorems of this section are left as exercises. Outlines are given as an aid to the student.

Outline of proof of Theorem 1. By performing the same suitable elementary row transformations on both $AX = B$ and $[A \mathbin{\vdots} B]$ and, if necessary, properly rearranging the subscripts of the unknowns, we eventually obtain the equivalent system:

$$\begin{cases} x_1 && + c_{1,k+1}x_{k+1} + c_{1,k+2}x_{k+2} + \cdots + c_{1n}x_n - d_1 &= 0, \\ & x_2 & + c_{2,k+1}x_{k+1} + c_{2,k+2}x_{k+2} + \cdots + c_{2n}x_n - d_2 &= 0, \\ && \cdots \\ && x_k + c_{k,k+1}x_{k+1} + c_{k,k+2}x_{k+2} + \cdots + c_{kn}x_n - d_k &= 0, \\ &&& - d_{k+1} = 0, \\ &&& - d_{k+2} = 0, \\ && \cdots \\ &&& - d_m = 0, \end{cases}$$

and the corresponding augmented matrix. If any one of the numbers $d_{k+1}, \ldots, d_m$ is different from zero, we have a contradiction and the system above is inconsistent. Hence the equivalent original system is inconsistent. But if $d_{k+1} = d_{k+2} = \cdots = d_m = 0$, the last $m - k$ equations are satisfied and so are the first k equations, since we can solve them for $x_1, \ldots, x_k$ in terms of $x_{k+1}, \ldots, x_n$. Therefore the system is consistent if and only if

$$d_{k+1} = d_{k+2} = \cdots = d_m = 0.$$

Since $|I_k| \neq 0$, the rank of the coefficient matrix is equal to k, and so is the rank of the augmented matrix when $d_{k+1} = d_{k+2} = \cdots = d_m = 0$. But if any one of these $m - k$ numbers is different from zero, the rank of the augmented matrix is greater than k. Hence the system is consistent if and only if the ranks of the coefficient and augmented matrices are the same.

Outline of proof of Theorem 2. In the outline of the above proof of Theorem 1 when $AX = B$ is consistent and the rank equals k, we can solve for certain x_j in terms of d_j and $n - k$ remaining unknowns, that is,

$$x_j = d_j - c_{j,k+1}x_{k+1} - c_{j,k+2}x_{k+2} - \cdots - c_{jn}x_n, \ (j = 1, 2, \ldots, k).$$

If the system has a unique solution, then $n - k = 0$ and hence $k = n$ which means that the rank of the system equals the number of unknowns. Conversely, if the rank of the system equals the number of unknowns then $k = n$ and hence $x_j = d_j$, which is a unique solution where $j = 1, 2, \ldots, n$.

EXERCISES

1. Determine whether the following systems are inconsistent, consistent with a unique solution, or consistent with an infinite number of solutions. Find r, if it exists, and state the relation between r and n.

(a) $\begin{cases} x_1 + 3x_2 + x_3 = 4, \\ x_1 + x_2 - x_3 = 1, \\ 2x_1 + 4x_2 = 0. \end{cases}$

(b) $\begin{cases} x_1 - x_2 + 6 = 0, \\ x_1 + 2x_2 - 5 = 0, \\ 3x_1 + 3x_2 - 4 = 0. \end{cases}$

(c) $\begin{cases} x_1 + 2x_2 + x_3 = 6, \\ x_1 - x_2 = 2, \\ x_1 - x_2 + x_3 = 0, \\ 3x_1 + 2x_3 = 8. \end{cases}$

(d) $\begin{cases} x_1 + x_2 + x_3 - 5 = 0, \\ x_1 - x_2 - x_3 - 4 = 0. \end{cases}$

(e) $\begin{bmatrix} 1 & 1 & 1 \\ 1 & -1 & 0 \\ 2 & 0 & 1 \end{bmatrix} \begin{bmatrix} x_1 \\ x_2 \\ x_3 \end{bmatrix} = \begin{bmatrix} 0 \\ 0 \\ 0 \end{bmatrix}.$

(f) $AX = 0$, where $A = \begin{bmatrix} 2 & 1 & 0 \\ 1 & -1 & 1 \\ 0 & 1 & -1 \end{bmatrix}$ and $X = \begin{bmatrix} x_1 \\ x_2 \\ x_3 \end{bmatrix}.$

(g) $\begin{cases} x_1 + x_2 + 2x_3 - x_4 = 2, \\ 2x_1 + 2x_3 = 0, \\ -x_1 - x_2 + x_3 = 0, \\ 2x_1 - x_3 + x_4 = -2. \end{cases}$

(h) $AX = B$, where $B = \begin{bmatrix} 2 \\ 0 \\ 4 \end{bmatrix}$, $A = \begin{bmatrix} 1 & 1 & -1 \\ 2 & 2 & -1 \\ 1 & 1 & 0 \end{bmatrix}$, $X = \begin{bmatrix} x_1 \\ x_2 \\ x_3 \end{bmatrix}.$

2. Which of the systems in Exercise 1 are homogeneous?

3. A certain system of linear equations with 6 unknowns is known to be con- .sistent and to have a unique solution. What can be said about the ranks of the augmented and coefficient matrices? What can be said about the number of equations? Give reasons.

4. The rank of the coefficient matrix of a certain inconsistent system of linear equations with 5 unknowns is found to be 4. What can be said about the rank of the augmented matrix? What can be said about the number of equations?

5. Suppose we are given 5 linear homogeneous equations in 5 unknowns. If det $A \neq 0$, what can we say about a solution?

6. Determine whether or not $x_1 = \frac{1}{2}$, $x_2 = -\frac{3}{2}$, $x_3 = 1$ is a solution of the following system:

$$\begin{cases} x_1 + x_2 + x_3 = 0, \\ x_1 - 3x_2 - 2x_3 = 3, \\ 2x_1 + 2x_2 - x_3 = 2. \end{cases}$$

7. The system $AX = B$ consists of m linear equations (which may or may not be homogeneous) in n unknowns. Assume that r exists for this system. Why is it always true that $r \leq m$ and $r \leq n$?

8. Give a complete proof in statement-reason form for: (*a*) Theorem 1; (*b*) Theorem 2.

8.2 INCONSISTENT SYSTEMS

As we have seen, inconsistent systems are identified by Theorem 1, and if the ranks of the coefficient and augmented matrices are found to be unequal, any search for a solution is abandoned immediately.

Example 1.

The system
$$\begin{cases} x_1 + 3x_2 - x_3 = 4, \\ x_1 + 2x_2 + x_3 = 2, \\ 3x_1 + 7x_2 + x_3 = 9, \end{cases}$$
is inconsistent because the rank of A is 2 and the rank of $[A \mid B]$ is 3.

Example 2. Geometrically, for inconsistent systems, when $n = 2$ and $m = 3$ we have three lines that do not intersect at a common point. (Fig. 8.3.)

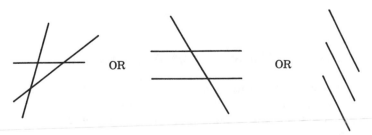

OR   OR

Figure 8.3

Homogeneous systems are never inconsistent because they always have at least the so-called *trivial solution*, $(0, 0, \ldots, 0)$. In other words, because $B = 0$, the ranks of the coefficient and augmented matrices are equal; therefore, by Theorem 1, any homogeneous system is consistent.

EXERCISES

1. Verify that the following systems are inconsistent and then sketch the graphs of the equations of each system.

(a) $\begin{cases} x_1 + x_2 = 4, \\ x_1 - x_2 = 0, \\ \qquad x_2 = 3. \end{cases}$
(b) $\begin{cases} x_1 + x_2 = 2, \\ x_1 - x_2 = 0, \\ 2x_1 + 2x_2 = 6. \end{cases}$

(c) $\begin{cases} 3x_1 - x_2 = 3, \\ 9x_1 - 3x_2 = 9, \\ -6x_1 + 2x_2 = 6. \end{cases}$
(d) $\begin{cases} 3x_1 + x_2 = 1, \\ 6x_1 + 2x_2 = 6. \end{cases}$

2. Suppose that four planes are represented by four linear homogeneous equations $AX = 0$, and the rank of A is found to be 3. Can the system be inconsistent? Why? If a solution exists, give a geometric interpretation.

3. Show that the following system is inconsistent by finding the rank of the augmented matrix only, and then state why you did not have to find the rank of the coefficient matrix.

$$\begin{cases} 2x + y = -4, \\ x - y = 4, \\ -3x + 3y = 2. \end{cases}$$

4. By inspection tell why the following systems cannot be inconsistent.

(a) $\begin{cases} 2x_1 - 3x_2 = 0, \\ 4x_1 - 5x_2 = 0. \end{cases}$
(b) $\begin{cases} 2x_1 = 4, \\ 3x_2 = 9. \end{cases}$

5. Discuss the consistency of the following system for various possible values of b.

$$\begin{cases} x_1 + x_2 = 4, \\ x_1 + x_2 = b. \end{cases}$$

8.3 CONSISTENT SYSTEM WITH A UNIQUE SOLUTION

The following example furnishes a geometric interpretation of a system of three linear equations in three unknowns which has exactly one solution. Obviously for a system with 4 unknowns such a geometric interpretation would be impossible.

Example 1.

Consider the system: $\begin{cases}(1) & x_1 + x_2 + x_3 = 3, \\ (2) & 2x_2 + x_3 = 2, \\ (3) & x_2 + 2x_3 = 2.\end{cases}$

If each of the planes representing these equations is drawn, Fig. 8.4 results. Note that the three planes intersect at a point $(\frac{5}{3}, \frac{2}{3}, \frac{2}{3})$. That is, the coordinates of only one point satisfy all three equations simultaneously.

In Section 8.1 we saw that systems with a unique solution are recognized by making use of Theorem 1 and Theorem 2. Obviously this requires a knowledge of whether r exists, and if so, whether it is equal to n. There is a method for determining this information and at the same time proceeding toward a solution (if there is one). This method will be called the *echelon method* and will be explained by means of examples.

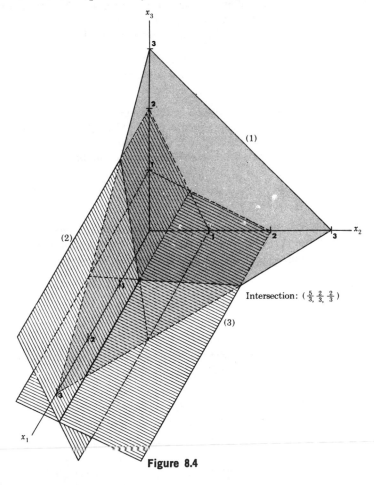

Figure 8.4

Example 2.

Consider
$$\begin{cases} x_1 + x_2 + x_3 = 4, \\ x_1 + 2x_2 + 2x_3 = 2, \\ -x_1 - x_2 + x_3 = 2. \end{cases}$$

The first step is to transform the augmented matrix of the system to an echelon matrix by means of elementary *row* operations, as was done in Example 2 of Section 7.1.

$$\begin{bmatrix} 1 & 1 & 1 & 4 \\ 1 & 2 & 2 & 2 \\ -1 & -1 & 1 & 2 \end{bmatrix} \underset{\substack{-R_1+R_2 \\ R_1+R_3}}{\sim} \begin{bmatrix} 1 & 1 & 1 & 4 \\ 0 & 1 & 1 & -2 \\ 0 & 0 & 2 & 6 \end{bmatrix} \underset{(\frac{1}{2})R_3}{\sim} \begin{bmatrix} 1 & 1 & 1 & 4 \\ 0 & 1 & 1 & -2 \\ 0 & 0 & 1 & 3 \end{bmatrix}.$$

The last matrix (echelon matrix) may be used to determine r, if it exists, and thus determine the type of system with which we are dealing. In this example it turns out that $r = 3$. (This can be found mentally by using elementary column operations to reduce the first three columns to the normal form I_3). Therefore, by the two theorems, we have a consistent system with exactly one solution. The resulting echelon matrix may also be used to express the equivalent system:

$$\begin{cases} x_1 + x_2 + x_3 = 4, \\ x_2 + x_3 = -2, \\ x_3 = 3. \end{cases}$$

By substitution the solution is quickly found to be $x_1 = 6$, $x_2 = -5$, $x_3 = 3$. A geometric interpretation of this example is given by three planes passing through the point $(6, -5, 3)$. The substitution at the end of the procedure could be avoided by continuing with elementary row transformations on the echelon matrix until

the matrix $\begin{bmatrix} 1 & 0 & 0 & 6 \\ 0 & 1 & 0 & -5 \\ 0 & 0 & 1 & 3 \end{bmatrix}$ is obtained. Thus $\begin{cases} x_1 = 6, \\ x_2 = -5, \\ x_3 = 3. \end{cases}$

The echelon method can be applied to solve consistent systems of equations with or without a unique solution. In fact the method can be used to recognize an inconsistent system; this will now be illustrated.

Example 3.

Consider
$$\begin{cases} x_1 + 3x_2 - x_3 = 4, \\ x_1 + 2x_2 + x_3 = 2, \\ 3x_1 + 7x_2 + x_3 = 9. \end{cases}$$

Applying the echelon method, we write the augmented matrix and then transform it to an echelon matrix by the elementary row operations.

$$\begin{bmatrix} 1 & 3 & -1 & 4 \\ 1 & 2 & 1 & 2 \\ 3 & 7 & 1 & 9 \end{bmatrix} \underset{\substack{-R_1+R_2 \\ -3R_1+R_3}}{\sim} \begin{bmatrix} 1 & 3 & -1 & 4 \\ 0 & -1 & 2 & -2 \\ 0 & -2 & 4 & -3 \end{bmatrix}$$

$$\underset{-R_2}{\sim} \begin{bmatrix} 1 & 3 & -1 & 4 \\ 0 & 1 & -2 & 2 \\ 0 & -2 & 4 & -3 \end{bmatrix} \underset{2R_2+R_3}{\sim} \begin{bmatrix} 1 & 3 & -1 & 4 \\ 0 & 1 & -2 & 2 \\ 0 & 0 & 0 & 1 \end{bmatrix}.$$

Because the last row contains zeros everywhere except in the last column, the rank of the coefficient matrix is less than the rank of the augmented matrix, and hence by Theorem 1 the system is not consistent.

Sometimes there are more equations than unknowns; that is, $m > n$. This situation is also easily handled by the echelon method.

Example 4.

Consider
$$\begin{cases} (1) & 2x_1 + x_2 = 1, \\ (2) & -4x_1 + 6x_2 = 6, \\ (3) & -2x_1 + 7x_2 = 7. \end{cases}$$

By the echelon method, the augmented matrix is transformed to an echelon matrix.

$$\begin{bmatrix} 2 & 1 & 1 \\ -4 & 6 & 6 \\ -2 & 7 & 7 \end{bmatrix} \underset{\substack{2R_1 + R_2 \\ R_1 + R_3}}{\sim} \begin{bmatrix} 2 & 1 & 1 \\ 0 & 8 & 8 \\ 0 & 8 & 8 \end{bmatrix} \underset{-R_2 + R_3}{\sim} \begin{bmatrix} 2 & 1 & 1 \\ 0 & 8 & 8 \\ 0 & 0 & 0 \end{bmatrix} \underset{\substack{(\frac{1}{2})R_1 \\ (\frac{1}{8})R_2}}{\sim} \begin{bmatrix} 1 & \frac{1}{2} & \frac{1}{2} \\ 0 & 1 & 1 \\ 0 & 0 & 0 \end{bmatrix}.$$

We can now easily find that $r = 2$, and hence we have a unique solution which can be found by substitution in the equivalent system

$$\begin{cases} x_1 + \frac{1}{2}x_2 = \frac{1}{2}, \\ \qquad x_2 = 1. \end{cases}$$

The solution is $(0, 1)$. A geometric interpretation of this example is three lines passing through the point $(0, 1)$. (See Fig. 8.5.)

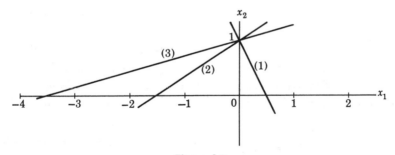

Figure 8.5

In order to refresh the student's memory, Example 1 of this section will be solved by the matrix inversion method that was presented in Chapter 6.

Example 5. Using matrix notation we had

$$AX = B \quad \text{or} \quad \begin{bmatrix} 1 & 1 & 1 \\ 0 & 2 & 1 \\ 0 & 1 & 2 \end{bmatrix} \begin{bmatrix} x_1 \\ x_2 \\ x_3 \end{bmatrix} = \begin{bmatrix} 3 \\ 2 \\ 2 \end{bmatrix}.$$

$$X = A^{-1}B \quad \text{or} \quad \begin{bmatrix} x_1 \\ x_2 \\ x_3 \end{bmatrix} = \frac{1}{3} \begin{bmatrix} 3 & -1 & -1 \\ 0 & 2 & -1 \\ 0 & -1 & 2 \end{bmatrix} \begin{bmatrix} 3 \\ 2 \\ 2 \end{bmatrix} = \begin{bmatrix} \frac{5}{3} \\ \frac{2}{3} \\ \frac{2}{3} \end{bmatrix}.$$

In order to apply this procedure it is necessary that A^{-1} exist. It will exist if $r = m = n$. Why? This method is useful for solving a set of systems, all with the same A but different B.

Remember that Cramer's rule may also be employed to solve the preceding example. The inversion method and Cramer's rule will not apply unless there is a unique solution.

If a homogeneous system has only one solution then that solution is the trivial solution $(0, 0, 0, \ldots, 0)$ or null vector.

EXERCISES

1. Each of the following matrices has been obtained from the augmented matrix of a given system of equations by using the echelon method. In each case, tell what you can about the solution of the equivalent original system.

(a) $\begin{bmatrix} 1 & 2 & 4 \\ 0 & 1 & 1 \end{bmatrix}$;

(b) $\begin{bmatrix} 1 & 2 & 0 \\ 0 & 1 & 0 \end{bmatrix}$;

(c) $\begin{bmatrix} 1 & 2 & 2 \\ 0 & 0 & 1 \end{bmatrix}$;

(d) $\begin{bmatrix} 1 & 2 & 0 \\ 0 & 0 & 1 \end{bmatrix}$;

(e) $\begin{bmatrix} 1 & 1 & 4 \\ 0 & 1 & 3 \\ 0 & 0 & 0 \end{bmatrix}$;

(f) $\begin{bmatrix} 1 & 0 & 0 \\ 0 & 1 & 0 \\ 0 & 0 & 1 \end{bmatrix}$.

2. For each of the following systems determine by the echelon method whether the system is consistent with a unique solution, and if it is, find that solution. Check your answers.

(a) $\begin{cases} x_1 + x_2 = 3, \\ 2x_1 - x_2 = 4. \end{cases}$

(b) $\begin{cases} x_1 \quad - \quad x_3 - 2 = 0, \\ \quad x_2 + 3x_3 - 1 = 0, \\ x_1 - 2x_2 \quad - 7 = 0. \end{cases}$

(c) $\begin{cases} x_1 + 2x_2 - x_3 = 6, \\ 2x_1 - x_2 + 3x_3 = -13, \\ 3x_1 - 2x_2 + 3x_3 = -16. \end{cases}$

(d) $\begin{cases} 6x_1 + 3x_2 + 2x_3 = 1, \\ 3x_1 \quad - 4x_3 = 4, \\ 5x_1 - x_2 \quad = 14. \end{cases}$

(e) $\begin{cases} 2x_1 + x_2 - x_3 = -4, \\ x_1 - x_2 + 3x_3 = 3, \\ x_1 + 2x_2 - 4x_3 = 1. \end{cases}$

(f) $\begin{cases} x_1 - x_2 - x_3 - x_4 = 5, \\ x_1 + 2x_2 + 3x_3 + x_4 = -2, \\ 2x_1 \quad + 2x_3 + 3x_4 = 3, \\ 3x_1 + x_2 \quad + 2x_4 = 1. \end{cases}$

(g) $\begin{cases} x_1 + 2x_2 + x_3 = 2, \\ 2x_1 \quad - 2x_3 + x_4 = 6, \\ 4x_2 + 3x_3 + 2x_4 = -1, \\ -x_1 + 6x_2 - x_3 - x_4 = 2. \end{cases}$

(h) $\begin{cases} x_1 - x_2 = 1, \\ 2x_1 + x_2 = \frac{19}{2}, \\ 4x_1 - 2x_2 = 9. \end{cases}$

Also draw a graph.

(i) $\begin{cases} x + y + 2z = 6, \\ x - y - 4z = -8, \\ 3x - 2y + 5z = 11, \\ 2x + 5y - 2z = 3. \end{cases}$

(j) $\begin{cases} x + 2y = 0, \\ 3x - y = 0. \end{cases}$

$$(k) \begin{cases} x_1 + 2x_2 + 3x_3 = 0, \\ 2x_1 - x_2 + x_3 = 0, \\ 2x_1 + 3x_2 + 4x_3 = 0. \end{cases} \qquad (l) \begin{cases} x_1 + x_2 + x_3 = 0, \\ x_1 - x_2 - 2x_3 = 0, \\ 2x_1 - x_3 = 0. \end{cases}$$

3. Explain what happens in the echelon matrix when the system is inconsistent.

4. Two alloys P and Q are manufactured by a certain factory, which sells its products by the ton but purchases some of the ingredients in 100 pound units. For each ton of P produced, 4 units of metal A and 4 units of metal B are required. Each ton of Q requires 7 units of A and 3 units of B. If the factory can obtain and wishes to use exactly 60 units of metal A and 40 units of metal B per day, how many tons of each alloy can it produce in a day?

5. A trucking company owns three types of trucks, numbered 1, 2, and 3, which are equipped to haul three different types of machines per load according to the following chart.

	Trucks		
	No. 1	No. 2	No. 3
Machine A	1	1	1
Machine B	0	1	2
Machine C	2	1	1

How many trucks of each type should be sent to haul exactly 12 of the type A machines, 10 of the type B machines, and 16 of the type C machines? Assume each truck is fully loaded.

6. To control a certain crop disease, it is determined that it is necessary to use 6 units of chemical A, 10 units of chemical B, and 8 units of chemical C. One barrel of commercial spray P contains 1, 3, and 4 units respectively of these chemicals. One barrel of commercial spray Q contains 3, 3, 3 units respectively, and spray R contains 2 units of A and 5 units of B. How much of each type of spray should be used to spread the exact amounts of chemicals needed to control the disease?

7. For the network diagrammed in Fig. 8.6,

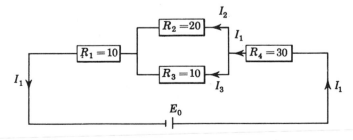

Figure 8.6

Kirchhoff's Laws yield the system of equations,

$$\begin{cases} I_1 - I_2 - I_3 = 0, \\ 20I_2 - 10I_3 = 0, \\ 40I_1 + 20I_2 = E_0. \end{cases}$$

Solve for the currents I_1, I_2, I_3.

8. Sketch the planes $x + 2y + 2z = 6$, $2x + y + z = 6$, and $3x + 2y + z = 9$. Estimate the point of intersection from your graph. Then solve these equations by the echelon method to accurately find the point common to the three planes.

8.4 CONSISTENT SYSTEM WITH AN INFINITE NUMBER OF SOLUTIONS

First, we give an example to show how there can be more than one solution to a system of equations.

Example 1. It can be verified that the system

$$\begin{cases} (1)\ x_1 + x_2 + x_3 = 3, \\ (2)\ x_1 \qquad - x_3 = 1, \\ (3)\qquad x_2 + 2x_3 = 2, \end{cases}$$

is consistent ($r = 2$), but by Theorem 2 there is not a unique solution. If we graph this system we find that the three planes representing the three equations intersect along a line; thus, there are an infinite number of points (or vectors) that satisfy this system. This is illustrated in Fig. 8.7.

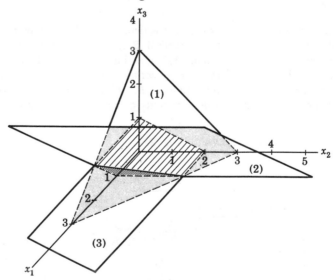

Figure 8.7

A consistent system with more than one solution also is identified by applying Theorems 1 and 2 (for such systems, r exists and $r < n$). The system may then be solved by expressing a certain set of r unknowns in terms of the other $n - r$ unknowns. (This was justified in the process of proving Theorem 2.) These $n - r$ unknowns are considered to be arbitrary parameters. The solution thus obtained is called a **complete solution.** A procedure for finding such a solution is best explained by the use of two examples.

Example 2.

Solve
$$\begin{cases} x_1 + x_2 + x_3 + x_4 = 4, \\ x_1 + 3x_2 + 3x_3 = 2, \\ x_1 + x_2 + 2x_3 - x_4 = 6. \end{cases}$$

The echelon method will be employed again. Transform the augmented matrix to an echelon matrix by means of elementary row operations.

$$\begin{bmatrix} 1 & 1 & 1 & 1 & 4 \\ 1 & 3 & 3 & 0 & 2 \\ 1 & 1 & 2 & -1 & 6 \end{bmatrix} \underset{\substack{-R_1 + R_2 \\ -R_1 + R_3}}{\sim} \begin{bmatrix} 1 & 1 & 1 & 1 & 4 \\ 0 & 2 & 2 & -1 & -2 \\ 0 & 0 & 1 & -2 & 2 \end{bmatrix}$$

$$\underset{(\frac{1}{2})R_2}{\sim} \begin{bmatrix} 1 & 1 & 1 & 1 & 4 \\ 0 & 1 & 1 & -\frac{1}{2} & -1 \\ 0 & 0 & 1 & -2 & 2 \end{bmatrix}$$

From the last matrix (an echelon matrix) we find that $r = 3$ and hence the system is consistent. It was obvious from the beginning that we could not have a unique solution because there were only three equations in four unknowns. From the echelon matrix we have the equivalent system

$$\begin{cases} x_1 + x_2 + x_3 + x_4 = 4, \\ x_2 + x_3 - \frac{1}{2}x_4 = -1, \\ x_3 - 2x_4 = 2, \end{cases}$$

or

$$\begin{cases} x_1 = 4 - x_4 - x_3 - x_2, \\ x_2 = -1 + \frac{1}{2}x_4 - x_3, \\ x_3 = 2 + 2x_4. \end{cases}$$

By substitution we arrive at the **complete solution**

$$\begin{cases} x_1 = 5 - \frac{3}{2}x_4, \\ x_2 = -3 - \frac{3}{2}x_4, \\ x_3 = 2 + 2x_4. \end{cases}$$

From the complete solution we may obtain what is called a **particular solution,** if we substitute values for the parameter (x_4 in this example).

$$\text{If } x_4 = 0, \quad \begin{cases} x_1 = 5, \\ x_2 = -3, \\ x_3 = 2. \end{cases}$$

Thus the vector $(5, -3, 2, 0)$ is a particular solution.

$$\text{If} \quad x_4 = 4, \quad \begin{cases} x_1 = -1, \\ x_2 = -9, \\ x_3 = 10. \end{cases}$$

Thus the vector $(-1, -9, 10, 4)$ is another particular solution. If the parameter can take on an infinite number of values, then there will be an infinite number of solutions.

In the previous example we could have modified our method to eliminate the necessity to substitute unknowns back in the preceding equations.

For example, when we had the echelon matrix $\begin{bmatrix} 1 & 1 & 1 & 1 & 4 \\ 0 & 1 & 1 & -\frac{1}{2} & -1 \\ 0 & 0 & 1 & -2 & 2 \end{bmatrix}$, we

could have continued using elementary row transformations to create a submatrix I_r. In this problem it is done as follows:

$$\underset{-R_2 + R_1}{\sim} \begin{bmatrix} 1 & 0 & 0 & \frac{3}{2} & 5 \\ 0 & 1 & 1 & -\frac{1}{2} & -1 \\ 0 & 0 & 1 & -2 & 2 \end{bmatrix} \underset{-R_3 + R_2}{\sim} \begin{bmatrix} 1 & 0 & 0 & \frac{3}{2} & 5 \\ 0 & 1 & 0 & \frac{3}{2} & -3 \\ 0 & 0 & 1 & -2 & 2 \end{bmatrix}.$$

The latter matrix is the augmented matrix of the system

$$\begin{cases} x_1 & + \frac{3}{2}x_4 = 5, \\ x_2 & + \frac{3}{2}x_4 = -3, \\ x_3 - 2x_4 = 2, \end{cases}$$

from which the complete solution follows easily. This method is sometimes called the **Gauss-Jordan elimination method.**

Example 3.

Solve $\qquad \begin{cases} x_1 + x_2 + 3x_3 = 8, \\ x_2 + 3x_3 = 6, \\ x_1 + 2x_2 + 6x_3 = 14. \end{cases}$

Transforming the augmented matrix to an echelon matrix, we have

$$\begin{bmatrix} 1 & 1 & 3 & 8 \\ 0 & 1 & 3 & 6 \\ 1 & 2 & 6 & 14 \end{bmatrix} \underset{-R_1 + R_3}{\sim} \begin{bmatrix} 1 & 1 & 3 & 8 \\ 0 & 1 & 3 & 6 \\ 0 & 1 & 3 & 6 \end{bmatrix} \underset{-R_2 + R_3}{\sim} \begin{bmatrix} 1 & 1 & 3 & 8 \\ 0 & 1 & 3 & 6 \\ 0 & 0 & 0 & 0 \end{bmatrix}.$$

From this we find that $r = 2$, and hence, by Theorems 1 and 2, we know that we have a consistent system with more than one solution. Also from this echelon matrix we recognize that an equivalent system is

$$\begin{cases} x_1 + x_2 + 3x_3 = 8, \\ x_2 + 3x_3 = 6, \end{cases} \quad \text{or} \quad \begin{cases} x_1 = 8 - (6 - 3x_3) - 3x_3, \\ x_2 = 6 - 3x_3; \end{cases}$$

therefore, the complete solution is

$$\begin{cases} x_1 = 2, \\ x_2 = 6 - 3x_3. \end{cases}$$

Or, by the Gauss-Jordan elimination method, the echelon matrix is equivalent

(by $-R_2 + R_1$) to $\begin{bmatrix} 1 & 0 & 0 & 2 \\ 0 & 1 & 3 & 6 \\ 0 & 0 & 0 & 0 \end{bmatrix}$, which is the augmented matrix for the system

$\begin{cases} x_1 \qquad = 2, \\ \quad x_2 + 3x_3 = 6. \end{cases}$ The complete solution follows immediately, $\begin{cases} x_1 = 2 + 0x_3, \\ x_2 = 6 - 3x_3. \end{cases}$

It is important to note that in Example 3 we can solve for x_1 and x_2 in terms of x_3, or we can solve for x_1 and x_3 in terms of x_2, but we *cannot* solve for x_2 and x_3 in terms of x_1. In some situations it might be best to know such information ahead of time; this is the purpose of Theorem 3.

Theorem 3.   *A consistent system of linear equations of rank r can be solved for r unknowns, say $x_{i_1}, x_{i_2}, \ldots, x_{i_r}$ in terms of the remaining $n - r$ unknowns, if and only if the submatrix of coefficients of $x_{i_1}, x_{i_2}, \ldots, x_{i_r}$ has rank r.*

An outline of the proof of this theorem is given after the next two examples.

Example 4.   In Example 3 the rank of the system was 2. The rank of the

matrix of coefficients for x_1 and x_2 was 2 since $\begin{bmatrix} 1 & 1 \\ 0 & 1 \\ 1 & 2 \end{bmatrix} \sim \begin{bmatrix} 1 & 0 \\ 0 & 1 \\ 0 & 0 \end{bmatrix}$.

This information could be obtained from the echelon matrix. It allows us to predict the solution of x_1 and x_2 in terms of x_3. However, the rank of the matrix of coefficients for x_2 and x_3 was 1 because

$$\begin{bmatrix} 1 & 3 \\ 1 & 3 \\ 2 & 6 \end{bmatrix} \sim \begin{bmatrix} 1 & 0 \\ 0 & 0 \\ 0 & 0 \end{bmatrix}.$$

This allows us to predict that we *cannot* solve for x_2 and x_3 in terms of x_1. Again this information could be obtained from the echelon matrix.

A homogeneous system is handled in the same way by this method.

Consider a consistent system of rank m with more unknowns than equations ($n > m$); when a complete solution is found and all the parameters are assigned the value zero, the resulting particular solution is called a **basic solution**. The m unknowns or variables (which can be determined by Theorem 3) not serving as parameters in a basic solution are called **basic variables**.

Example 5. The system

$$\begin{cases} x_1 + x_2 + 3x_3 - x_4 = 6, \\ x_1 + 2x_2 + 2x_3 - x_4 = 2, \end{cases}$$

can be shown to have a complete solution

$$\begin{cases} x_1 \phantom{{}={}} = 10 - 4x_3 + x_4, \\ x_2 = -4 + x_3. \end{cases}$$

When the parameters x_3 and x_4 are both zero, there results a basic solution $(10, -4, 0, 0)$. Here the basic variables are x_1 and x_2. This, of course, is not the only basic solution. For a complete solution in which x_2 and x_3 are the parameters, there is a different basic solution.

Basic solutions and basic variables will play a big part in our discussion of linear programming in Chapter 12.

Outline of proof of Theorem 3. Assume that the rank of the submatrix of coefficients of r of the unknowns is r. We have already shown in the process of proving Theorem 2 that these unknowns can be found in terms of the remaining $n - r$ unknowns.

Conversely, if we assume that r of the unknowns, $x_{i_1}, x_{i_2}, \ldots, x_{i_r}$, can be found in terms of the other $n - r$ unknowns, the rank of this system must be r. Hence the rank of the coefficient matrix of this system is r, and by elementary operations r can be shown to equal the rank of the submatrix of coefficients of $(x_{i_1}, x_{i_2}, \ldots, x_{i_r})$ in the original system.

EXERCISES

1. The following echelon matrices have been obtained from the augmented matrices of various systems by using the echelon method. What can you tell about the solution of the equivalent, original system in each case?

$$(a) \begin{bmatrix} 1 & 2 & 2 \\ 0 & 0 & 0 \end{bmatrix}, \qquad (b) \begin{bmatrix} 1 & 2 & 0 \\ 0 & 0 & 0 \end{bmatrix}, \qquad (c) \begin{bmatrix} 1 & 2 & 0 \\ 0 & 0 & 1 \end{bmatrix},$$

$$(d) \begin{bmatrix} 1 & 3 & 0 \\ 0 & 1 & 0 \end{bmatrix}.$$

2. By the Gauss-Jordan elimination method or the echelon method, determine whether the system is consistent and has more than one solution. If so, find a complete solution and one particular solution.

$$(a) \begin{cases} x_1 + x_2 - x_3 = 4, \\ x_1 - x_2 + x_3 = 2. \end{cases} \qquad (b) \begin{cases} 2x_1 + x_2 - x_3 = 3, \\ x_1 + x_2 \phantom{{}- x_3} = 2, \\ x_1 \phantom{{}+ x_2} - x_3 = 1. \end{cases}$$

(c) $\begin{cases} 3x_1 - x_2 + x_3 = 4, \\ x_1 - x_2 = 0, \\ 2x_1 + x_3 = 4, \\ 4x_1 - 2x_2 + x_3 = 4. \end{cases}$ (d) $\begin{cases} x_1 + 2x_2 - x_3 + x_4 = 1, \\ x_1 - x_2 + x_3 - x_4 = 2. \end{cases}$

(e) $\begin{cases} x_1 - 2x_2 + x_3 - x_4 = 3, \\ 2x_1 - 3x_2 = 3, \\ x_1 - x_2 - x_3 + x_4 = 0. \end{cases}$ (f) $\begin{cases} x_1 + x_3 = 2, \\ x_2 + x_3 = 6, \\ x_2 + x_4 = 0, \\ x_1 + x_2 + x_3 + x_4 = 2. \end{cases}$

(g) $2x_1 + x_2 = 4.$ (h) $\begin{cases} 2x_1 - x_2 = 0, \\ -4x_1 + 2x_2 = 0. \end{cases}$ (i) $\begin{cases} x_1 - 3x_2 + 2x_3 = 0, \\ -x_1 - 2x_2 + 2x_3 = 0, \\ -2x_1 + x_2 = 0. \end{cases}$

3. Explain what happens in the echelon matrix when the system is consistent and has an infinite number of solutions.

4. In a homogeneous system, can we always be assured that the null vector will be a particular solution?

5. In the following consistent system, can we solve for x_1 and x_2 in terms of x_3? Why?

$$\begin{cases} x_1 + x_2 + x_3 = 4, \\ -x_1 - x_2 = 2, \\ 2x_1 + 2x_2 + 2x_3 = 8. \end{cases}$$

6. Without solving the system, state which unknowns can be expressed in terms of the others.

$$\begin{cases} x_1 - x_2 - 3x_3 - 2x_4 = 4, \\ x_1 + x_2 - 3x_3 - 2x_4 = 2. \end{cases}$$

State reasons for your conclusions.

7. (a) Determine one basic solution for

$$\begin{cases} -x_1 + x_2 + x_3 = 4, \\ 2x_1 - 2x_2 + x_4 = 5. \end{cases}$$

(b) Determine which sets of unknowns may serve as basic variables.

8. (a) In the following system, the ranks of the coefficient and augmented matrices are 2. Solve the system in terms of z and w.

$$\begin{cases} x + y + z + 2w = 1, \\ 2x + 2y + 2z + 4w = 2, \\ 2x - y + 2z + w = 2. \end{cases}$$

(b) Use the complete solution found as an answer to part (a) to find a basic solution.

9. Use a graph to explain why the system $\begin{cases} x + y = 2, \\ 3x + 3y = 6, \end{cases}$ has an infinite number of solutions.

10. Demonstrate graphically that the system

$$\begin{cases} x \quad\;\; + z = 1, \\ x + y + z = 3, \\ \quad\;\; y \quad\;\;\; = 2, \end{cases}$$

has an infinite number of solutions. Then using the echelon method, find the complete solution and three particular solutions (be sure that the particular solutions agree with your graph).

11. (*a*) A trucking company owns three types of trucks which are equipped to haul two different types of machines per load according to the following chart.

	Trucks		
	No. 1	No. 2	No. 3
Machine A	1	1	1
Machine C	2	1	1

How many trucks of each type could be sent to haul exactly 12 of the type A machines and 16 of the type C machines? Assume each truck is fully loaded. (See Exercise 5 of Section 8.3)

(*b*) Why are there not an infinite number of solutions to part (*a*)?

12. To control a certain crop disease, it is determined that it is necessary to use 6 units of chemical A and 10 units of chemical B. One barrel of commercial spray P contains 1 unit of A and 3 units of B. One barrel of spray Q contains 3 units of A and 3 units of B, and spray R contains 2 units of A and 5 units of B. How much of each type of spray could be used to spread the exact amount of chemicals needed to control the disease? (See Exercise 6 of Section 8.3)

13. Give a complete proof in statement–reason form for Theorem 3.

8.5 A GEOMETRIC SUMMARY WHEN $n = 3$ (Optional)

For those who are interested in the geometric ramifications of the first four sections of this chapter, the following outline is presented.

I. Inconsistent system, $n = 3$.

(1) If $\begin{cases} \text{rank of } [A \mid B] = 4, \\ \text{rank of} \quad\;\; A \quad\;\; = 3, \end{cases}$ then at least three of the m planes intersect at a unique point, and at least one plane does not pass through that point.

(2) If $\begin{cases} \text{rank of } [A \mid B] = 3, \\ \text{rank of} \quad A \quad = 2, \end{cases}$ then at least two of the m planes intersect along a unique line, and at least one plane does not pass through that line.

(3) If $\begin{cases} \text{rank of } [A \mid B] = 2, \\ \text{rank of} \quad A \quad = 1, \end{cases}$ then there are m parallel planes where at least one of them is not coplanar with all the others. (Here "parallel" includes the coincident case.)

II. Consistent system, $n = 3$.

(1) If $r = 3$, then m planes intersect at a unique point.

(2) If $r = 2$, then m planes intersect along a unique line.

(3) If $r = 1$, then m planes intersect along a plane, that is, they are coincident.

EXERCISES

1. In a form not containing i or j, write the system of equations represented by the expression $\sum_{j=1}^{2} a_{ij}x_j = b_i$, where $i = 1, 2, \ldots, m$. Using this system, complete the following chart. In the third column indicate whether the system has a unique solution, infinitely many solutions, or no solution.

Rank of coefficient matrix.	Rank of augmented matrix.	Number of solutions	Give a geometric interpretation.
2	3		
2	2		
1	1		

8.6 SUMMARY

The system of linear equations $AX = B$ is either consistent or it is not. Our first task is to devise a procedure to determine which is the case (Theorem 1). Next, a consistent system either has a unique solution or it does not. Our second task is to devise a procedure for deciding which of these cases exists (Theorem 2). Thus, we have one of three situations: the system has (1) no solution or (2) exactly one solution or (3) more than one solution. Finally, if solutions exist, what are the methods for finding them? The echelon method has the advantage of supplying the information needed to employ Theorems 1, 2, and 3 while proceeding toward a solution (if one exists); moreover it will supply a solution to any consistent system of linear equations. When a unique solution exists, Cramer's rule or matrix inversion also may be employed by selecting a certain n of the m equations.

A homogeneous system is always consistent; the null vector is always a solution.

For a consistent system with more unknowns than equations, when a complete solution is found and all parameters are assigned the value zero, the resulting particular solution is called a basic solution; the unknowns or variables not serving as parameters are called basic variables.

EXERCISES

Answer the following questions for each of the systems given below. Do not calculate a specific solution for any system.

(a) Does the system have a solution? Why?

(b) Does the system have a unique solution? Why?

(c) If a solution does exist and yet is not unique, write the general form of a complete solution such as,

$$\begin{cases} x_1 = f_1(x_2, x_5), \\ x_3 = f_2(x_2, x_5), \quad \text{State how you know that your solution can be found.} \\ x_4 = f_3(x_2, x_5). \end{cases}$$

1. $\begin{cases} x_1 + x_2 \quad\quad = 4, \\ 3x_1 \quad\quad + x_3 = 1, \quad \text{The rank of the augmented matrix is 3.} \\ 2x_1 - x_2 + x_3 = 0. \end{cases}$

2. $\begin{cases} x_1 + x_2 \quad\quad + x_4 = 0, \\ x_1 - x_2 + x_3 + x_4 = 0, \quad \text{The rank of the coefficient matrix is 3.} \\ 2x_1 \quad\quad + x_3 + x_4 = 0. \end{cases}$

3. $\begin{cases} 2x_1 + 2x_2 = 4, \\ x_1 + x_2 = 2, \\ x_1 - 2x_2 = 1, \\ 2x_1 - x_2 = 3. \end{cases}$ The augmented matrix is equivalent to $\begin{bmatrix} I_2 & \vdots & 0 \\ \cdots & \vdots & \cdots \\ 0 & \vdots & 0 \end{bmatrix}$.

NEW VOCABULARY

homogeneous linear system 8.1	trivial solution 8.2
nonhomogeneous linear system 8.1	echelon method 8.3
	complete solution 8.4
consistent system 8.1	particular solution 8.4
inconsistent system 8.1	Gauss–Jordan elimination method 8.4
unique solution 8.1	basic solution 8.4
rank of the system 8.1	basic variables 8.4

9

Vector Spaces

9.1 DEFINITION

In Chapter 2 the student was introduced to an element called a vector, and it was defined to be an ordered set of scalars $(a_1, a_2, \ldots, a_n)$. At that time the discussion was largely confined to vectors with constant components and certain operations among these vectors.

Example 1. Given $\alpha = (2, 1, 6), \beta = (4, 2, 0)$ and a scalar c.

$$\alpha + \beta = (2 + 4, 1 + 2, 6 + 0) = (6, 3, 6),$$

$$\alpha \cdot \beta = 2 \cdot 4 + 1 \cdot 2 + 6 \cdot 0 = 8 + 2 + 0 = 10,$$

$$c\alpha = (c \cdot 2, c \cdot 1, c \cdot 6) = (2c, c, 6c).$$

In this chapter we wish to broaden our concepts of vectors by introducing a new mathematical system called a **vector space**.

Definition. *A set of elements forms a **vector space** if:*

(1) Any two of the elements can be added in a unique way and their sum is also an element of the set.

(2) Any element b of the set can be multiplied by an arbitrary scalar s to produce a unique element sb of the set.

(3) The following laws are satisfied: If a, b, c represent arbitrary elements of the set and r, s represent arbitrary scalars,

$$a + b = b + a;$$
$$a + (b + c) = (a + b) + c;$$

there exists an element 0 in the set such that

$$a + 0 = a;$$

141

there exists an element $-a$ *in the set such that*
$$a + (-a) = 0;$$
$$r(a + b) = ra + rb;$$
$$(r + s)a = ra + sa;$$
$$r(sa) = (rs)a;$$

there exists a scalar 1, known as the identity element for multiplication, such that

$$1 \cdot a = a.$$

In this definition, by a scalar we mean an element of a field (see Section 3.6). For the remainder of this text, however, we shall be concerned only with the situation where the scalars are members of the real number field.

Example 2. The set of all vectors in the $x_1 x_2$-plane forms a vector space. Members of this vector space can be graphed on a two-dimensional graph. (See Fig. 9.1.) The vectors belonging to this particular vector space can be thought of as "creatures of two-space or two dimensions." Note that the sum of any two vectors also belongs to the set, and that the product of any real number by any of these vectors is in the set.

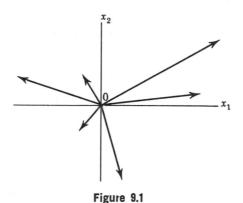

Figure 9.1

Example 3. The set of all vectors in three-space forms a vector space. Geometrically, members of this vector space can be graphed on a three-dimensional graph. (See Fig. 9.2.) This is an example of what we will later call a three-dimensional vector space. These members may be thought of as "creatures of three-space."

The two preceding examples suggest the following fact which a review of Sections 3.4 and 3.5 should make apparent: The set of all n-dimensional vectors forms a vector space.

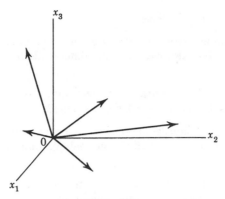

Figure 9.2

Example 4. The set of all vectors that originate at the origin and are parallel to the vector $(3, 1)$ forms a vector space which can be described geometrically as shown in Fig. 9.3. This is an example of what later will be called a one-dimensional vector space.

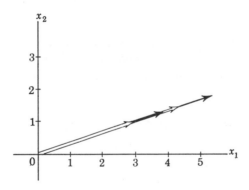

Figure 9.3

Example 5. The set of vectors in the x_1x_2-plane with integral components does not form a vector space because postulate (2) of the definition is not satisfied. For example, $\frac{2}{3}(6, 4) = (4, \frac{8}{3})$ does not belong to the set because $\frac{8}{3}$ is not an integer.

The elements of a vector space do *not* have to be limited to vectors as defined in Chapter 2. The student should observe that the set of all 2 by 2 matrices with scalar entries forms a vector space because all the requirements of the definition are satisfied.

EXERCISES

1. Show that the set of vectors of Example 3 satisfies all the requirements of a vector space as given in the definition.

2. Repeat Exercise 1 for Example 4.

3. From the definition, show that the set of all 2 by 2 matrices with real entries forms a vector space where the operations of addition and scalar multiplication are defined as usual.

4. Will the set of all 3 by 2 matrices with real entries form a vector space where addition and scalar multiplication are defined as usual?

5. Will the set of all binomials $(cx + d)$ where c and d are real numbers form a vector space if the operations of addition and multiplication by a scalar are defined as usual?   Show why.

6. Will the set of three vectors $(2, 3)$, $(1, 1)$, and $(0, 0)$ form a vector space (usual operations)?   Give sufficient reasons for your answer.

7. Show that the set of ordinary real numbers forms a vector space under addition and multiplication.

8. Do all of the vectors in the plane of $i + j + k$ and $2i - j$ form a vector space where addition and multiplication of a vector by a scalar are defined as usual? Why?

9. Verify that the vector $(0, 0)$ forms a vector space under the usual operations of addition and scalar multiplication of a vector.   Will any one vector with two components other than $(0, 0)$ form a vector space?   Why?

10. Why do the elements of any vector space form an Abelian group under addition?

9.2 LINEAR DEPENDENCE AND INDEPENDENCE

In the remainder of this chapter only vectors as they were defined in Chapter 2, namely ordered sets of scalars, will be considered as elements of our vector spaces; keep in mind, however, that other elements exist which will serve as elements of a vector space.

Certain vectors in a vector space can be combined to produce other vectors in the same vector space.

Example 1.   Any vector γ in the x_1x_2-plane can be produced by a proper choice of scalar coefficients in the following equation.

$$\gamma = k_1(1, 2) + k_2(3, 4).$$

We say that γ is a *linear combination* of $(1, 2)$ and $(3, 4)$.

Definition.   *If $\alpha_1, \alpha_2, \cdots, \alpha_n$ are vectors and $k_1, k_2, \cdots, k_n$ are scalars, the vector*

$$\gamma = k_1 \alpha_1 + k_2 \alpha_2 + \cdots + k_n \alpha_n$$

*is said to be a **linear combination** of the vectors*

$$\alpha_1, \alpha_2, \cdots, \alpha_n.$$

Definition. *A set of vectors α_1, α_2, $\cdots$, α_n is said to **span** a vector space provided that they belong to the vector space and that every vector in the space can be expressed as a linear combination of them.*

Example 2. The vectors $\alpha_1 = (1, 0, 0)$, $\alpha_2 = (0, 1, 0)$, and $\alpha_3 = (0, 0, 1)$ span the vector space consisting of all three-dimensional real vectors, because by appropriate choice of coefficients, any three-dimensional vector γ can be written as a linear combination of α_1, α_2, and α_3. See Figure 9.4.

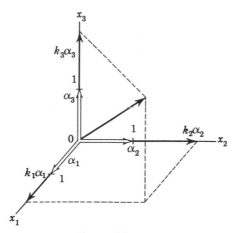

Figure 9.4

Example 3. The vectors $\beta_1 = (1, 0, 0)$, $\beta_2 = (0, 1, 0)$, and $\beta_3 = (1, 1, 0)$ do ***not*** span the vector space consisting of all three-dimensional vectors because there is no choice of the k's that will enable us to express any vector not in the x_1x_2-plane in terms of β_1, β_2, and β_3. That is, any linear combination of $(1, 0, 0)$, $(0, 1, 0)$, and $(1, 1, 0)$ will be in the x_1x_2-plane (Fig. 9.5). Therefore, these three vectors do not span three-space. (It can be verified, however, that the set of all three-dimensional vectors which terminate in the x_1x_2-plane form a vector space and that β_1, β_2, β_3 span this vector space.)

In Example 2 we have an illustration of a concept known as **linear independence,** that is, the vectors α_1, α_2, and α_3 are linearly independent because none of them can be expressed as a linear combination of the other two. However, these vectors together with $\gamma = k_1\alpha_1 + k_2\alpha_2 + k_3\alpha_3$, are not linearly independent because, by its very form, γ can be expressed as a linear combination of α_1, α_2, and α_3. In Example 3 the vectors β_1, β_2, and β_3 are *not* linearly independent, because it is quite obvious that β_3 can be expressed as a linear combination of β_1 and β_2. We say that β_1, β_2, and β_3 are **linearly dependent.** It can be shown that this fact was significant in determining that β_1, β_2, β_3 did not span the vector space consisting of all three-dimensional vectors.

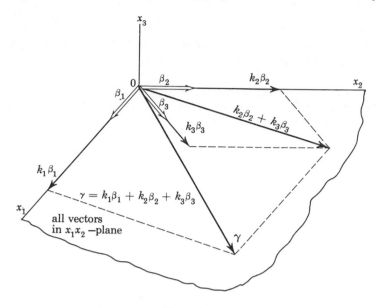

Figure 9.5

The concepts of linear dependence and linear independence are now defined formally.

Definition.   *The n vectors $\alpha_1, \alpha_2, \ldots, \alpha_n$ are said to be **linearly dependent** if there exists a set of scalars $k_1, k_2, \ldots, k_n$, not all zero, such that $k_1\alpha_1 + k_2\alpha_2 + \cdots + k_n\alpha_n = 0$.*

In other words if the vectors are linearly dependent, a vector α_i whose coefficient is not zero can be expressed as a linear combination of the other vectors by transposing them to the other side of the equation and then dividing by k_i.

Definition.   *A set of vectors $\alpha_1, \alpha_2, \ldots, \alpha_n$ which is not linearly dependent is said to be **linearly independent**. That is, if $\alpha_1, \alpha_2, \ldots, \alpha_n$ are linearly independent and if*

$$k_1\alpha_1 + k_2\alpha_2 + \cdots + k_n\alpha_n = 0,$$

then $k_1 = k_2 = \cdots = k_n = 0$.

Example 4.   The vectors $(1, 1, 0)$, $(3, 2, 1)$, and $(2, 1, 1)$ are *linearly dependent* because there exists a set of scalars k_1, k_2, k_3, not all zero, such that $k_1(1, 1, 0) + k_2(3, 2, 1) + k_3(2, 1, 1) = (0, 0, 0)$.   We know this and can find these k's by considering the system of homogeneous equations resulting from the addition of corresponding components.

$$\begin{cases} k_1 + 3k_2 + 2k_3 = 0, \\ k_1 + 2k_2 + k_3 = 0, \\ \phantom{k_1 + {}}k_2 + k_3 = 0. \end{cases}$$

First of all we know that some nonzero k's exist because the rank of the system is 2, and hence by what we learned in the preceding chapter, there is a solution other than $(0, 0, 0)$ for the homogeneous system. We can find such a solution by first finding a complete solution, $\begin{cases} k_1 = k_3, \\ k_2 = -k_3. \end{cases}$ Let $k_3 = 1$; then a particular solution is $k_1 = 1$, $k_2 = -1$, $k_3 = 1$. Thus $(1)\alpha_1 + (-1)\alpha_2 + (1)\alpha_3 = 0$, and any one of these vectors can be written as a linear combination of the other two. For example, $\alpha_1 = \alpha_2 - \alpha_3$.

Example 5. The vectors $(3, 2, 1)$, $(0, 1, 2)$, and $(1, 0, 2)$ are *linearly independent* because if $k_1(3, 2, 1) + k_2(0, 1, 2) + k_3(1, 0, 2) = (0, 0, 0)$, then $k_1 = k_2 = k_3 = 0$. We know this because the linear homogeneous system

$$\begin{cases} 3k_1 + \quad\quad k_3 = 0, \\ 2k_1 + k_2 \quad\quad = 0, \\ k_1 + 2k_2 + 2k_3 = 0, \end{cases}$$

has rank 3 and hence the only solution is $k_1 = 0$, $k_2 = 0$, $k_3 = 0$.

The student should observe at this point that if the number of vectors exceeds the number of components of the vectors involved, then the set of vectors must be linearly dependent. For example, the vectors $(1, 1)$, $(3, 2)$, $(1, 2)$ must be linearly dependent because

$$k_1(1, 1) + k_2(3, 2) + k_3(1, 2) = (0, 0),$$

yields the homogeneous linear system

$$\begin{cases} k_1 + 3k_2 + k_3 = 0, \\ k_1 + 2k_2 + 2k_3 = 0, \end{cases}$$

for which the rank must be less than 3, and therefore a solution other than $(0, 0, 0)$ must exist.

EXERCISES

1. Determine whether the following sets of vectors are linearly dependent or independent. If they are linearly dependent, find a set of k's, and then express one of the vectors as a linear combination of the others.

(a) $(2, -1)$, $(-4, 2)$;

(b) $(1, 1)$, $(2, 1)$;

(c) $(2, 1, 0)$, $(1, 3, 2)$, $(0, 9, 1)$;

(d) $(1, 0, -3)$, $(3, 1, 1)$, $(2, 1, 4)$;

(e) $(2, 1)$, $(1, 4)$, $(6, 9)$;

(f) $(2, 1, 6)$, $(4, 5, 0)$;

(g) $(6, 9, 1)$, $(0, 1, 0)$, $(1, 0, 0)$;

(h) $(2, 0, 3)$, $(0, 1, 1)$, $(2, 1, 4)$.

2. Express $\begin{bmatrix} 3 \\ 4 \end{bmatrix}$ as a linear combination of $\begin{bmatrix} 2 \\ 1 \end{bmatrix}$ and $\begin{bmatrix} 1 \\ 1 \end{bmatrix}$. Illustrate your answer graphically.

3. Show how any vector (a, b, c) in three-space can be expressed as a linear combination of $(1, 0, 0)$, $(0, 1, 0)$, and $(0, 0, 1)$.

4. Do the vectors $(2, 3)$ and $(2, -1)$ span the vector space consisting of all vectors in two-space? Would $(2, 3)$ and $(-4, -6)$ span the same space?

5. Do the vectors $(3, 4, 6)$ and $(4, 9, 1)$ span the vector space consisting of all vectors in three-space? Why?

6. Do the vectors $(4, 9, 1, 0)$, $(0, 4, 9, 1)$, and $(1, 0, 0, 1)$ span the vector space consisting of all vectors in four-space?

7. (*a*) Is it possible for three vectors in two-space to be linearly independent?
(*b*) Is it possible for three vectors in two-space to be linearly dependent?
(*c*) Is it possible for two vectors in three-space to be linearly independent?
(*d*) Is it possible for two vectors in three-space to be linearly dependent?

8. Show that $(4, 2)$ cannot be expressed as a linear combination of $(-3, 2)$ and $(9, -6)$.

9. In each part describe geometrically the vector space spanned by the given set of vectors:

$$(a)\ \begin{bmatrix} 0 \\ 2 \\ 1 \end{bmatrix}, \begin{bmatrix} 1 \\ 1 \\ 1 \end{bmatrix}, \begin{bmatrix} 2 \\ 1 \\ 4 \end{bmatrix}; \qquad (b)\ \begin{bmatrix} 0 \\ 1 \\ 4 \end{bmatrix}, \begin{bmatrix} 0 \\ 3 \\ 2 \end{bmatrix}, \begin{bmatrix} 0 \\ 2 \\ 4 \end{bmatrix}; \qquad (c)\ \begin{bmatrix} 2 \\ 1 \\ 3 \end{bmatrix}, \begin{bmatrix} 4 \\ 1 \\ 6 \end{bmatrix}.$$

10. If a set of vectors spans a vector space, must it be a linearly independent set? One part of Exercise 9 illustrates the correct answer to this question. Which part is it?

11. Would the vector $(0, 0)$ by itself be linearly independent or linearly dependent? Answer the same question for the vector $(1, 2)$.

12. Write out a proof for the fact that a set of nonzero vectors (all having the same number of components) is linearly dependent, if and only if one of them can be expressed as a linear combination of the others.

13. Suppose you are given a set of vectors all having the same number of components. Prove that the set of all linear combinations of these vectors is a vector space.

9.3 BASIS

Before we give the important definition of a **basis** of a vector space, consider another example in connection with the spanning of a vector space.

Example 1. The linearly independent vectors $\delta_1 = (0, 1, 1)$ and $\delta_2 = (1, 1, 0)$ do *not* span the vector space consisting of all vectors in three-space because any linear combination of these vectors,

$$\gamma = k_1(0, 1, 1) + k_2(1, 1, 0),$$

is in the plane in which these two vectors lie (Fig. 9.6).

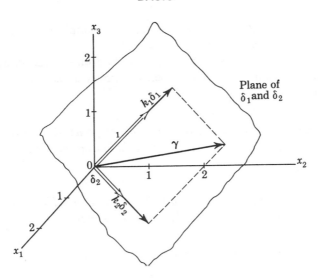

Figure 9.6

Intuitively, it would seem that in order for a set of vectors to span n-dimensional space the set must contain at least n vectors.

Definition. *A basis of a vector space is any set of vectors which (a) are linearly independent and (b) span the vector space.*

Example 2. The set of vectors in Example 1 does *not* form a basis of the vector space consisting of vectors in three-space because it does not span the space. The set is, however, linearly independent.

Example 3. The set of vectors $(0, 1)$, $(1, 0)$, and $(1, 1)$ does *not* form a basis for the vector space consisting of all vectors in the x_1x_2-plane because the set is not linearly independent. The set does, however, span the space.

Example 4. The set of vectors $(1, 0, 0)$, $(0, 1, 0)$, and $(0, 0, 1)$ is a basis for the vector space consisting of all vectors in three-space. The set is linearly independent; the set spans the space. Likewise, $(1, 2, 3)$, $(3, 2, 1)$, and $(1, 1, 0)$ form a basis for the same vector space.

It can be proved that there are the same number of vectors in every basis of a specific vector space. For example, if there are three vectors in a basis of a certain vector space, then there are three vectors in any other basis of that same vector space.

Definition. *The **dimension** of a vector space is the number of vectors in any basis of the space. A vector space consisting of the zero vector only is said to have dimension zero.*

For example, the vector space mentioned in Example 4 of this section is a three-dimensional vector space.

The concept of basis of a vector space is important in the study of linear programming. Examples 5 and 6 below furnish a background for such an application.

Definition. *A vector space is said to be* **generated** *by a certain set of vectors if the vector space consists of all of the linear combinations of vectors of that set.*

Definition. *The vector space consisting of the set of all linear combinations of columns of a matrix A is called the* **column space** *of A.*

Example 5. Consider each column of matrix A as a vector.

$$A = \begin{bmatrix} 2 & 6 & 1 & 0 & 5 \\ 0 & 2 & 0 & 1 & 6 \end{bmatrix}.$$

The set of vectors which can be written as a linear combination of these vectors forms a vector space, called the *column space* of A. The third and fourth vectors form a basis of this column space; we say that these vectors *generate* the column space. Is this the only basis?

Example 6. Suppose we are given a consistent system of equations

$$\begin{cases} x_1 + x_2 + 3x_3 + x_4 & = 6, \\ x_1 - 3x_2 - x_3 + x_5 & = 1, \\ x_1 + x_3 + x_6 = 2. \end{cases}$$

This system may be written

$$x_1 \begin{bmatrix} 1 \\ 1 \\ 1 \end{bmatrix} + x_2 \begin{bmatrix} 1 \\ -3 \\ 0 \end{bmatrix} + x_3 \begin{bmatrix} 3 \\ -1 \\ 1 \end{bmatrix} + x_4 \begin{bmatrix} 1 \\ 0 \\ 0 \end{bmatrix} + x_5 \begin{bmatrix} 0 \\ 1 \\ 0 \end{bmatrix} + x_6 \begin{bmatrix} 0 \\ 0 \\ 1 \end{bmatrix} = \begin{bmatrix} 6 \\ 1 \\ 2 \end{bmatrix}.$$

The vectors $\begin{bmatrix} 1 \\ 0 \\ 0 \end{bmatrix}$, $\begin{bmatrix} 0 \\ 1 \\ 0 \end{bmatrix}$, and $\begin{bmatrix} 0 \\ 0 \\ 1 \end{bmatrix}$ form a basis for the column space of the aug-

mented matrix of the system. The vector $\begin{bmatrix} 6 \\ 1 \\ 2 \end{bmatrix}$ on the right side can be expressed as a

linear combination of this basis by assigning values to the scalar multipliers, that is, $x_1 = 0$, $x_2 = 0$, $x_3 = 0$, $x_4 = 6$, $x_5 = 1$, $x_6 = 2$. This was called a basic solution in

Chapter 8. If we add three times the first equation to the second equation, we get

$$\begin{cases} x_1 + x_2 + 3x_3 + x_4 & = 6, \\ 4x_1 & + 8x_3 + 3x_4 + x_5 & = 19, \\ x_1 & + x_3 & + x_6 = 2, \end{cases}$$

or

$$x_1 \begin{bmatrix} 1 \\ 4 \\ 1 \end{bmatrix} + x_2 \begin{bmatrix} 1 \\ 0 \\ 0 \end{bmatrix} + x_3 \begin{bmatrix} 3 \\ 8 \\ 1 \end{bmatrix} + x_4 \begin{bmatrix} 1 \\ 3 \\ 0 \end{bmatrix} + x_5 \begin{bmatrix} 0 \\ 1 \\ 0 \end{bmatrix} + x_6 \begin{bmatrix} 0 \\ 0 \\ 1 \end{bmatrix} = \begin{bmatrix} 6 \\ 19 \\ 2 \end{bmatrix}.$$

Now another basic solution may be obtained by treating the second, fifth, and sixth

vectors as a basis and expressing the vector $\begin{bmatrix} 6 \\ 19 \\ 2 \end{bmatrix}$ as a linear combination of them by

assigning the values $x_1 = 0$, $x_2 = 6$, $x_3 = 0$, $x_4 = 0$, $x_5 = 19$, $x_6 = 2$. Note that the new member of the basis was introduced by an elementary row transformation.

Problems similar to Example 6 will be pursued further in Chapter 12.

EXERCISES

1. Verify that the vectors $\begin{bmatrix} 2 \\ 1 \end{bmatrix}$ and $\begin{bmatrix} 4 \\ 0 \end{bmatrix}$ form a basis for the set of all vectors with two components.

2. Express $\begin{bmatrix} 6 \\ 1 \end{bmatrix}$ as a linear combination of the basis vectors in Exercise 1.

3. Which of the following sets of vectors are not a basis of the vector space consisting of all three-dimensional vectors? State why they are not a basis.

(a) $\begin{bmatrix} 1 \\ 0 \\ 1 \end{bmatrix}$, $\begin{bmatrix} 2 \\ 0 \\ 1 \end{bmatrix}$, $\begin{bmatrix} 0 \\ 0 \\ 1 \end{bmatrix}$;

(b) $\begin{bmatrix} 2 \\ 1 \\ 4 \end{bmatrix}$, $\begin{bmatrix} 1 \\ 1 \\ 1 \end{bmatrix}$;

(c) $\begin{bmatrix} 1 \\ 2 \\ 1 \end{bmatrix}$, $\begin{bmatrix} 3 \\ 1 \\ 0 \end{bmatrix}$, $\begin{bmatrix} 1 \\ 0 \\ 0 \end{bmatrix}$;

(d) $\begin{bmatrix} 1 \\ 1 \\ 1 \end{bmatrix}$, $\begin{bmatrix} 0 \\ 0 \\ 1 \end{bmatrix}$, $\begin{bmatrix} 1 \\ 0 \\ 0 \end{bmatrix}$, $\begin{bmatrix} 0 \\ 1 \\ 0 \end{bmatrix}$;

(e) $\begin{bmatrix} 1 \\ 2 \\ 1 \end{bmatrix}$, $\begin{bmatrix} 1 \\ 3 \\ 0 \end{bmatrix}$, $\begin{bmatrix} 0 \\ 1 \\ -1 \end{bmatrix}$.

4. Write two sets of columns which will serve as a basis of the column space of A.

$$A = \begin{bmatrix} 2 & -4 & 1 & 2 \\ 1 & -2 & 0 & 0 \end{bmatrix}.$$

Find two sets of two columns which will not serve and state why they will not serve.

5. Would any three vectors of a three-dimensional vector space be a basis of that vector space? Why?

6. A certain vector space is spanned by four linearly independent vectors. What can be said about the dimension of this vector space?

7. A certain vector space is spanned by four linearly dependent vectors. What can be said about the dimension of this vector space?

8. What is the dimension of the vector space spanned by the vectors $\begin{bmatrix} 2 \\ 1 \\ 4 \end{bmatrix}$ and $\begin{bmatrix} 2 \\ 1 \\ 1 \end{bmatrix}$?

9. What is the dimension of the column space of each of the following matrices?

(a) $\begin{bmatrix} 1 \\ 2 \end{bmatrix}$;

(b) $\begin{bmatrix} 2 & -1 \\ 1 & -1 \end{bmatrix}$;

(c) $\begin{bmatrix} 0 & 2 & -1 \\ 0 & 4 & -2 \end{bmatrix}$;

(d) $\begin{bmatrix} 1 & 1 \\ 1 & 2 \\ 1 & 3 \end{bmatrix}$;

(e) $\begin{bmatrix} 1 & 0 & 0 \\ 0 & 0 & 1 \\ 0 & 3 & 0 \end{bmatrix}$;

(f) I_4.

10. For the system $\begin{cases} x_1 + 2x_2 + x_3 = 4, \\ x_1 - x_2 + x_4 = 5, \end{cases}$ write a set of columns which forms a basis for the column space of the coefficient matrix A. Then assign values to x_1, x_2, x_3, and x_4 which will enable you to write $\begin{bmatrix} 4 \\ 5 \end{bmatrix}$ as a linear combination of the columns of A.

11. Define the *row space* of a matrix.

12. If a subset of the elements of a vector space forms another vector space under the original operations, we say that this subset forms a *subspace*.

(a) Give two examples of subspaces of the vector space consisting of all vectors with two components.

(b) Give two examples of subsets of the same vector space as in (a) which do not form subspaces.

(c) How would the dimension of a subspace compare with the dimension of the whole vector space?

(d) Would a basis of a vector space also be a basis for any subspace of that vector space?

NEW VOCABULARY

vector space   9.1
linear combination   9.2
span   9.2
linearly dependent   9.2
linearly independent   9.2

basis   9.3
dimension   9.3
column space   9.3
row space   9.3
subspace   9.3

10

Linear Transformations

10.1 GEOMETRIC INTERPRETATION OF A MAPPING

The transformation of the elements of one set into the elements of another set is a very important concept in mathematics. Such a procedure frequently is called a *mapping*. For example, the scalar x can be mapped into the scalar x^3. The transformation represented by T can be expressed as "the cube of" and denoted in the following ways:

$$T(x) = x^3, \quad \text{or} \quad x \xrightarrow{\text{T}} x^3.$$

The element x^3 is called the *image* of x.

In a mapping of the elements of a set U into the elements of a set V, the set U is called the *domain* of the mapping. The subset of elements of V, each of which is actually an image of at least one element of U, is called the *range* of the mapping. Another transformation, "the magnitude of," maps a real vector α into a scalar $|\alpha|$,

$$T(\alpha) = |\alpha|, \quad \text{or} \quad \alpha \xrightarrow{\text{T}} |\alpha|.$$

Here the domain is the set of n-dimensional real vectors, and the range is the set of nonnegative real numbers.

Still other transformations map vectors into vectors. We shall devote the rest of this section to a geometric discussion of such mappings (in two dimensions) in order to illustrate a variety of types of vector transformations. All vectors used in the following examples will originate at the origin. The following transformations may be considered as *vector functions* of a vector variable.

154

Example 1. Let T map each nonzero vector α into the vector which has the same direction but twice the magnitude of α (Fig. 10.1).

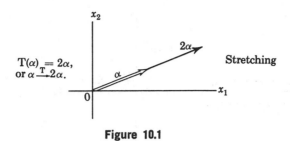

Figure 10.1

Such a transformation may be referred to as a "stretching."

Example 2. Let T map each nonzero vector α into the vector having the same magnitude and the opposite direction (Fig. 10.2).

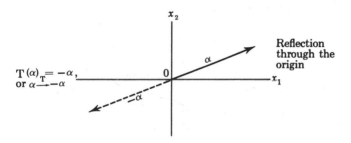

Figure 10.2

Such a transformation may be referred to as a "reflection through the origin."

Example 3. Let T be the mapping which reflects each vector $\alpha = (a_1, a_2)$ through the x_1-axis ($a_2 \neq 0$) (Fig. 10.3).

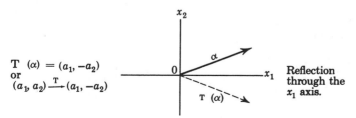

Figure 10.3

Example 4. Let T be a mapping which gives a 90° rotation, with respect to the origin, to each nonzero vector $\alpha = (a_1, a_2)$ (Fig. 10.4).

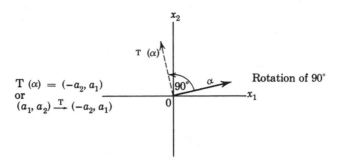

$$T(\alpha) = (-a_2, a_1)$$
or
$$(a_1, a_2) \xrightarrow{\text{T}} (-a_2, a_1)$$

Rotation of 90°

Figure 10.4

Example 5. Let T be a mapping which slides the terminal point of a vector $\alpha = (a_1, a_2)$ parallel to the x_1-axis a distance of $3a_2$ units while the initial point remains fixed $(a_2 \neq 0)$ (Fig. 10.5).

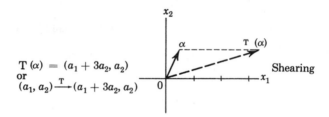

$$T(\alpha) = (a_1 + 3a_2, a_2)$$
or
$$(a_1, a_2) \xrightarrow{\text{T}} (a_1 + 3a_2, a_2)$$

Shearing

Figure 10.5

Such a transformation may be referred to as a "shear."

EXERCISES

1. Find the image of β under the mapping $\beta \xrightarrow{\text{T}} -2\beta$, or $T(\beta) = -2\beta$. Then graph β and the image of β.

(a) Let $\beta = \begin{bmatrix} 1 \\ -2 \end{bmatrix}$;

(b) let $\beta = \begin{bmatrix} 0 \\ 3 \end{bmatrix}$;

(c) let $\beta = -2 \begin{bmatrix} 1 \\ 1 \end{bmatrix}$.

In Exercises 2–9, what are the domain and range for the following mappings?

Let x and y represent real numbers.

2. $T(x) = x^2 + 1$.

3. $x \xrightarrow{\text{T}} (x, 2x)$.

4. $T(\alpha) = \alpha^2$, where $\alpha = (x, y)$.

5. $\begin{bmatrix} x \\ y \end{bmatrix} \xrightarrow{\text{T}} \begin{bmatrix} 0 \\ y \end{bmatrix}$.

6. $T(A) = A^2$, where $A = \begin{bmatrix} x & x \\ x & x \end{bmatrix}$.

7. $T(x) = \sqrt{1 - x^2}$.

8. $T(x) = -\sqrt{1 - x^2}$.

9. $T(x) = \sqrt{x^2 - 1} + 1$.

In Exercises 10–15, describe the geometric effect of each of the following transformations. State this effect in words and illustrate with a graph.

10. $\begin{bmatrix} x_1 \\ x_2 \end{bmatrix} \xrightarrow{\text{T}} \begin{bmatrix} 2x_1 \\ x_2 \end{bmatrix}$.

11. $T(\alpha) = -2\alpha$, where $\alpha = \begin{bmatrix} a_1 \\ a_2 \end{bmatrix}$.

12. $\begin{bmatrix} x_1 \\ x_2 \end{bmatrix} \xrightarrow{\text{T}} \begin{bmatrix} x_1 \\ 0 \end{bmatrix}$.

13. $\begin{bmatrix} x_1 \\ x_2 \end{bmatrix} \xrightarrow{\text{T}} \begin{bmatrix} x_1 + x_2 \\ x_2 \end{bmatrix}$.

14. $(x_1, x_2) \xrightarrow{\text{T}} (x_1 + 2, x_2 + 3)$.

15. $\begin{bmatrix} x_1 \\ x_2 \end{bmatrix} \xrightarrow{\text{T}} \begin{bmatrix} -2x_2 \\ 2x_1 \end{bmatrix}$.

10.2 MATRIX TRANSFORMATIONS

The various transformations performed in Examples 1–5 of Section 10.1 can be expressed by making use of matrix multiplication.

Example 1. If we use a column matrix to represent α, the "stretching" transformation $\alpha \xrightarrow{\text{T}} 2\alpha$ may be expressed as

$$\begin{bmatrix} a_1 \\ a_2 \end{bmatrix} \xrightarrow{\text{T}} \begin{bmatrix} 2 & 0 \\ 0 & 2 \end{bmatrix} \begin{bmatrix} a_1 \\ a_2 \end{bmatrix} = \begin{bmatrix} 2a_1 \\ 2a_2 \end{bmatrix}.$$

Example 2. Likewise the "reflection through the origin" transformation $\alpha \xrightarrow{\text{T}} -\alpha$ may be expressed as

$$\begin{bmatrix} a_1 \\ a_2 \end{bmatrix} \xrightarrow{\text{T}} \begin{bmatrix} -1 & 0 \\ 0 & -1 \end{bmatrix} \begin{bmatrix} a_1 \\ a_2 \end{bmatrix} = \begin{bmatrix} -a_1 \\ -a_2 \end{bmatrix}.$$

Example 3. The "reflection through the x_1-axis" transformation $(a_1, a_2) \xrightarrow{\text{T}} (a_1, -a_2)$ may be expressed as

$$\begin{bmatrix} a_1 \\ a_2 \end{bmatrix} \xrightarrow{\text{T}} \begin{bmatrix} 1 & 0 \\ 0 & -1 \end{bmatrix} \begin{bmatrix} a_1 \\ a_2 \end{bmatrix} = \begin{bmatrix} a_1 \\ -a_2 \end{bmatrix}.$$

Example 4. The "rotation of 90°" of a nonzero vector was expressed as

$$(a_1, a_2) \overset{T}{\rightarrow} (-a_2, a_1).$$

This transformation may be written

$$\begin{bmatrix} a_1 \\ a_2 \end{bmatrix} \overset{T}{\rightarrow} \begin{bmatrix} 0 & -1 \\ 1 & 0 \end{bmatrix} \begin{bmatrix} a_1 \\ a_2 \end{bmatrix} = \begin{bmatrix} -a_2 \\ a_1 \end{bmatrix}.$$

Example 5. The "shearing" transformation

$$(a_1, a_2) \overset{T}{\rightarrow} (a_1 + 3a_2, a_2)$$

may be expressed as

$$\begin{bmatrix} a_1 \\ a_2 \end{bmatrix} \overset{T}{\rightarrow} \begin{bmatrix} 1 & 3 \\ 0 & 1 \end{bmatrix} \begin{bmatrix} a_1 \\ a_2 \end{bmatrix} = \begin{bmatrix} a_1 + 3a_2 \\ a_2 \end{bmatrix}.$$

A transformation of vectors is called a ***matrix transformation*** if it can be expressed by multiplying the vector by a matrix. That is, $\alpha \overset{T}{\rightarrow} A\alpha$. We are concerned only with a square, real matrix A. Examples 1 to 5, above, are illustrations of matrix transformations.

The introduction of new variables expressed as linear combinations of the original variables is an important example of a matrix transformation.

Consider
$$\begin{cases} \bar{x}_1 = a_{11}x_1 + a_{12}x_2 + \cdots + a_{1n}x_n, \\ \bar{x}_2 = a_{21}x_1 + a_{22}x_2 + \cdots + a_{2n}x_n, \\ \qquad\qquad \cdots \\ \bar{x}_n = a_{n1}x_1 + a_{n2}x_2 + \cdots + a_{nn}x_n, \end{cases}$$

or $\bar{X} = AX$, or $X \overset{T}{\rightarrow} AX$.

Here we have mapped any point in the X coordinate system into an image in the $\bar{X}$ coordinate system. The $\bar{X}$ coordinate system ***need not*** be considered different from the X coordinate system. Actually two interpretations of this transformation may be given. They are illustrated in the following example.

Example 6. Consider the effect of the transformation of rotation through the angle θ on the point (x_1, x_2) in the x_1x_2-plane. This transformation yields the image $(\bar{x}_1, \bar{x}_2)$ in the $\bar{x}_1\bar{x}_2$-plane according to the equations

$$\begin{cases} \bar{x}_1 = (\cos \theta)x_1 + (-\sin \theta)x_2, \\ \bar{x}_2 = (\sin \theta)x_1 + (\cos \theta)x_2, \end{cases}$$

or
$$\begin{bmatrix} \bar{x}_1 \\ \bar{x}_2 \end{bmatrix} = \begin{bmatrix} \cos \theta & -\sin \theta \\ \sin \theta & \cos \theta \end{bmatrix} \begin{bmatrix} x_1 \\ x_2 \end{bmatrix},$$

or
$$\bar{X} = AX, \qquad \text{or} \qquad X \overset{T}{\rightarrow} AX.$$

Specifically, let $\theta = 30°$ and let $(x_1, x_2) = (2, 0)$. Then

$$\begin{bmatrix} \bar{x}_1 \\ \bar{x}_2 \end{bmatrix} = \begin{bmatrix} \frac{1}{2}\sqrt{3} & -\frac{1}{2} \\ \frac{1}{2} & \frac{1}{2}\sqrt{3} \end{bmatrix} \begin{bmatrix} 2 \\ 0 \end{bmatrix} = \begin{bmatrix} \sqrt{3} \\ 1 \end{bmatrix}.$$

Thus the image of $(2, 0)$ is $(\sqrt{3}, 1)$. This transformation may be interpreted in two ways:

(1) Let the $\bar{x}_1\bar{x}_2$-plane be the same as the x_1x_2-plane and thus the point $(2, 0)$ has been mapped into another point $(\sqrt{3}, 1)$ in the same plane (Fig. 10.6).

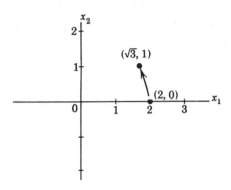

Figure 10.6

(2) Let the point remain fixed and consider the original axes as having been rotated by $-30°$. Therefore the same point that has the coordinates $(2, 0)$ in the original x_1x_2-plane has the coordinates $(\sqrt{3}, 1)$ in the image $\bar{x}_1\bar{x}_2$-plane (Fig. 10.7).

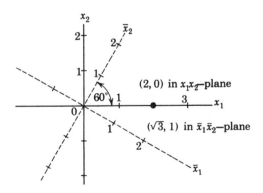

Figure 10.7

The introduction of a single new variable into a system of linear equations is another example of a matrix transformation. This type of transformation will be useful in Chapter 12.

Example 7. Consider the system of equations

$$\begin{cases} (1) & x_1 - 2x_2 = 0, \\ (2) & x_1 \qquad\;\; = 0, \\ (3) & \qquad\;\; x_2 = 0. \end{cases}$$

The introduction of the new variable $\bar{x}_1 = x_1 - 2x_2$ transforms the system to

$$\begin{cases} (1') & \bar{x}_1 \qquad\;\; = 0, \\ (2') & \bar{x}_1 + 2x_2 = 0, \\ (3') & \qquad\;\; x_2 = 0. \end{cases}$$

Figures 10.8 and 10.9 show the graphs before and after the transformation, respectively. This transformation may be effected by the postmultiplication of the original

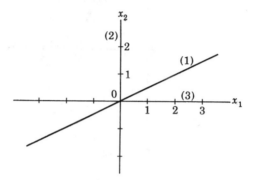

Figure 10.8

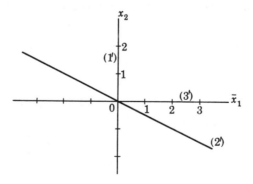

Figure 10.9

augmented matrix by an elementary matrix (designed to add twice the first column to the second column) to produce the final augmented matrix.

$$\begin{bmatrix} 1 & -2 & 0 \\ 1 & 0 & 0 \\ 0 & 1 & 0 \end{bmatrix} \begin{bmatrix} 1 & 2 & 0 \\ 0 & 1 & 0 \\ 0 & 0 & 1 \end{bmatrix} = \begin{bmatrix} 1 & 0 & 0 \\ 1 & 2 & 0 \\ 0 & 1 & 0 \end{bmatrix}.$$

$$\begin{bmatrix} \text{original} \\ \text{augmented} \\ \text{matrix} \end{bmatrix} \begin{bmatrix} \text{elementary} \\ \text{matrix} \end{bmatrix} = \begin{bmatrix} \text{final} \\ \text{augmented} \\ \text{matrix} \end{bmatrix}.$$

In this example we have mapped a matrix into another matrix by matrix multiplication.

In the preceding example the x_1 and $\bar{x}_1$-axes were considered the same and the net result was the rotation of two of the three lines. It is also possible to perform a rotation and translation.

Example 8. Consider the inconsistent system

$$\begin{cases} (1) & x_1 + x_2 = 1, \\ (2) & x_1 \quad\quad = 0, \\ (3) & \quad\quad x_2 = 0. \end{cases}$$

The introduction of the new variable $\bar{x}_1 = x_1 + x_2 - 1$ transforms the system to

$$\begin{cases} (1') & \bar{x}_1 \quad\quad = 0, \\ (2') & \bar{x}_1 - x_2 = -1, \\ (3') & \quad\quad x_2 = 0. \end{cases}$$

Figures 10.10 and 10.11 show the graphs before and after the transformation, respectively. This transformation could have been accomplished by postmultiplying the original augmented matrix by a product of elementary matrices [designed to add (-1) times the first column to the second column and also to add (-1) times the first column to the third column] to produce the final augmented matrix.

$$\begin{bmatrix} 1 & 1 & 1 \\ 1 & 0 & 0 \\ 0 & 1 & 0 \end{bmatrix} \begin{bmatrix} 1 & -1 & -1 \\ 0 & 1 & 0 \\ 0 & 0 & 1 \end{bmatrix} = \begin{bmatrix} 1 & 0 & 0 \\ 1 & -1 & -1 \\ 0 & 1 & 0 \end{bmatrix}.$$

$$\begin{bmatrix} \text{original} \\ \text{augmented} \\ \text{matrix} \end{bmatrix} \begin{bmatrix} \text{product of} \\ \text{elementary} \\ \text{matrices} \end{bmatrix} = \begin{bmatrix} \text{final} \\ \text{augmented} \\ \text{matrix} \end{bmatrix}.$$

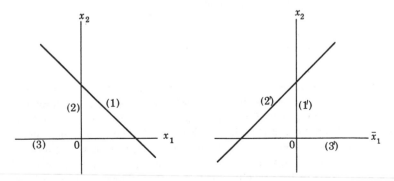

Figure 10.10   Figure 10.11

The benefits of the transformations performed in the last two examples will become apparent in Sections 12.6 and 12.9.

Note that in a system of linear equations, a change in variables may be effected by elementary *column* operations; the resulting system *is not* equivalent to the original system. On the other hand, elementary *row* operations maintain the same variables and the resulting system *is* equivalent to the original system.

EXERCISES

1. The mapping $\beta \rightarrow k\beta$ is the "stretching" transformation described in Example 1 of Section 10.1. This can be thought of as a change of scale and hence the number k is the scale factor or "scalar." Determine the matrix A such that

$$\beta \xrightarrow{T} A\beta = k\beta, \quad \text{where} \quad \beta = \begin{bmatrix} b_1 \\ b_2 \end{bmatrix}.$$

2. Determine the image of $\alpha = \begin{bmatrix} a_1 \\ a_2 \end{bmatrix}$ under the matrix transformation $\alpha \xrightarrow{T} A\alpha$

for each A, and describe the geometric effect of the transformation.

(a) $A = \begin{bmatrix} 1 & 0 \\ 0 & 1 \end{bmatrix}$; (b) $A = \begin{bmatrix} 2 & 0 \\ 0 & 1 \end{bmatrix}$; (c) $A = \begin{bmatrix} 0 & 0 \\ 0 & 1 \end{bmatrix}$;

(d) $A = \begin{bmatrix} 0 & -3 \\ 3 & 0 \end{bmatrix}$; (e) $A = \begin{bmatrix} 1 & 1 \\ 0 & 1 \end{bmatrix}$; (f) $A = \begin{bmatrix} 1 & 1 \\ 1 & 1 \end{bmatrix}$.

3. Find a matrix A such that the following transformations are accomplished by $T(\alpha) = A\alpha$.

(a) α is projected on the x_1-axis.
(b) α is reflected through the x_1-axis and the magnitude is doubled.
(c) α is rotated $45°$ in the x_1x_2-plane.

4. (a) Consider the system of equations $\begin{cases} x_1 + 2x_2 = 2, \\ x_1 \qquad\quad = 0, \\ \qquad\quad x_2 = 0, \end{cases}$ and introduce the new

variable $\bar{x}_1 = x_1 + 2x_2 - 2$. What is the new system? Graph both systems.

(b) This transformation could be accomplished by elementary column operations on the augmented matrix. These operations are (i) add -2 times the first column to the second column and (ii) add -2 times the first column to the third column. What are the two elementary matrices which accomplish these operations?

(c) Express the transformation of part (a) as $T(F) = FQ = G$, where F is the augmented matrix of the original system, G is the augmented matrix of the second system, and Q is a product of elementary matrices.

10.3 LINEAR TRANSFORMATIONS

The purpose of this section is to define a linear transformation, which is the type of transformation with which we are primarily concerned, and then to show that the transformations of Section 10.2 are of this type.

Definition. *A transformation* T *of a vector space* V *into* V *is said to be a linear transformation if*

$$T(\alpha + \beta) = T(\alpha) + T(\beta), \quad and \quad T(k\alpha) = kT(\alpha),$$

where k *is a scalar and* α *and* β *are arbitrary vectors belonging to* V.

We can obtain a multitude of examples of linear transformations if we can show that the matrix transformations discussed in Section 10.2 are linear. Let a matrix transformation which transforms a vector space V into itself be

$$A\alpha = \beta, \quad or \quad \alpha \xrightarrow{T} A\alpha = \beta,$$

where A is an n by n matrix, α is an element of the vector space V, and its image β is also an element of V. Now let γ also belong to the vector space V. Since

$$A(\alpha + \gamma) = A\alpha + A\gamma, \quad and \quad A(k\alpha) = k(A\alpha),$$

the requirements of a linear transformation of V are met, and we have the following theorem. (Reasons for the last two statements are left as an exercise for the student.)

Theorem 1. *Every matrix transformation is a linear transformation.*

Thus all of the examples of the preceding section can be considered as examples of linear transformations. The elementary row transformations of Chapter 7 are also examples of linear transformations. There the elements of the vector spaces were matrices rather than vectors. An example of a transformation that is not linear may be enlightening.

Example 1. Let the transformation T map a two-dimensional vector (a, b) into $(a + 2, b)$. This transformation is not linear because

$$T\{ k(a, b) \} = T\{ (ka, kb) \} = (ka + 2, kb),$$

whereas $\quad kT\{ (a, b) \} = k(a + 2, b) = (ka + 2k, kb),$

and these two results are not equal in general. Furthermore,

$$T\{ (a, b) + (c, d) \} = T\{ (a + c, b + d) \} = (a + c + 2, b + d),$$

whereas $T\{ (a, b) \} + T\{ (c, d) \} = (a + 2, b) + (c + 2, d) = (a + c + 4, b + d),$

and these two results are not equal.

EXERCISES

1. Show that the following transformation is not linear.

$$(a, b) \xrightarrow{\text{T}} (a, 2), \quad \text{or} \quad T(a, b) = (a, 2).$$

2. In Exercise 1, is it possible to express the transformation as

$$\begin{bmatrix} a \\ b \end{bmatrix} \to A \begin{bmatrix} a \\ b \end{bmatrix} = \begin{bmatrix} a \\ 2 \end{bmatrix}, \text{ where } A \text{ is a 2 by 2 matrix?} \quad \text{Why?}$$

3. Show by definition that the following transformation is linear.

$$(a, b) \xrightarrow{\text{T}} (-2a, 2b), \quad \text{or} \quad T(a, b) = (-2a, 2b).$$

4. Find out which of the following transformations are linear and justify your answer.

(a) $(a, b) \xrightarrow{\text{T}} (a + 1, b)$;

(b) $\begin{bmatrix} a \\ b \end{bmatrix} \xrightarrow{\text{T}} \begin{bmatrix} a + b \\ a - b \end{bmatrix}$;

(c) $T(a, b) = (3a, 2b)$;

(d) $\begin{bmatrix} a \\ b \end{bmatrix} \xrightarrow{\text{T}} \frac{1}{2} \left(\begin{bmatrix} a \\ b \end{bmatrix} + \begin{bmatrix} 2 \\ 1 \end{bmatrix} \right)$;

(e) $T(\alpha) = |\alpha|\alpha$, where $\alpha = (a_1, a_2)$;
(f) $T(a, b) = (0, 0)$.

5. Give reasons for the proof of Theorem 1.

6. Let V be the vector space consisting of all two-dimensional real vectors. Prove that if T is a linear transformation from V into V then $T(0, 0) = (0, 0)$. How could this result have been used in parts (a) and (d) of Exercise 4 above?

NEW VOCABULARY

Convex Sets

11.1 LINEAR INEQUALITIES

In Chapter 8 we were concerned with systems of linear equations. Now we will consider systems of linear inequalities. First we review a few of the properties that the student should remember about inequalities. The elements considered below are real numbers.

I. The sense of an inequality is not changed if the same real number is added to (or subtracted from) both sides. That is, if

$$a \geq b \text{ then } a + n \geq b + n \quad (\text{or } a - n \geq b - n).$$

II. The sense of an inequality is not changed if both sides are multiplied or divided by the same positive number n. That is, if $a \geq b$ and $n > 0$, then $an \geq bn$ and $\dfrac{a}{n} \geq \dfrac{b}{n}$.

III. The sense of an inequality is *reversed* if both sides are multiplied or divided by the same negative number m. That is, if $a \geq b$ and $m < 0$, then $am \leq bm$ and $\dfrac{a}{m} \leq \dfrac{b}{m}$.

An inequality which fails to be true for certain values of the variables involved is called a *conditional inequality*. The *solution* of a conditional inequality involving one variable is the set of all values of that variable for which the inequality is true.

Example 1. Consider the inequality $3 - 2x \geq 5$. By Statement I, we can obtain $-2x \geq 5 - 3$, or $-2x \geq 2$. By Statement III, $x \leq -1$ which is called the solution of the given conditional inequality. Notice that the solution consists of an infinite number of values of x.

When we graph a linear equation involving two variables, such as

$$x_1 + x_2 = 1,$$

a straight line is the result (Fig. 11.1). This means that any point whose coordinates satisfy the equation will lie on the line, and any point whose coordinates do not satisfy the equation does not lie on the line.

When we graph a linear inequality involving two variables, such as

$$x_1 + x_2 \geq 1,$$

a straight line and the set of points on one side of the line is the solution (Fig. 11.2). The question arises: How do we determine which side of

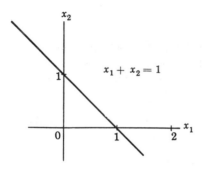

Figure 11.1

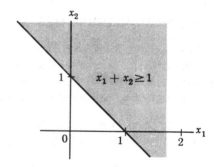

Figure 11.2

the line contains the points whose coordinates satisfy the inequality? This can be done by testing any point not on the line. For example the co-ordinates of the point $(0, 0)$ do not satisfy the inequality in the problem above; therefore we shade the plane on the opposite side of the line. A set of points so determined by a linear inequality in two dimensions is called a *half-plane*. A half-plane is said to be *closed* or *open* depending upon whether the bounding line is included ($\leq$ or $\geq$) or is *not* included ($<$ or $>$).

Now consider the following system of two inequalities

$$\begin{cases} x_1 + x_2 \geq 1, \\ x_1 + 2x_2 \leq 2. \end{cases}$$

Geometrically, we obtain what is called the *intersection* of two half-planes, which consists of the set of all points (or vectors) whose coordinates satisfy both inequalities; this set is pictured in Fig. 11.3 as the shaded portion of the graph.

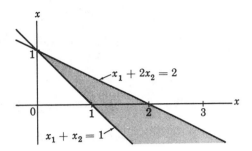

Figure 11.3

For certain purposes this set of points (or vectors) which is the solution of the system, is called the *feasible set* of the system. The student should contrast the solution of a consistent system of two linear equations and the solution of a consistent system of two linear inequalities.

So far this discussion has been concerned with inequalities in two dimensions. In three dimensions the boundaries are planes.

For n dimensions we have the following definition.

Definition. *The set of all points $\rho = (x_1, x_2, \ldots, x_n)$ whose coordinates satisfy the linear equation*

$$c_1 x_1 + c_2 x_2 + \cdots + c_n x_n = d$$

is called a hyperplane. This can be expressed as the scalar product $\gamma \cdot \rho = d$ where $\gamma = (c_1, c_2, \ldots, c_n)$. The c_i and x_i are real numbers.

Example 2. $4x_1 + 3x_2 + x_3 - x_4 + x_5 = 4$ defines a hyperplane.

A hyperplane involving n unknowns divides the n-space into three distinct sets:

(1) $c_1 x_1 + c_2 x_2 + \cdots + c_n x_n = d$ or $\gamma \cdot \rho = d,$

(2) $c_1 x_1 + c_2 x_2 + \cdots + c_n x_n < d$ or $\gamma \cdot \rho < d,$

(3) $c_1 x_1 + c_2 x_2 + \cdots + c_n x_n > d$ or $\gamma \cdot \rho > d.$

The set of all ρ that satisfy (2) and the set of all ρ that satisfy (3) are called *open half-spaces*. The set of all ρ that satisfy $\gamma \cdot \rho \leq d$ and the set of all ρ that satisfy $\gamma \cdot \rho \geq d$ are called *closed half-spaces*.

Definition. *Let A be an m by n real matrix and let B be an m by 1 real* *matrix.   A real vector* $X = \begin{bmatrix} x_1 \\ x_2 \\ \cdot \\ \cdot \\ \cdot \\ x_n \end{bmatrix}$ *which satisfies a system of linear inequalities,*

$AX \geq B$ *(or* $AX \leq B$*), is called a **feasible vector** for the system of inequalities.*

Example 3.   Describe graphically the feasible set (that is, the set of feasible vectors) for the system

$$\begin{cases} x_1 + x_2 \leq 1, \\ \qquad x_2 \geq 0, \\ x_1 + x_2 \leq 2, \\ x_1 - x_2 \geq 0. \end{cases}$$

If we graph each inequality separately we obtain figures 11.4, 11.5, 11.6, and 11.7.

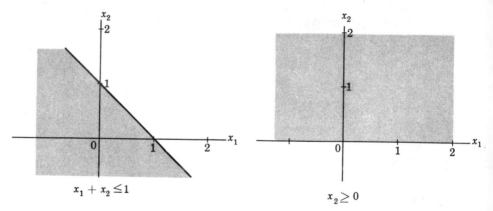

$x_1 + x_2 \leq 1$

Figure 11.4

$x_2 \geq 0$

Figure 11.5

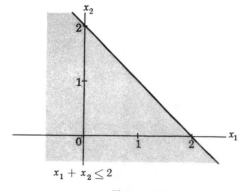

$x_1 + x_2 \leq 2$

Figure 11.6

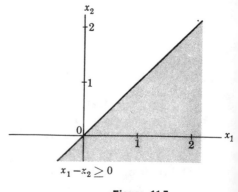

$x_1 - x_2 \geq 0$

Figure 11.7

Graphing all of the inequalities simultaneously, we get Fig. 11.8.   All points in the shaded triangle of Fig. 11.8 belong to the feasible set.   Notice that the third inequality is superfluous.

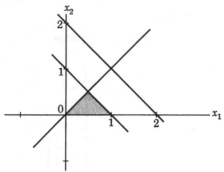

Figure 11.8

In this example notice that if the sense of the third inequality had been reversed there would have been no solution of the system.   In such a case we say that the system is *inconsistent.*

Example 4.   Describe graphically the feasible set defined by

$$\begin{cases} (1) & x_1 + x_2 + 2x_3 \leq 2, \\ (2) & x_1 + 2x_2 + x_3 \leq 2, \\ & x_1 \geq 0, \\ & x_2 \geq 0, \\ & x_3 \geq 0. \end{cases}$$

As shown in Fig. 11.9, all points inside the shaded solid and on the bounding planes belong to the feasible set.

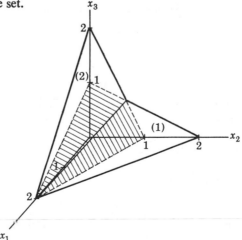

Figure 11.9

EXERCISES

1. Solve for x: $6 - 3x \geq 12$.

2. Solve for x: $x + 6 < -2x - 4$.

In Exercises 3–7, show on a graph the feasible set for the given system of inequalities.

3. $\begin{cases} 2x_1 + 3x_2 \leq 12, \\ 2x_1 + x_2 \leq 8. \end{cases}$

4. $\begin{bmatrix} 1 & 1 \\ -1 & 1 \\ -1 & 0 \\ 0 & -1 \end{bmatrix} \begin{bmatrix} x_1 \\ x_2 \end{bmatrix} \leq \begin{bmatrix} 2 \\ 1 \\ 0 \\ 0 \end{bmatrix}.$

5. $\begin{cases} x_1 - x_2 \geq 0, \\ x_2 \geq 0, \\ x_1 \leq 2. \end{cases}$

6. $\begin{bmatrix} 3 & 2 \\ 2 & 4 \\ 1 & 0 \\ 0 & 1 \end{bmatrix} \begin{bmatrix} x_1 \\ x_2 \end{bmatrix} \geq \begin{bmatrix} 6 \\ 4 \\ 0 \\ 0 \end{bmatrix}.$

7. $\begin{cases} x_1 + x_2 \geq 1, \\ x_2 + x_3 \geq 1, \\ x_1 \geq 0, \\ x_2 \geq 0, \\ x_3 \geq 0. \end{cases}$

In Exercises 8 and 9 find the intersections of the given half-spaces.

8. $\begin{cases} x_1 + 2x_2 \geq 20, \\ 3x_1 + x_2 \geq 15, \\ x_1 \geq 0, \\ x_2 \geq 0. \end{cases}$

9. $\begin{cases} x_1 + x_2 + x_3 \leq 1, \\ 2x_3 \leq 1, \\ x_1 \geq 0, \\ x_2 \geq 0, \\ x_3 \geq 0. \end{cases}$

10. Find any superfluous inequalities in the following set:

$$\begin{cases} x_1 + x_2 < 2, \\ x_1 + x_2 < 0, \\ x_1 \geq 0, \\ x_2 \leq 2. \end{cases}$$

11. For the hyperplane $x_1 + 2x_2 - 3x_3 + x_4 = 2$, find in which half-space the point $(1, 4, 2, 1)$ is located.

12. Solve for x: $\dfrac{x + 2}{3} \leq \dfrac{-6x + 3}{-2}$.

13. Solve for x: $\dfrac{1}{x} > \dfrac{2 - x}{x}$.

14. Solve graphically: $\begin{cases} 2x_1 + 3x_2 = 12, \\ 2x_1 + x_2 = 8. \end{cases}$ Compare with Exercise 3 above.

15. Solve graphically by shading the appropriate half-plane:

(a) $x_1 + 3x_2 \geq 6$.   (b) $x_1 + 3x_2 > 6$.

(c) $x_1 + 2x_2 \geq -6$.   (d) $x_1 - 2x_2 > -6$.

In each case, tell whether the solution is a closed or open half-plane.

16. (a) In two dimensions, what is the graph of a hyperplane?
    (b) In three dimensions, what is the graph of a hyperplane?

11.2 CONVEX SETS

Definition. *A set of points in n-space is said to be* **convex** *if for every pair of points* α, β, *in the set, the line segment joining these points is also in the set.* (*By a line segment from* β *to* α *in n-space we mean the set of all points* ρ *such that* $\rho = t\alpha + (1 - t)\beta$ *for* $0 \leq t \leq 1$. *Note that when* $t = 0$, $\rho = \beta$, *and when* $t = 1$, $\rho = \alpha$.) *A set is considered to be convex if it contains fewer than two points.*

Example 1. Figures 11.10 through 11.13 illustrate the meaning of the preceding definition in two-space.

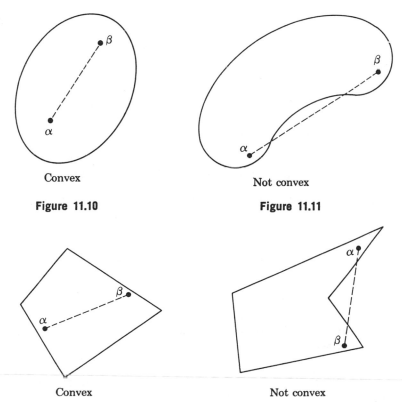

Convex   Not convex

Figure 11.10   **Figure 11.11**

Convex   Not convex

Figure 11.12   **Figure 11.13**

Theorem 1.   *The intersection of two or more convex sets is convex.*

Proof.   Let A and B be two convex sets (in n-space) and let p and q be *any* two points (or vectors) that *belong to both sets, that is to the* **intersection** (Fig. 11.14).   If the intersection consists of less than two points, it is convex by definition.

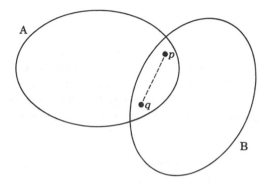

Figure 11.14

STATEMENT	REASON
(1) Line segment pq lies in A.	(1) A is convex.
(2) Line segment pq lies in B.	(2) B is convex.
(3) Line segment pq lies in both A and B and hence in their intersection.	(3) Steps (1) and (2).
(4) Intersection of A and B is convex.	(4) Definition of convex set.

(5) By the same reasoning the intersection of more than two convex sets is convex.

As an exercise, the student should show that a half-space is a convex set. Then by Theorem 1 we have the following theorem.

Theorem 2.   *The intersection of two or more half-spaces is a convex set.*

Definition.   *The intersection of a finite number of closed half-spaces is called a* **polyhedral convex set.**

Definition.   *A point (or vector)* τ *is an* **extreme point** *(or extreme vector) of the polyhedral convex set C when:*

(1) *The point τ belongs to C,* and

(2) *The point τ is the intersection of n bounding hyperplanes of C where n is the dimension of the space involved.*

Example 2.   For the system of linear inequalities

$$\begin{cases} x_1 + x_2 + \ x_3 \le 1, \\ x_1 + x_2 + 4x_3 \le 2, \\ x_1 \qquad\qquad \ge 0, \\ \qquad x_2 \qquad\quad \ge 0, \\ \qquad\qquad x_3 \ge 0, \end{cases}$$

the feasible set is the polyhedral convex set pictured in Fig. 11.15. The extreme points are designated $\tau_1, \tau_2, \tau_3, \tau_4, \tau_5, \tau_6$. Each of these extreme points is the intersection of a certain three planes in three-space.

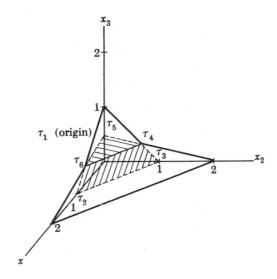

Figure 11.15

A polyhedral convex set in n-space is said to be **bounded** if n positive numbers $k_1, k_2, \ldots, k_n$ exist such that the set is contained in an intersection of the half-spaces $-k_i \le x_i \le k_i$ for $i = 1, 2, \ldots, n$. This can be illustrated by the preceding example. There the polyhedral convex set in three-space is bounded because the set is contained within the "box" defined by the intersection of $x_1 \le 2$, $x_1 \ge -2$, $x_2 \le 2$, $x_2 \ge -2$, $x_3 \le 1$, and $x_3 \ge -1$. This is graphed in Fig. 11.16. If the set is not bounded, we say that it is **unbounded** or **infinite in extent.**

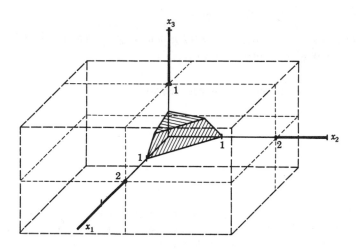

Figure 11.16

Example 3.   Given $\begin{cases} 2x_1 + x_2 \geq 2, \\ x_1 + 2x_2 \geq 2, \\ x_1 \geq 0, \\ \phantom{2x_1 + {}}x_2 \geq 0. \end{cases}$

The feasible set for this system is a polyhedral convex set which is *infinite in extent*. The extreme points are the intersections of the lines in two-space, namely $A(0, 2)$, $B(2, 0)$, and $C(\frac{2}{3}, \frac{2}{3})$.   (Fig. 11.17).

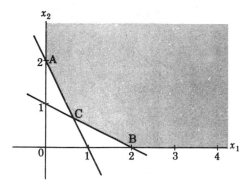

Figure 11.17

EXERCISES

1. Which of the following are convex sets?   Which are polyhedral convex sets? Give reasons:

(*a*) the edges and interior of a rectangle;

(*b*) the interior of a sphere;

(*c*) the boundaries and interior of a triangular pyramid;

(*d*) the boundaries and interior of an equilateral triangle;

(*e*) a torus formed by revolving a circle about an axis exterior to the circle (shaped like a doughnut).

2. In Exercise 1 describe the extreme points where possible.   Where it is not possible, state why it is not.

3. Construct two examples to show that a convex set with extreme points $(0, 2)$, $(1, 1)$, and $(1, 0)$ may or may not be infinite in extent.

4. Is a nonempty polyhedral convex set formed by the intersection of two half-planes always infinite in extent?

5. A certain manufacturer makes 2 products A and B in two factories P and Q. Factory P produces 1 unit of each product per hour.   Factory Q produces 2 units of A per hour but no units of B.   If this manufacturer must produce 12 units of A and 6 units of B, what is the convex set of hours that he could operate each factory to meet production?   What are the extreme points?   (*Hint:* Let x_1 = the number of hours that factory P could operate and let x_2 = the number of hours that factory Q could operate.)

6. A fruit grower ships three varieties of fruit from Florida to Vermont.   A certain truck will hold 800 boxes of fruit.   Assume that this truck is filled.   If the grower must ship at least 200 boxes of oranges, at least 100 boxes of grapefruit, and at least 200 boxes of tangerines, what is the convex set of ways in which he can load the truck for the trip?   What are the extreme points?   (*Hint:* Let x_1 = the number of boxes of oranges, x_2 = the number of boxes of grapefruit, and $x_3 = 800 - x_1 - x_2$ = the number of boxes of tangerines.)

7. Repeat Exercise 6, except that the shipment can have *at most* 200 boxes of tangerines.

11.3 MAXIMUM AND MINIMUM OF A LINEAR FUNCTION OVER A CONVEX POLYGON

For simplicity we shall confine our discussion in this section to two dimensions.   The results of this section, however, can be extended to n dimensions. In two dimensions a bounded polyhedral convex set is called a *convex polygon.*

In the problems in the next chapter we shall define a linear function over a convex set and then seek the maxima and minima of that function over the specified convex set.

Example 1.   Let $f = x_1 + x_2$.   Let the convex polygon be defined by

$$\begin{cases} x_1 + 2x_2 \leq 2, \\ x_1 \qquad\;\; \geq 0, \\ \qquad x_2 \geq 0. \end{cases}$$

On a graph the convex polygon is the interior and boundaries of a triangle as shown in Fig. 11.18. If f could be evaluated at every point in the convex set we would find that f is a maximum over the feasible set at $x_1 = 2$ and $x_2 = 0$, and f is a minimum when $x_1 = 0$, $x_2 = 0$. Theorem 5, later in this section, will justify these statements.

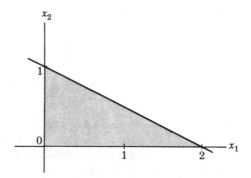

Figure 11.18

The purpose of this section is to show that maximum or minimum values of f on a convex set will occur at extreme points if they occur at all. The advantage of this accomplishment is that there are a finite number of extreme points for a convex polygon. We shall use our knowledge of vectors to achieve our goal. Theorem 3 is needed in the proof of Theorem 4 and Theorem 4 is used to prove Theorem 5.

Theorem 3. *Given three distinct vectors α, β, γ, with a common origin in two-space: If γ terminates on the line segment between the terminals of α and β, then there exists a real number t such that $0 < t < 1$ and*

$$\gamma = t\alpha + (1 - t)\beta.$$

Proof.

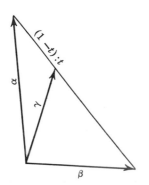
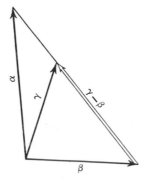
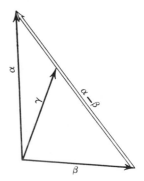

Figure 11.19   **Figure 11.20**   **Figure 11.21**

Let γ divide the line drawn from the terminal of α to the terminal of β in the ratio $(1 - t):t$; thus $0 < t < 1$.   See figures 11.19, 11.20, and 11.21.

STATEMENT	REASON
(1) $(\gamma - \beta) = t(\alpha - \beta)$ where $0 < t < 1$.	(1) Vector subtraction and interpretation of a scalar times a vector.
(2) $\gamma = \beta + t(\alpha - \beta)$.	(2) Transpose β in (1).
(3) $\gamma = t\alpha + (1 - t)(\beta)$.	(3) Rearrange terms.

Theorem 4.   *If a point* (p_1, p_2) *lies on the line-segment between two points* (a_1, a_2) *and* (b_1, b_2), *then the value of a linear function* $f(x_1, x_2) = k_1 x_1 + k_2 x_2$ *evaluated at* (p_1, p_2) *is between distinct values of f at the end points of the line segment.*

Proof.   Making use of vectors, let:

$$(a_1, a_2) = \alpha, \ (b_1, b_2) = \beta, \text{ and } (p_1, p_2) = \rho.$$

Also let:

the value of f at (a_1, a_2) be called $f(\alpha)$;
the value of f at (b_1, b_2) be called $f(\beta)$;
the value of f at (p_1, p_2) be called $f(\rho)$.

Since $f = k_1 x_1 + k_2 x_2$, f can be thought of as the dot product of $(k_1, k_2) = \lambda$ and $(x_1, x_2) = X$.

STATEMENT	REASON
(1) $f(\alpha) = k_1 a_1 + k_2 a_2 = \lambda \cdot \alpha$.	(1) Definition of dot product.
(2) $f(\beta) = k_1 b_1 + k_2 b_2 = \lambda \cdot \beta$.	(2) Same.
(3) $f(\rho) = k_1 p_1 + k_2 p_2 = \lambda \cdot \rho$.	(3) Same.
(4) $\rho = t\alpha + (1 - t)\beta$, where $0 < t < 1$.	(4) Theorem 3.
(5) $\lambda \cdot \rho = \lambda \cdot (t\alpha) + \lambda \cdot (1 - t)\beta$.	(5) Dot product of vectors is distributive.
(6) $\lambda \cdot \rho = t(\lambda \cdot \alpha) + (1 - t)(\lambda \cdot \beta)$.	(6) Theorem 11, Section 3.4.
(7) $f(\rho) = t f(\alpha) + (1 - t)f(\beta)$.	(7) Statements (1), (2), and (3).
(8) $f(\rho) - f(\beta) + t [f(\alpha) - f(\beta)]$.	(8) Rearrange terms.
(9) $f(\rho)$ is between $f(\alpha)$ and $f(\beta)$.	(9) Because $0 < t < 1$.

In statement (7) of the above proof notice that if $f(\alpha) = f(\beta)$ (that is, if the values of the function are the same at the end-points) then $f(\rho) = f(\beta) = f(\alpha)$.

Theorem 5.   *A linear function* $f = k_1x_1 + k_2x_2$ *defined at every point of a convex polygon assumes its minimum and maximum values (for the polygon) at extreme points of the convex polygon.*

Proof. In Fig. 11.22, let τ_1 be chosen so that $f(\tau_1)$ is greater than or equal to f at any other extreme point. Also let τ_2 be chosen so that $f(\tau_2)$ is less than or equal to f at any other extreme point. Let ρ be any interior point belonging to the convex polygon. Draw a line from τ_1 to ρ and extend it until it cuts a bounding line of the polygon at α, and let τ_4 and τ_5 be the extreme points on this bounding line.

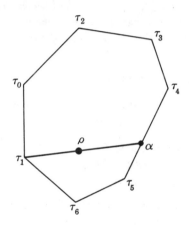

Figure 11.22

STATEMENT	REASON
(1) $f(\tau_1) \geq f(\tau_4) \geq f(\tau_2)$. $\quad\;\; f(\tau_1) \geq f(\tau_5) \geq f(\tau_2)$.	(1) By assumption.
(2) $f(\alpha)$ is between or equal to $f(\tau_4)$ and $f(\tau_5)$.	(2) Theorem 4 and the possibility that α is an extreme point.
(3) $f(\tau_1)$ is the greatest value assumed by f on the boundary, and $f(\tau_2)$ is the smallest value assumed by f on the boundary.	(3) Statements (2) and then (1).
(4) $f(\tau_1) \geq f(\rho) \geq f(\alpha)$.	(4) Theorem 4.
(5) $f(\tau_1) \geq f(\rho) \geq f(\tau_2)$.	(5) Statements (4) and then (3).

If the convex set is infinite in extent, then either maximum f or minimum f or both maximum f and minimum f may fail to exist. If they do exist, however, it can be shown by a similar argument that they occur at extreme points.

EXERCISES

1. Prove the converse of Theorem 3. (That is, if $\gamma = t\alpha + (1 - t)\beta$ where $0 < t < 1$, then γ terminates on a line between the terminals of α and β. All three vectors have a common origin.)

2. In each of the parts (a), (b), (c), let a polyhedral convex set be defined by the given system of inequalities. Let a linear function be defined over the convex set. Make use of Theorem 5 to determine the maximum and/or minimum values of the function over the convex set.

(a) $f = 2x_1 + x_2$ where the convex set is defined by

$$\begin{cases} x_1 + 2x_2 \leq 2, \\ x_1 \qquad \geq 0, \\ \qquad x_2 \geq 0. \end{cases}$$

(b) $f = x_1 - x_2$ where the convex set is defined by

$$\begin{cases} x_1 + x_2 \geq 1, \\ -x_1 + 2x_2 \leq 1, \\ x_1 \qquad \leq 1. \end{cases}$$

(c) $f = x_1 + x_2$ where the convex set is defined by

$$\begin{cases} x_1 + 2x_2 \leq 4, \\ 3x_1 + x_2 \leq 6, \\ x_1 \qquad \geq 0, \\ \qquad x_2 \geq 0. \end{cases}$$

3. Let α be the vector from $(0, 0)$ to $(0, 3)$, β the vector from $(0, 0)$ to $(6, 0)$, and γ the vector from $(0, 0)$ to $(4, 1)$. Find the number t mentioned in Theorem 3.

4. Prove: A linear function $f = k_1x_1 + k_2x_2$ defined at every point of a convex set, infinite in extent in two-space, assumes its minimum (or maximum) value (for the set), if it exists, at an extreme point of the set.

NEW VOCABULARY

12

Linear Programming

12.1 INTRODUCTION

Consider the problem of finding the minimum or maximum of a linear function of the form

$$f = a_1x_1 + a_2x_2 + \cdots + a_nx_n + b_1$$

over a convex set. Problems of this type have attracted considerable attention in recent years; these problems are frequently concerned with decision-making and occur in management science in connection with production schedules, optimum inventories, shipping schedules, and in many other areas. Linear programming is a mathematical method for solving certain of these problems. The following example will demonstrate a very simple problem and its solution.

Example 1. There are two factories that manufacture three different grades of paper. There is some demand for each grade. The company that controls the factories has contracts to supply 16 tons of low grade, 5 tons of medium grade, and 20 tons of high grade paper. It costs $1000 per day to operate the first factory and $2000 per day to operate the second factory. Factory number one produces 8 tons of low grade, 1 ton of medium grade, and 2 tons of high grade paper in one day's operation. Factory number two produces 2 tons of low grade, 1 ton of medium grade, and 7 tons of high grade paper per day. How many days should each factory be operated in order to fill the orders most economically?

	Factory 1	Factory 2	Tons Needed
Low-Grade	8 tons per day	2 tons per day	16
Medium-Grade	1 ton per day	1 ton per day	5
High-Grade	2 tons per day	7 tons per day	20
Daily Cost	$1000	$2000	

The table shows the information stated in the problem. The entries in the table indicate the production of each grade of paper by the factories, the minimum requirements to fill the orders, and the daily cost of operating each factory. Let x_1 be the number of days that Factory 1 operates, and let x_2 be the number of days that Factory 2 operates in order to produce the required amounts.

(1) $8x_1 + 2x_2 \geq 16$.   (At least 16 tons of low grade paper are required.)

(2) $x_1 + x_2 \geq 5$.   (At least 5 tons of medium grade paper are required.)

(3) $2x_1 + 7x_2 \geq 20$.   (At least 20 tons of high grade paper are required.)

(4) $x_1 \geq 0$,   (5) $x_2 \geq 0$.   (Number of days operated must be nonnegative.)

The five inequalities above represent five restrictions on our variables. We wish to minimize the total operating cost of the factories,

$$f(x_1, x_2) = 1000x_1 + 2000x_2.$$

Geometric Solution. First we will determine a geometric solution of the problem. Consider $8x_1 + 2x_2 \geq 16$ or equivalently $4x_1 + x_2 \geq 8$. This represents all points *on* and *above* the line (1) $4x_1 + x_2 = 8$. Likewise, graph the other inequalities. All points in the shaded region in Fig. 12.1 satisfy the five inequalities and represent the feasible set of solutions.

The cost function is $f(x_1, x_2) = 1000x_1 + 2000x_2$ or $f = 1000x_1 + 2000x_2$. If f is assigned arbitrary values, the equation in each case represents a straight line of slope $-\frac{1}{2}$. With f as a parameter, $1000x_1 + 2000x_2 = f$ is the equation of a family of parallel lines. The lines correspond to increasing values of f as they go up from the origin. From the figure it appears that the line corresponding to $f = 7000$ is the "lowest" line that has a point in common with the shaded region. Any lower line does not intersect the feasible set, and higher lines represent larger values of f than the minimum. Hence the point $(3, 2)$, which is the intersection of (2) $x_1 + x_2 = 5$ and (3) $2x_1 + 7x_2 = 20$, gives the minimum f which is $(1000)(3) + (2000)(2) = 7000$. Thus if Factory 1 operates three days, and Factory 2 operates two days, the requirements will be met at less cost than with any other combination.

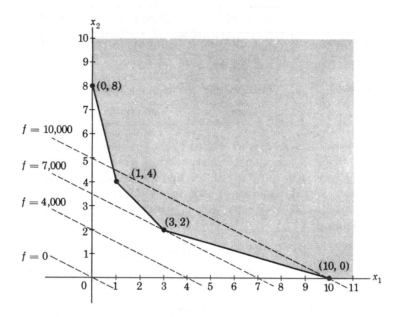

Figure 12.1

Notice that if $x_1 = 3$, $x_2 = 2$, then $8x_1 + 2x_2 = 28$, or 28 tons of low grade paper are produced. This is more than the minimum requirement, but any other combination of operating days (including fractions) will result in a greater cost. At first it seems strange that a surplus is obtained at minimum cost.

EXERCISES

Solve the following by the geometric method taught in this section:

1. Minimize $f = x_1 + x_2$, subject to $\begin{cases} x_1 + 2x_2 \geq 12, \\ x_1 \qquad \geq 6, \\ \qquad x_2 \geq 0. \end{cases}$

(The feasible set here is the convex set of Exercise 5 in Section 11.2.)

2. Minimize $f = 2x_1 + x_2$, subject to $\begin{cases} x_1 + x_2 \geq 1, \\ x_1 - x_2 \geq -1, \\ x_1 + 2x_2 \leq 4, \\ \qquad x_2 \geq 0. \end{cases}$

3. Maximize $f = 2x_1 + x_2$, subject to the same restrictions as in Exercise 2.

4. Maximize $f = x_1 - 3x_2$, subject to $\begin{cases} -x_1 + x_2 \leq 1, \\ x_1 + x_2 \leq 1, \\ x_1 \qquad \geq 0, \\ \qquad x_2 \geq 0. \end{cases}$

5. Minimize $f = x_1 + 2x_2$, subject to
$$\begin{cases} 2x_1 + x_2 \geq 8, \\ x_1 + x_2 \geq 6, \\ x_1 + 2x_2 \geq 9, \\ x_1 \geq 0, \\ x_2 \geq 0. \end{cases}$$

6. Let $f = 8x_1 + 6x_2$ and let the feasible set be defined by
$$\begin{cases} 4x_1 + 3x_2 \geq 18, \\ 2x_1 + 5x_2 \geq 16, \\ x_1 \geq 0, \\ x_2 \geq 0. \end{cases}$$

Show that more than one extreme point will yield minimum f, and give a geometrical explanation of that fact.

7. Show that $g = 4x_1 - 5x_2$ has no maximum or minimum when defined over the feasible set of Exercise 6.

12.2 HISTORY AND APPLICATIONS

Linear programming is a relatively new field in mathematics. Most of the basic work was done in the 1940's by such men as F. L. Hitchcock, L. Kantorovitch (Russian), T. C. Koopmans, and G. B. Dantzig. Much of this basic work was spurred by the economic theories of J. Von Neumann and W. Leontief in the 1930's. In 1947 Dantzig, who was a member of a group studying allocation problems for the U. S. Air Force, formulated the general linear programming problem and developed the simplex method of solution. Since that time the subject has received widespread attention in such diverse fields as nutrition, engineering, economics, agriculture, and many others.

In general, a problem of linear programming is that of finding nonnegative values of a number of variables for which a certain linear function of those variables assumes the greatest (or the least) possible value while subject to certain linear constraints.

To give the student an idea of how linear programming can be applied in various fields, the data of the paper problem in the previous section will be applied to four hypothetical, oversimplified problems. The student should also observe that the basic mathematical model can assume various disguises.

Example 1. The minimum requirements of the amount of certain chemicals necessary to grow a certain crop successfully have been found. Knowing the content and cost of two special types of commercial fertilizers, packaged in 100 pound bags, a grower wants to know how many bags of each type should be applied to his crop to assure proper growth at minimum cost.

	Fertilizer 1	Fertilizer 2	Units needed
Chemical A	8 units per bag	2 units per bag	16
Chemical B	1 unit per bag	1 unit per bag	5
Chemical C	2 units per bag	7 units per bag	20
Cost Per Bag	1000¢	2000¢	

Let x_1 be the number of bags of Fertilizer 1 that are applied.
Let x_2 be the number of bags of Fertilizer 2 that are applied.

Example 2. A nutritionist working for a space craft designer is faced with the problem of minimizing weight subject to certain nutritional requirements. He is considering two foods which are packaged in tubes.

	Food 1	Food 2	Requirements
Carbohydrates	8 units per tube	2 units per tube	16
Fats	1 unit per tube	1 unit per tube	5
Proteins	2 units per tube	7 units per tube	20
Wt. (grams) per tube	1000	2000	

Let x_1 be the number of tubes of Food 1 sent on space craft.
Let x_2 be the number of tubes of Food 2 sent on space craft.

Example 3. An office manager must assign his two groups of employees in such a way that each of three tasks is performed a certain number of times and the time to do them is held to a minimum.

	Group 1	Group 2	Times needed
Task A	8 times per assignment	2 times per assignment	16
Task B	1 time per assignment	1 time per assignment	5
Task C	2 times per assignment	7 times per assignment	20
Minutes taken per assignment	1000	2000	

Let x_1 be the number of times employee Group 1 is assigned to work.
Let x_2 be the number of times employee Group 2 is assigned to work.

Example 4. A fruit buyer needs a certain number of units of various varieties of fruit. Two suppliers can supply his needs but will sell the fruit only in full truck-loads consisting of a specified number of units of each variety (let one unit equal 10 boxes). How many loads should the buyer order from each supplier in order to save time and money by holding the shipping distance to a minimum?

	Supplier 1	Supplier 2	Units needed
Variety A	8 units per load	2 units per load	16
Variety B	1 unit per load	1 unit per load	5
Variety C	2 units per load	7 units per load	20
Distance in miles	1000	2000	

Let x_1 be the number of truckloads ordered from Supplier 1.
Let x_2 be the number of truckloads ordered from Supplier 2.

The student should observe that in Examples 2 and 4, the solution vector had to have integral components. When applied problems of this type are encountered and if such a solution vector is not obtained by our methods, then techniques beyond the scope of this text must be employed. The study of such problems is a very interesting branch of Linear Programming.

The petroleum industry has found linear programming useful in refining procedures. Agriculture may use it to secure proper mixes of feed, fertilizer, seed and the like. The transportation industry is interested in the problem of minimizing shipping costs while supplying many consumers with specified requirements. Some of these problems are more complicated than those treated in this text and the interested reader should refer to other books. There are, of course, many other possible applications of linear programming, many yet unknown.

EXERCISES

Draw a chart and solve the following linear programming problems:

1. Two oil refineries produce three grades of gasoline A, B, and C. At each refinery, the various grades of gasoline are produced in a single operation so that they are in fixed proportions. Assume that one operation at Refinery 1 produces 1 unit of A, 3 units of B, and 1 unit of C. One operation at Refinery 2 produces 1 unit of A, 4 units of B, and 5 units of C. Refinery 1 charges $300 for what is produced in one operation, and Refinery 2 charges $500 for the production of one operation. A consumer needs 100 units of A, 340 units of B, and 150 units of C. How should the orders be placed if the consumer is to meet his needs most econo-mically?

2. Suppose a certain company has two methods, M_1 and M_2, of manufacturing three automobile gadgets G_1, G_2, and G_3. The first method will produce one of each gadget in 3 hours. The second method will produce 3 G_1's and 1 G_3 in 4 hours. The company has an order for 6 G_1's, 2 G_2's, and 4 G_3's. How many times should we employ each method to fill the order and minimize the time we spend in production?

3. A trucking company owns 2 types of trucks. Type A has 20 cubic yards of refrigerated space and 30 cubic yards of nonrefrigerated space. Type B has 20 cubic yards of refrigerated space and 10 cubic yards of nonrefrigerated space. A customer wants to haul some produce a certain distance and will require 160 cubic yards of refrigerated space and 120 cubic yards of nonrefrigerated space. The trucking company figures it will take 300 gallons of gas for the type A truck to make the trip and 200 gallons of gas for the type B truck. Find the number of trucks of each type that the company should allow for the job in order to minimize gas consumption.

4. A nutritionist in a large institution wishes to serve food that provides the necessary vitamins and minerals for the inhabitants. Foods F_1 and F_2 contain the following amounts of vitamins and minerals per pound of food eaten.

	F_1	F_2
Vitamins	2 units	4 units
Minerals	5 units	2 units

At least 80 units of vitamins and at least 60 units of minerals must be provided. If the costs of F_1 and F_2 are $1 and $.80 per pound, respectively, how many pounds of each food should be ordered to meet minimum diet requirements while also minimizing the total cost of the foods purchased?

5. A local television network is faced with the following problem. It has been found that Program A with 20 minutes of music and 1 minute of advertisement draws 30,000 viewers while Program B with 10 minutes of music and 1 minute of advertisement draws 10,000 viewers. Within one week the advertiser insists that at least 6 minutes be devoted to his advertisement and the network can afford no more than 80 minutes of music. How many times per week should each program be given in order to obtain the maximum number of viewers?

6. A fruit dealer ships 800 boxes of fruit north on a certain truck. If he must ship at least 200 boxes of oranges at 20¢ a box profit, at least 100 boxes of grapefruit at 10¢ a box profit and at *most* 200 boxes of tangerines at 30¢ a box profit, how should he load his truck for maximum profit? (*Hint:* See Exercise 6 of Section 11.2.)

12.3 MATRIX NOTATION

The linear programming problem can be expressed in matrix notation. In order to illustrate this we shall use the paper production problem of Section

12.1.   We let

$$X = \begin{bmatrix} x_1 \\ x_2 \end{bmatrix}$$ be a 2-component column matrix.

Then from the table,

Paper	Factory 1	Factory 2	Tons Needed
Low-Grade	8	2	16
Medium-Grade	1	1	5
High-Grade	2	7	20
Daily Cost	1000	2000	

we define matrices $A = \begin{bmatrix} 8 & 2 \\ 1 & 1 \\ 2 & 7 \end{bmatrix}$, $R = \begin{bmatrix} 16 \\ 5 \\ 20 \end{bmatrix}$,   and $C = [1000 \ \ 2000]$.

Hence our restrictions $\begin{cases} 8x_1 + 2x_2 \geq 16, \\ x_1 + x_2 \geq 5, \\ 2x_1 + 7x_2 \geq 20, \end{cases}$ and $\begin{cases} x_1 \geq 0, \\ x_2 \geq 0, \end{cases}$

can be written as $\begin{bmatrix} 8 & 2 \\ 1 & 1 \\ 2 & 7 \end{bmatrix} \begin{bmatrix} x_1 \\ x_2 \end{bmatrix} \geq \begin{bmatrix} 16 \\ 5 \\ 20 \end{bmatrix}$ and $\begin{bmatrix} x_1 \\ x_2 \end{bmatrix} \geq \begin{bmatrix} 0 \\ 0 \end{bmatrix}$,

or $AX \geq R$ and $X \geq 0$.   (Be sure all inequality symbols in the first set of restrictions have the same sense.)   The first matrix inequality indicates the required amounts to be produced and the second matrix inequality states that the number of days of production is nonnegative.

Our purpose is to minimize $1000x_1 + 2000x_2$, or

$$[1000 \ \ 2000] \begin{bmatrix} x_1 \\ x_2 \end{bmatrix}, \quad \text{or} \quad CX.$$

Therefore the statement of the problem using matrix notation is:

Minimize CX subject to the restrictions $AX \geq R$ and $X \geq 0$, where A, X, R, and C are defined above.

It will be necessary in our discussion of the simplex method (Sections 12.6–12.10) to express the maximum problem so that the relation of the first matrix inequality is ($\leq$) rather than ($\geq$), as in the minimum problem; this convention will be adhered to in the following example.

Example 1. In matrix notation, the problem: Maximize $-2z_1 + z_2$ subject to

$$\begin{cases} z_1 + 2z_2 \geq 2, \\ z_1 - z_2 \leq 1, \end{cases} \text{ and } \begin{cases} z_1 \geq 0, \\ z_2 \geq 0, \end{cases} \text{ is written: Maximize } [-2 \quad 1]\begin{bmatrix} z_1 \\ z_2 \end{bmatrix} \text{ subject to}$$

$$\begin{bmatrix} -1 & -2 \\ 1 & -1 \end{bmatrix}\begin{bmatrix} z_1 \\ z_2 \end{bmatrix} \leq \begin{bmatrix} -2 \\ 1 \end{bmatrix} \text{ and } \begin{bmatrix} z_1 \\ z_2 \end{bmatrix} \geq \begin{bmatrix} 0 \\ 0 \end{bmatrix}.$$ Notice that the sense of the first

inequality $z_1 + 2z_2 \geq 2$ had to be reversed to get the desired form. If the sense of second inequality $z_1 - z_2 \leq 1$ had been reversed, the problem could be expressed in matrix notation, but the sense of the resulting *matrix inequality* would not conform to our convention.

EXERCISES

Set up the following problems using matrix notation.

1. Exercise 1 of Section 12.1.　　　　2. Exercise 2 of Section 12.1.

3. Exercise 3 of Section 12.1.　　　　4. Exercise 4 of Section 12.1.

5. Exercise 5 of Section 12.1.　　　　6. Exercise 6 of Section 12.1.

7. Exercise 1 of Section 12.2.　　　　8. Exercise 2 of Section 12.2.

9. Exercise 3 of Section 12.2.　　　　10. Exercise 4 of Section 12.2.

11. Exercise 5 of Section 12.2.　　　　12. Exercise 6 of Section 12.2.

12.4 A GENERAL LINEAR PROGRAMMING PROBLEM

Suppose that m different goods are produced by n different factories. Let a_{ij} be the number of units of Product i produced by Factory j; for example, a_{23} represents the number of units of Product 2 produced by Factory 3. We can represent this by a table with m rows and n columns, and the entries of the table may be thought of as an m by n matrix A.

$$A = \begin{bmatrix} a_{11} & a_{12} & \cdots & a_{1n} \\ a_{21} & a_{22} & \cdots & a_{2n} \\ \cdot & \cdot & \cdot & \cdot \\ \cdot & \cdot & \cdot & \cdot \\ \cdot & \cdot & \cdot & \cdot \\ a_{m1} & a_{m2} & \cdots & a_{mn} \end{bmatrix} \begin{matrix} \text{Product 1} \\ \text{Product 2} \\ \cdot \\ \cdot \\ \cdot \\ \text{Product } m \end{matrix}$$

Factory 1　　Factory 2　　　Factory n

Suppose we are given certain minimal requirements to meet, such as the number of each product to be produced. Let these requirements form an

m-component column vector $R = \begin{bmatrix} r_1 \\ \cdot \\ \cdot \\ \cdot \\ r_m \end{bmatrix}$. The costs of production at the n

factories are given and may be represented by an n-component row vector
$C = [c_1 c_2 \ldots c_n]$. Let $x_1, x_2, \ldots, x_n$ be the number of days the factories

operate and let $X = \begin{bmatrix} x_1 \\ x_2 \\ \cdot \\ \cdot \\ \cdot \\ x_n \end{bmatrix}$.

Since $x_1 \geq 0$, $x_2 \geq 0, \ldots, x_n \geq 0$, then $X \geq 0$ (the number of days of
operation is nonnegative). Since

$$\begin{cases} a_{11}x_1 + \cdots + a_{1n}x_n \geq r_1, \\ a_{21}x_1 + \cdots + a_{2n}x_n \geq r_2, \\ \qquad \qquad \vdots \\ a_{m1}x_1 + \cdots + a_{mn}x_n \geq r_m, \end{cases} \qquad \text{then} \qquad AX \geq R.$$

(The minimal requirements are met or exceeded.)   The total cost of production is $c_1x_1 + c_2x_2 + \cdots + c_nx_n$ or CX.

Thus our general problem is to minimize CX subject to $X \geq 0$ and $AX \geq R$,
where A, X, R, and C are as stated above.

12.5 THE DUAL PROBLEM

In Sections 12.6 to 12.10 we shall consider the *Simplex Method* of solving
Linear Programming problems. As presented in this book, the application
of the Simplex Method to a minimum problem requires that we write the
dual, maximum problem. Also the *Duality Theorem* which appears later
in this section will be used to justify many steps that we take in the
succeeding sections.

Every linear programming problem has associated with it another linear
programming problem called its **dual.** For example, suppose the paper
company of Section 12.1 wants to assign values for each grade of paper.
That is, the low grade paper is worth z_1 units of money per ton, the medium
grade paper is worth z_2 units of money per ton, etc. These values are called
shadow prices and have no necessary relation to market prices, although they
may help to determine them. Actually, the set of prices chosen as the solution of the dual reflects both the demand for the product and the operating
costs but not necessarily the quality of the product.

In our previous illustration, then, the shadow price of the paper demands

is $16z_1 + 5z_2 + 20z_3$ or $R^T Z$ where Z is the column vector $\begin{bmatrix} z_1 \\ z_2 \\ z_3 \end{bmatrix}$, and the row vector R^T is the transpose of the column vector $R = \begin{bmatrix} 16 \\ 5 \\ 20 \end{bmatrix}$, as given in

Section 12.3.   Now naturally the company wants to make this value as high as possible in order to justify its market prices.   However, suppose the shadow price of each factory's output must not exceed the cost of operating the factory, that is,

$$\begin{cases} 8z_1 + z_2 + 2z_3 \leq 1000 & \text{for Factory 1,} \\ 2z_1 + z_2 + 7z_3 \leq 2000 & \text{for Factory 2,} \end{cases}$$

or $A^T Z \leq C^T.$

Also, of course, these shadow prices must be nonnegative, $Z \geq 0$.

Therefore the company is faced with another problem:

Maximize $R^T Z$ subject to the restrictions $\begin{cases} A^T Z \leq C^T, \\ Z \geq 0. \end{cases}$

This maximum problem is the dual of the minimum problem.   Since we have three unknowns to solve for, the geometric approach used previously would be rather cumbersome; if we use a method which is explained in

Section 12.7, we find $\begin{bmatrix} z_1 \\ z_2 \\ z_3 \end{bmatrix} = \begin{bmatrix} 0 \\ 600 \\ 200 \end{bmatrix}$. Also, maximum $R^T Z = 7000$, which

we notice is equal to minimum CX.   This remarkable result leads us to the principal theorem of linear programming.   It is called the Duality Theorem, whose proof* is beyond the scope of this book, but which we state as follows:

Theorem 1.   (*The Duality Theorem*)   *A feasible vector X_0 exists and is a solution of the minimum problem (Minimize CX subject to $AX \geq R$ and $X \geq 0$) if and only if a feasible vector Z_0 exists and is a solution of the maximum problem (Maximize $R^T Z$ subject to $A^T Z \leq C^T$ and $Z \geq 0$).   Moreover $R^T Z_0 = CX_0$ if and only if X_0 and Z_0 are solutions.*

From this theorem we see that for every linear programming problem there is another, the dual problem, and the solution of one exists if and only if the other has a solution.   These two problems are:

THE MAXIMUM PROBLEM	THE MINIMUM PROBLEM
Maximize $R^T Z$,	Minimize CX,
subject to $A^T Z \leq C^T$,	subject to $AX \geq R$,
$Z \geq 0$.	$X \geq 0$.

And Max $R^T Z$ = Min CX.

---

* A proof may be found in a book entitled *The Theory of Games and Linear Programming* by S. Vajda, (London, Methuen and Co., and New York, John Wiley & Sons, Inc.), pages 72–75.

The maximum problem can be thought of as the dual of the minimum problem or the minimum problem can be thought of as the dual of the maximum problem. In either event, one problem is referred to as the *primal* and the other as the *dual*.

NOTES:

(1) Since in the preceding illustration we found $z_1 = 0$, then economically we may maintain that the low grade paper was a by-product.

(2) An economic interpretation of the 2-component column vector $A^T Z$ would be that each component gives the total shadow price of the production of each factory.

(3) In our illustration the dual problem amounts to this: the company wants to assign shadow prices to each of the goods it produces in such a way that as much as possible of the value of the total production is assigned to the goods actually in demand by the customers, and as little as possible to those goods that are not desired.

When A is a 2 by 2 matrix, the dual problems can be written:

MAXIMUM PROBLEM

Maximize f, where
$$a_1 z_1 + b_1 z_2 \leq c_1,$$
$$a_2 z_1 + b_2 z_2 \leq c_2,$$
$$r_1 z_1 + r_2 z_2 = f.$$

MINIMUM PROBLEM

Minimize g, where
$$a_1 x_1 + a_2 x_2 \geq r_1,$$
$$b_1 x_1 + b_2 x_2 \geq r_2,$$
$$c_1 x_1 + c_2 x_2 = g.$$

Example 1. Suppose we are given a maximum problem:

$$\text{Maximize} \quad f = 4z_1 + 5z_2,$$

$$\text{subject to} \quad \begin{cases} z_1 + 3z_2 \leq 4, \\ z_1 + z_2 \leq 2, \end{cases} \quad \text{and} \quad \begin{cases} z_1 \geq 0, \\ z_2 \geq 0. \end{cases}$$

Then there exists the dual to this problem.

$$\text{Minimize} \quad g = 4x_1 + 2x_2,$$

$$\text{subject to} \quad \begin{cases} x_1 + x_2 \geq 4, \\ 3x_1 + x_2 \geq 5, \end{cases} \quad \text{and} \quad \begin{cases} x_1 \geq 0, \\ x_2 \geq 0. \end{cases}$$

If we were given the minimum problem, then we would say that its dual was the maximum problem. The following chart may be helpful in remembering how to write the dual in either case.

MAXIMUM PROBLEM	MINIMUM PROBLEM		
$1z_1 + 3z_2 \leq 4$	$1x_1$	$3x_1$	$4x_1$
	$+$	$+$	$+$
$1z_1 + 1z_2 \leq 2$	$1x_2$	$1x_2$	$2x_2$
	VI	VI	$\parallel$
$4z_1 + 5z_2 = f$	4	5	g

If these problems were solved we would find that $z_1 = 1$, $z_2 = 1$; and $x_1 = \frac{1}{2}$, $x_2 = \frac{7}{2}$; therefore as was to be expected maximum f = minimum g.

$$\text{Maximum } f = 4(1) + 5(1) = 9.$$

$$\text{Minimum } g = 4(\tfrac{1}{2}) + 2(\tfrac{7}{2}) = 9.$$

EXERCISES

Set up the *dual* of each of the following problems. Do not solve.

1. Minimize $g = x_1 + x_2$,

   subject to $\begin{cases} x_1 + 2x_2 \geq 12, \\ x_1 + 3x_2 \geq 6, \end{cases}$ and $\begin{cases} x_1 \geq 0, \\ x_2 \geq 0. \end{cases}$

2. Minimize $g = x_1 + 2x_2$,

   subject to $\begin{cases} 2x_1 + x_2 \geq 8, \\ x_1 + x_2 \geq 6, \\ x_1 + 2x_2 \geq 9, \end{cases}$ and $\begin{cases} x_1 \geq 0, \\ x_2 \geq 0. \end{cases}$

3. Maximize $f = 2z_1 + z_2$,

   subject to $\begin{cases} z_1 + z_2 \geq 1, \\ z_1 - z_2 \geq -1, \\ z_1 + 2z_2 \leq 4, \end{cases}$ and $\begin{cases} z_1 \geq 0, \\ z_2 \geq 0. \end{cases}$

4. Maximize $f = 100z_1 + 200z_2$,

   subject to $\begin{cases} z_1 - z_2 \leq 4, \\ z_1 + z_2 \leq 5, \\ z_1 - z_2 \geq 2, \end{cases}$ and $\begin{cases} z_1 \geq 0, \\ z_2 \geq 0. \end{cases}$

Set up and solve the dual of the following problems by the geometric procedure taught previously.

5. Minimize $g = 16x_1 + 30x_2$,

   subject to $\begin{cases} 2x_1 + 3x_2 \geq 2, \\ 2x_1 + 5x_2 \geq 3, \end{cases}$ and $\begin{cases} x_1 \geq 0, \\ x_2 \geq 0. \end{cases}$

6. Maximize $f = 5z_1 + 6z_2 + 2z_3$,

subject to $\begin{cases} z_1 + z_2 + z_3 \leq 1, \\ z_1 + 2z_2 \qquad \leq 3, \end{cases}$ and $\begin{cases} z_1 \geq 0, \\ z_2 \geq 0, \\ z_3 \geq 0. \end{cases}$

Set up and interpret the dual of each of the following problems.

7. Exercise 2 of Section 12.2.

8. Exercise 3 of Section 12.2.

9. Exercise 4 of Section 12.2.

10. In each of parts (a) and (b), set up the dual of the given system, solve the given system and its dual, and compare the solutions in the light of the Duality Theorem.

(a) Minimize $6x_1 + 5x_2$,

subject to $\begin{cases} x_1 + x_2 \geq 3, \\ 3x_1 + 2x_2 \geq 8, \end{cases}$ and $\begin{cases} x_1 \geq 0, \\ x_2 \geq 0. \end{cases}$

(b) Maximize $R^T Z$ subject to $A^T Z \leq C^T$,
$$Z \geq 0,$$

where $Z = \begin{bmatrix} z_1 \\ z_2 \end{bmatrix}$, $R = \begin{bmatrix} 1 \\ 1 \end{bmatrix}$, $A = \begin{bmatrix} -1 & 2 \\ 1 & -1 \end{bmatrix}$, $C = [-1 \quad 4]$.

12.6 INTRODUCTION TO THE SIMPLEX METHOD

Obviously when the number of unknowns exceeds 3, a geometric solution is impossible; therefore a general method of attack must be developed. The purpose of this section is to introduce such a method, called the "simplex method."

For the sake of simplicity we will confine our discussion of the simplex method to problems of the type: minimize CX, subject to $AX \geq R$, $X \geq 0$, and maximize $R^T Z$, subject to $A^T Z \leq C^T$, $Z \geq 0$, where $C \geq 0$. If, however, problems are confronted where C has negative entries, or if some of the restrictions are equalities, then more comprehensive works should be consulted. In practical problems, the limitation that $C \geq 0$ is not severe.

To begin with if we introduce m new nonnegative variables,

$$z_{n+1}, z_{n+2}, \ldots, z_{n+m},$$

called *slack variables,* then in the maximum problem we can replace the restrictions given in the form of inequalities

$$\begin{cases} b_{11}z_1 + \cdots + b_{1n}z_n \leq c_1, \\ b_{21}z_1 + \cdots + b_{2n}z_n \leq c_2, \\ \qquad \cdots \\ b_{m1}z_1 + \cdots + b_{mn}z_n \leq c_m, \end{cases}$$

by equivalent restrictions in the form of equations

$$\begin{cases} b_{11}z_1 + \cdots + b_{1n}z_n + z_{n+1} & = c_1, \\ b_{21}z_1 + \cdots + b_{2n}z_n + z_{n+2} & = c_2, \\ \quad\quad \cdots \\ b_{m1}z_1 + \cdots + b_{mn}z_n \quad\quad\quad + z_{n+m} = c_m. \end{cases}$$

The augmented matrix of this system then is $[B \mid I_m \mid C^T]$. If the equation giving the function to be maximized,

$$r_1z_1 + r_2z_2 + \cdots + r_nz_n + 0z_{n+1} + \cdots + 0z_{n+m} = f,$$

is added to the system, then the augmented matrix becomes

$$\begin{bmatrix} B & \vdots & I_m & \vdots & C^T \\ \text{---} & \vdots & \text{---} & \vdots & \text{---} \\ R^T & \vdots & 0 & \vdots & f \end{bmatrix}$$

Example 1.   For the maximum problem (dual of example in Section 12.1):

Subject to $\quad\begin{cases} 8z_1 + z_2 + 2z_3 + z_4 & = 1000, \\ 2z_1 + z_2 + 7z_3 \quad\quad + z_5 = 2000, \end{cases}$

maximize $\quad 16z_1 + 5z_2 + 20z_3 \quad\quad = f,$

the augmented matrix is

$$\begin{bmatrix} 8 & 1 & 2 & \vdots & 1 & 0 & \vdots & 1000 \\ 2 & 1 & 7 & \vdots & 0 & 1 & \vdots & 2000 \\ \text{---} & \text{---} & \text{---} & \vdots & \text{---} & \text{---} & \vdots & \text{---} \\ 16 & 5 & 20 & \vdots & 0 & 0 & \vdots & f \end{bmatrix}.$$

Now an obvious basic solution (see Section 8.4 for what is meant by a basic solution) of the system

$$\begin{cases} 8z_1 + z_2 + 2z_3 + z_4 & = 1000, \\ 2z_1 + z_2 + 7z_3 \quad\quad + z_5 = 2000, \end{cases}$$

is $(0, 0, 0, 1000, 2000)$ where the basic variables are z_4 and z_5. For this basic solution, $f = 0$, which is not the maximum f. The object is to find the basic solution (with all the variables having nonnegative values) that yields the largest f. Because there is a finite number of basic solutions this is possible, and the procedures taught in Chapter 8 furnish the tools to do the job. Of course having to find all the basic solutions in a large problem would be quite a task; therefore we are motivated to find some rules which will guide us as quickly as possible to the maximum f and assure us that it is indeed the maximum. Such rules may be discovered by considering the dual minimum problem.

The dual of Example 1 where $Z \geq 0$ is:

$$\text{Subject to} \quad \begin{cases} 8x_1 + 2x_2 \geq 16, \\ x_1 + x_2 \geq 5, \\ 2x_1 + 7x_2 \geq 20, \\ x_1 \qquad\quad \geq 0, \\ \qquad x_2 \geq 0, \end{cases}$$

$$\text{minimize} \quad 1000x_1 + 2000x_2 = g.$$

If we define the augmented matrix of the system above to be

$$M = \begin{bmatrix} 8 & 2 & \vdots & 16 \\ 1 & 1 & \vdots & 5 \\ 2 & 7 & \vdots & 20 \\ \hline 1 & 0 & \vdots & 0 \\ 0 & 1 & \vdots & 0 \\ \hline 1000 & 2000 & \vdots & g \end{bmatrix},$$

we notice that, with the exception of the lower right-hand entry, M is the

transpose of $\begin{bmatrix} B & \vdots & I_m & \vdots & C^T \\ \hline R^T & \vdots & 0 & \vdots & f \end{bmatrix}$. Thus the elementary row operations that we

will have to perform on $\begin{bmatrix} B & \vdots & I_m & \vdots & C^T \\ \hline R^T & \vdots & 0 & \vdots & f \end{bmatrix}$ to obtain basic solutions of the

associated system $\begin{cases} 8z_1 + z_2 + 2z_3 + z_4 \qquad\quad = 1000, \\ 2z_1 + z_2 + 7z_3 \qquad\quad + z_5 = 2000, \end{cases}$ can be interpreted as

column operations on matrix M above. These column operations have the effect of introducing new variables which transform one system into another as illustrated in Examples 7 and 8 of Section 10.2. The object will be to perform these transformations in such a way that we maintain nonnegative entries of the transformed C and make the entries of the last column of matrix M nonpositive, because then the origin will be an obvious solution of the corresponding minimum problem. The method we use for finding these transformations or changes of variables will be discussed in Section 12.9. It turns out that the dual, minimum problem of Example 1 can be transformed into a corresponding minimum problem by introducing three new variables $\bar{x}_1, \bar{\bar{x}}_1, \bar{x}_2$, in the order listed, by the substitutions

$$\bar{x}_1 = x_1 + \tfrac{1}{4}x_2 - 2,$$
$$\bar{\bar{x}}_1 = \bar{x}_1 + \tfrac{3}{4}x_2 - 3,$$
$$\bar{x}_2 = \tfrac{2}{5}\bar{\bar{x}}_1 + x_2 - 2.$$

Each introduction amounts to an elementary column operation on M,

or to an elementary row operation on $\begin{bmatrix} B & \vdots & I_m & \vdots & C^T \\ \cdots & \vdots & \cdots & \vdots & \cdots \\ R^T & \vdots & 0 & \vdots & f \end{bmatrix}$. Exactly how this is

accomplished will be explained in detail in Section 12.9. The result, however, is the following problem with the corresponding graph shown in Fig. 12.2.

$$\text{Minimize } 600\bar{x}_1 + 1000\bar{x}_2, \text{ subject to } \begin{cases} \tfrac{52}{5}\bar{\bar{x}}_1 - 6\bar{x}_2 \geq -12, \\ \bar{\bar{x}}_1 \geq 0, \\ 5\bar{x}_2 \geq 0, \\ \tfrac{7}{5}\bar{\bar{x}}_1 - \bar{x}_2 \geq -3, \\ -\tfrac{2}{5}\bar{\bar{x}}_1 + \bar{x}_2 \geq -2. \end{cases}$$

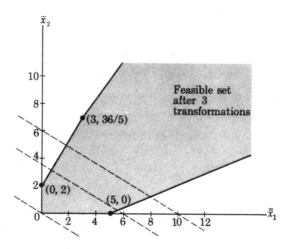

Figure 12.2

Note that all entries to the right of the inequalities are nonpositive and the entries of the transformed C are nonnegative. As the graph illustrates, this situation requires that minimum $600\bar{x}_1 + 1000\bar{x}_2$ occur at $(0, 0)$. The student should be sure to understand why this is true. Then by using $\bar{\bar{x}}_1 = 0$ and $\bar{x}_2 = 0$ and retracing our steps, we find $x_1 = 3$ and $x_2 = 2$; these values will yield minimum g and hence the corresponding basic solution of the system associated with the maximum problem will yield maximum f. This statement can be justified with some effort by making use of the duality theorem.

To summarize, we are looking for the basic solution to the system, for which $[B \; \vdots \; I_m \; \vdots \; C^T]$ is the augmented matrix, which will maximize f. We

will have this specific basic solution when the matrix $\begin{bmatrix} B & \vdots & I_m & \vdots & C^T \\ \cdots & \vdots & \cdots & \vdots & \cdots \\ R^T & \vdots & 0 & \vdots & f \end{bmatrix}$ is transformed such that the entries of the last row are nonpositive. At the same time, however, we must maintain nonnegative entries in the last column. Thus elementary row operations, with certain stipulations, will be employed on

$$\left[\begin{array}{c|c|c} B & I_m & C^T \\ \hline R^T & 0 & f \end{array}\right].$$

In the next section we shall list the mechanical steps which will allow us to find that basic solution, with nonnegative components, which will maximize f.

EXERCISES

1. Express the following systems of inequalities as systems of equations:

(a) $\begin{cases} z_1 + 2z_2 \leq 5, \\ z_1 + 3z_2 \leq 7. \end{cases}$

(b) $\begin{cases} z_1 + z_2 \leq 4, \\ z_1 + 4z_2 \leq 7, \\ 2z_2 \leq 3. \end{cases}$

2. (a) Represent graphically the system of inequalities in Exercise 1(a) and the additional restriction $Z \geq 0$.

(b) The resulting feasible set has 4 bounding lines; find the 6 points which are common to any 2 of these lines. Which of these points are extreme points?

(c) The system of equations, consisting of the answer to Exercise 1(a), will have 6 basic solutions. Find these basic solutions and show that they correspond to the 6 points found in part (b) of this problem. How can one distinguish which of the basic solutions represent extreme points?

3. (a) Let $B = \begin{bmatrix} 3 & 4 & 2 \\ 1 & 3 & 1 \end{bmatrix}$, $C = [6 \quad 8]$, and $R^T = [7 \quad 8 \quad 9]$. What does the matrix $[B \mid I_m \mid C^T]$ represent for the linear programming problem: maximize $f = R^T Z$ subject to $BZ \leq C^T$, $Z \geq 0$?

(b) What does the matrix $\left[\begin{array}{c|c|c} B & I_m & C^T \\ \hline R^T & 0 & f \end{array}\right]$ represent?

4. For a two-dimensional problem, (minimize $g = CX$, subject to $AX \geq R$, $X \geq 0$), explain why the origin is always the extreme point which yields minimum g when $C \geq 0$ and $R \leq 0$.

12.7 SIMPLEX METHOD

Authors frequently vary to a considerable extent in the method of presentation of the simplex algorithm. Often this variation is because of the mathematical background of the prospective readers. Our account of the method will be split into three parts: (A) setting up the proper matrix, (B) performing the operations on the matrix, and (C) interpreting the final matrix.

Part A: *Set up the maximum problem (by use of the dual if necessary).*

If the original problem is a maximum problem it should be written in the form:

Maximize $f = r_1 z_1 + r_2 z_2 + \cdots + r_n z_n$,

subject to
$$\begin{cases} b_{11} z_1 + \cdots + b_{1n} z_n \leq c_1, \\ b_{21} z_1 + \cdots + b_{2n} z_n \leq c_2, \\ \quad \vdots \\ b_{m1} z_1 + \cdots + b_{mn} z_n \leq c_m, \end{cases}$$
and
$$\begin{cases} z_1 \geq 0, \\ z_2 \geq 0, \\ \vdots \\ z_n \geq 0, \end{cases}$$

or maximize $f = R^T Z$, subject to $BZ \leq C^T$, and $Z \geq 0$, where

$$R^T = [r_1 \cdots r_n], \quad Z = \begin{bmatrix} z_1 \\ \vdots \\ z_n \end{bmatrix}, \quad B = \begin{bmatrix} b_{11} & \cdots & b_{1n} \\ & \vdots & \\ b_{m1} & \cdots & b_{mn} \end{bmatrix}, \quad C^T = \begin{bmatrix} c_1 \\ \vdots \\ c_m \end{bmatrix}.$$

If the original problem is a minimum problem it should be written in the form:

Minimize $g = c_1 x_1 + c_2 x_2 + \cdots + c_m x_m$,

subject to
$$\begin{cases} a_{11} x_1 + \cdots + a_{1m} x_m \geq r_1, \\ a_{21} x_1 + \cdots + a_{2m} x_m \geq r_2, \\ \quad \vdots \\ a_{n1} x_1 + \cdots + a_{nm} x_m \geq r_n, \end{cases}$$
and
$$\begin{cases} x_1 \geq 0, \\ x_2 \geq 0, \\ \vdots \\ x_m \geq 0. \end{cases}$$

And then the dual should be formed. The dual problem would be

maximize $f = r_1 z_1 + r_2 z_2 + \cdots + r_n z_n$,

subject to
$$\begin{cases} a_{11} z_1 + \cdots + a_{n1} z_n \leq c_1, \\ a_{12} z_1 + \cdots + a_{n2} z_n \leq c_2, \\ \quad \vdots \\ a_{1m} z_1 + \cdots + a_{nm} z_n \leq c_m, \end{cases}$$
and
$$\begin{cases} z_1 \geq 0, \\ z_2 \geq 0, \\ \vdots \\ z_n \geq 0, \end{cases}$$

or maximize $R^T Z$, subject to $\begin{cases} A^T Z \leq C^T, \\ Z \geq 0. \end{cases}$

Thus, regardless of whether the original problem is a maximum problem or a minimum problem we can arrive at the form:

$$\text{Maximize } f = R^T Z, \qquad \text{subject to } \begin{cases} BZ \leq C^T, \\ Z \geq 0, \end{cases}$$

where $B = A^T$ in the minimum problem. From this form, create a matrix

$$\left[\begin{array}{c|c|c} B & I_m & C^T \\ \hline R^T & 0 & f \end{array} \right].$$

Example 1. Consider the paper problem of the first section of this chapter.

$$\text{Minimize } 1000x_1 + 2000x_2, \text{ subject to } \begin{cases} 8x_1 + 2x_2 \geq 16, \\ x_1 + x_2 \geq 5, \\ 2x_1 + 7x_2 \geq 20, \end{cases} \text{ and } \begin{cases} x_1 \geq 0, \\ x_2 \geq 0. \end{cases}$$

Since this is a minimum problem we must consider the dual:

$$\text{Maximize } 16z_1 + 5z_2 + 20z_3, \text{ subject to } \begin{cases} 8z_1 + z_2 + 2z_3 \leq 1000, \\ 2z_1 + z_2 + 7z_3 \leq 2000, \end{cases} \text{ and } \begin{cases} z_1 \geq 0, \\ z_2 \geq 0, \\ z_3 \geq 0, \end{cases}$$

or maximize $R^T Z$, subject to $\begin{cases} BZ \leq C^T, \\ Z \geq 0, \end{cases}$ where

$$R^T = [16 \quad 5 \quad 20], \qquad Z = \begin{bmatrix} z_1 \\ z_2 \\ z_3 \end{bmatrix}, \qquad B = \begin{bmatrix} 8 & 1 & 2 \\ 2 & 1 & 7 \end{bmatrix}, \qquad C^T = \begin{bmatrix} 1000 \\ 2000 \end{bmatrix}.$$

Therefore,
$$\left[\begin{array}{c|c|c} B & I_2 & C^T \\ \hline R^T & 0 & f \end{array} \right] = \left[\begin{array}{ccc|cc|c} 8 & 1 & 2 & 1 & 0 & 1000 \\ 2 & 1 & 7 & 0 & 1 & 2000 \\ \hline 16 & 5 & 20 & 0 & 0 & f \end{array} \right].$$

Part B: *Perform the following steps on the matrix* $\left[\begin{array}{c|c|c} B & I_m & C^T \\ \hline R^T & 0 & f \end{array} \right].$

Step I. Choose any column (except the *last*) whose last entry is positive. The purpose here is to begin making all entries of the last row nonpositive. (The last entry of the last row is considered to be zero throughout the procedure.)

Step II. Find a *pivot* entry by dividing each nonzero entry (except the last) of the chosen column into the corresponding entry of the last column, and selecting as the pivot, the entry which yields the smallest of the resulting nonnegative ratios. The row which includes the pivot is called the pivot row. The purpose here is to keep the entries of the last column nonnegative.

Step III. By adding multiples of the entries of the pivot row to those of the other rows (third elementary row operation), make all other entries of the chosen column zero. This makes the variable associated with this column a basic variable. *We emphasize that the pivot row must be used to perform the transformations.*

Step IV. Repeat the first three steps until all entries in the last row are nonpositive. (Remember the last entry on the last row is always considered to be zero.)

Step V. By using only the first two elementary row operations, (multiply a row by a nonzero scalar and interchange two rows) create a submatrix I_m in part of the space formerly occupied by $[B \mid I_m]$. The columns deleted to form this submatrix I_m may be interior columns. This last step makes the nonzero components of Z appear in the last column in order.

Example 1 (continued). At each step after selecting a pivot we mark it with an asterisk. We had formed the matrix

$$\begin{bmatrix} 8^* & 1 & 2 & \vdots & 1 & 0 & \vdots & 1000 \\ 2 & 1 & 7 & \vdots & 0 & 1 & \vdots & 2000 \\ \hline 16 & 5 & 20 & \vdots & 0 & 0 & \vdots & f \end{bmatrix}.$$

Step I. Arbitrarily select column one. (Column two or column three could have been selected.)

Step II. Form the ratios $1000/8$ and $2000/2$. Obviously $1000/8$ is smaller, therefore 8 is the pivot and is designated with an asterisk.

Step III. Make the other entries of column 1 zero by applying the elementary row operations $(-\frac{1}{4}R_1 + R_2)$ and $(-2R_1 + R_3)$

$$\begin{bmatrix} 8 & 1^* & 2 & \vdots & 1 & 0 & \vdots & 1000 \\ 0 & \frac{3}{4} & \frac{13}{2} & \vdots & -\frac{1}{4} & 1 & \vdots & 1750 \\ \hline 0 & 3 & 16 & \vdots & -2 & 0 & \vdots & f-2000 \end{bmatrix}.$$

Step IV. Select the second column; 1 becomes the pivot because $1000/1$ is less than $1750/\frac{3}{4}$. Perform the elementary row operations $(-\frac{3}{4}R_1 + R_2)$ and $(-3R_1 + R_3)$ and we obtain an equivalent matrix,

$$\begin{bmatrix} 8 & 1 & 2 & \vdots & 1 & 0 & \vdots & 1000 \\ -6 & 0 & 5^* & \vdots & -1 & 1 & \vdots & 1000 \\ \hline -24 & 0 & 10 & \vdots & -5 & 0 & \vdots & f-5000 \end{bmatrix}.$$

We find 5 is the pivot since we must select the third column. The elementary row operations $(-\frac{2}{5}R_2 + R_1)$ and $(-2R_2 + R_3)$ give us

$$\begin{bmatrix} \frac{52}{5} & 1 & 0 & \vdots & \frac{7}{5} & -\frac{2}{5} & \vdots & 600 \\ -6 & 0 & 5 & \vdots & -1 & 1 & \vdots & 1000 \\ \hline -12 & 0 & 0 & \vdots & -3 & -2 & \vdots & f-7000 \end{bmatrix}.$$

Step V. Divide the second row by 5 and thus obtain I_2 in the space formerly occupied by the second and third columns of $[B \mid I_2]$.

$$Q = \begin{bmatrix} \frac{52}{5} & 1 & 0 & \vdots & \frac{7}{5} & -\frac{2}{5} & \vdots & 600 \\ -\frac{6}{5} & 0 & 1 & \vdots & -\frac{1}{5} & \frac{1}{5} & \vdots & 200 \\ \hdashline -12 & 0 & 0 & \vdots & -3 & -2 & \vdots & f - 7000 \end{bmatrix}.$$

Part C: *After completion of the preceding five steps, upon proper interpretation the resulting equivalent matrix will yield:*

(1) *the solution of the minimum problem,* $X = \begin{bmatrix} x_1 \\ \cdot \\ \cdot \\ \cdot \\ x_m \end{bmatrix}$,

(2) *the solution of the maximum problem,* $Z = \begin{bmatrix} z_1 \\ \cdot \\ \cdot \\ \cdot \\ z_n \end{bmatrix}$,

and (3) *the value of* $f = $ *maximum* $R^T Z = $ *minimum* CX.

To find X: In the matrix obtained in Step V, $-X^T$ occupies the position formerly occupied by the null vector in the last row of the original matrix,

$$\begin{bmatrix} B & \vdots & I_m & \vdots & C^T \\ \hdashline R^T & \vdots & 0 & \vdots & f \end{bmatrix}.$$

Thus, for Example 1, from matrix Q, $-X^T = [-3 \quad -2]$ and $X = \begin{bmatrix} 3 \\ 2 \end{bmatrix}$.

To find Z: Because of the various steps, there will occur m columns with one entry which is the number 1 and *all* of the other entries are 0. If the ith column is such a column, then z_i is equal to the last entry in the same row with the 1. If the ith column is not such a column, then $z_i = 0$. Thus, for Example 1, in Q, the second column and the third column have one entry which is a 1 and the other entries are 0; but the first column is not of this form. Therefore

$$z_1 = 0, \, z_2 = 600, \, z_3 = 200, \text{ and } Z = \begin{bmatrix} 0 \\ 600 \\ 200 \end{bmatrix}.$$

To find $f = Max \, R^T Z = Min \, CX$: Consider the entry in the lower right hand corner of the final matrix. Set it equal to zero and solve for f. Thus, in Example 1, from Q we have $f - 7000 = 0$ or $f = 7000$, which completes the solution.

As a summary, a diagram is given in Fig. 12.3 which illustrates how Part C was applied to the matrix Q on Page 201. Notice that the first three columns correspond to z_1, z_2, and z_3 respectively and that $z_2 = 600$ and $z_3 = 200$ since 600 and 200 are in the same rows as the unit entries in the z_2 and z_3 columns.

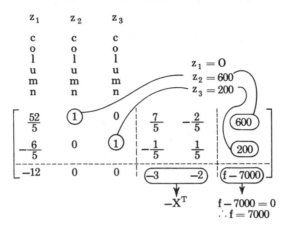

Figure 12.3

From the matrix in Fig. 12.3, we read $-X^T = [-3 \quad -2]$, therefore

$$X = \begin{bmatrix} 3 \\ 2 \end{bmatrix}. \quad \text{Also } Z = \begin{bmatrix} 0 \\ 600 \\ 200 \end{bmatrix}, \quad \text{and } f = 7000.$$

More reasons for performing some of the above steps are explained in sections 12.9 and 12.10.

Example 2.

Maximize $3z_1 + 2z_2$, subject to
$$\begin{cases} z_1 + 2z_2 \leq 6, \\ z_1 + z_2 \leq 4, \\ -z_1 + z_2 \geq -2, \\ z_1 \qquad\quad \geq 0, \\ \qquad z_2 \geq 0. \end{cases}$$

PART A: To get the problem in proper form we must multiply the third inequality by (-1), in order to reverse the sense of the inequality. Notice that our requirement that $C \geq 0$ is met. Now we have: maximize $R^T Z$, subject to $\begin{cases} BZ \leq C^T, \\ Z \geq 0, \end{cases}$

where $R^T = [3 \quad 2]$, $\quad Z = \begin{bmatrix} z_1 \\ z_2 \end{bmatrix}$, $\quad B = \begin{bmatrix} 1 & 2 \\ 1 & 1 \\ 1 & -1 \end{bmatrix}$, $\quad C^T = \begin{bmatrix} 6 \\ 4 \\ 2 \end{bmatrix}$.

Therefore,

$$\begin{bmatrix} B & \vdots & I_3 & \vdots & C^T \\ \text{---} & \vdots & \text{---} & \vdots & \text{---} \\ R^T & \vdots & 0 & \vdots & f \end{bmatrix} = \begin{bmatrix} 1 & 2 & \vdots & 1 & 0 & 0 & \vdots & 6 \\ 1 & 1 & \vdots & 0 & 1 & 0 & \vdots & 4 \\ 1 & -1 & \vdots & 0 & 0 & 1 & \vdots & 2 \\ \text{---} & & \vdots & \text{---} & & \vdots & \text{---} \\ 3 & 2 & \vdots & 0 & 0 & 0 & \vdots & f \end{bmatrix}.$$

PART B:

Step I. Arbitrarily select column one.

Step II. Form the ratios $6/1, 4/1, 2/1$. Obviously $2/1$ is the smallest, thus the 1 in the third row and first column is the pivot.

Step III. We perform the operations $(-R_3 + R_1)$, $(-R_3 + R_2)$, and $(-3R_3 + R_4)$, hence

$$\begin{bmatrix} 1 & 2 & \vdots & 1 & 0 & 0 & \vdots & 6 \\ 1 & 1 & \vdots & 0 & 1 & 0 & \vdots & 4 \\ 1^* & -1 & \vdots & 0 & 0 & 1 & \vdots & 2 \\ \text{---} & & \vdots & & & \vdots & \\ 3 & 2 & \vdots & 0 & 0 & 0 & \vdots & f \end{bmatrix} \sim \begin{bmatrix} 0 & 3 & \vdots & 1 & 0 & -1 & \vdots & 4 \\ 0 & 2^* & \vdots & 0 & 1 & -1 & \vdots & 2 \\ 1 & -1 & \vdots & 0 & 0 & 1 & \vdots & 2 \\ \text{---} & & \vdots & & & \vdots & \\ 0 & 5 & \vdots & 0 & 0 & -3 & \vdots & f-6 \end{bmatrix}.$$

Step IV. Select the second column and 2 becomes the pivot since $2/2$ is less than $4/3$ ($2/-1$ is not considered because it is negative). Perform the operations $(-\frac{3}{2}R_2 + R_1)$, $(\frac{1}{2}R_2 + R_3)$, and $(-\frac{5}{2}R_2 + R_4)$ and we obtain an equivalent matrix,

$$\begin{bmatrix} 0 & 0 & \vdots & 1 & -\frac{3}{2} & \frac{1}{2} & \vdots & 1 \\ 0 & 2 & \vdots & 0 & 1 & -1 & \vdots & 2 \\ 1 & 0 & \vdots & 0 & \frac{1}{2} & \frac{1}{2} & \vdots & 3 \\ \text{---} & & \vdots & & & \vdots & \\ 0 & 0 & \vdots & 0 & -\frac{5}{2} & -\frac{1}{2} & \vdots & f-11 \end{bmatrix}.$$

Step V. Divide the second row by 2. Interchange the first and third rows. I_3 is thus obtained in the first, second, and third columns. The resulting equivalent matrix has the following form, where the entries significant in the solution are printed in heavy type:

$$\begin{bmatrix} \mathbf{1} & 0 & \vdots & 0 & \frac{1}{2} & \frac{1}{2} & \vdots & \mathbf{3} \\ 0 & \mathbf{1} & \vdots & 0 & \frac{1}{2} & -\frac{1}{2} & \vdots & \mathbf{1} \\ 0 & 0 & \vdots & \mathbf{1} & -\frac{3}{2} & \frac{1}{2} & \vdots & \mathbf{1} \\ \text{---} & & \vdots & & & \vdots & \\ 0 & 0 & \vdots & \mathbf{0} & -\frac{5}{2} & -\frac{1}{2} & \vdots & f-11 \end{bmatrix}.$$

PART C: From the final matrix we read $-X^T = [0 \quad -\frac{5}{2} \quad -\frac{1}{2}]$,

therefore $X = \begin{bmatrix} 0 \\ \frac{5}{2} \\ \frac{1}{2} \end{bmatrix}$. Also $Z = \begin{bmatrix} 3 \\ 1 \end{bmatrix}$ and $f = 11$. See Fig 12.4.

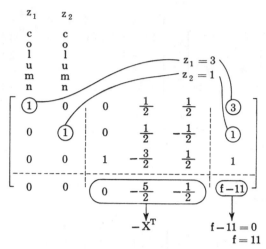

Figure 12.4

Example 3. The purpose of this example is to amplify Step V. Consider the problem:

$$\text{Maximize } f = 4z_1 - 2z_2 - 3z_3, \text{ subject to } \begin{cases} 2z_1 + z_2 & \leq 2, \\ -2z_1 + z_2 + z_3 \leq 1, \\ 4z_1 + 3z_2 & \leq 5, \end{cases} \text{ and } Z \geq 0.$$

PART A:

$$\begin{bmatrix} B & \vdots & I_3 & \vdots & C^T \\ \hline R^T & \vdots & 0 & \vdots & f \end{bmatrix} = \begin{bmatrix} 2^* & 1 & 0 & \vdots & 1 & 0 & 0 & \vdots & 2 \\ -2 & 1 & 1 & \vdots & 0 & 1 & 0 & \vdots & 1 \\ 4 & 3 & 0 & \vdots & 0 & 0 & 1 & \vdots & 5 \\ \hline 4 & -2 & -3 & \vdots & 0 & 0 & 0 & \vdots & f \end{bmatrix}.$$

PART B:

Step I. We must select column one.

Step II. Form the ratios 2/2, 5/4, and since 2/2 is the smaller, the first entry is the pivot.

Step III. The matrix above is equivalent to

$$\begin{bmatrix} 2 & 1 & 0 & \vdots & 1 & 0 & 0 & \vdots & 2 \\ 0 & 2 & 1 & \vdots & 1 & 1 & 0 & \vdots & 3 \\ 0 & 1 & 0 & \vdots & -2 & 0 & 1 & \vdots & 1 \\ \hline 0 & -4 & -3 & \vdots & -2 & 0 & 0 & \vdots & f-4 \end{bmatrix}.$$

Note that all entries of the last row are nonpositive, and hence Step IV is not needed.

Step V. Divide the first row by 2 and submatrix I_3 is formed by columns one, five, and six. (These columns are in bold print for emphasis.)

$$\begin{bmatrix} \mathbf{1} & \frac{1}{2} & 0 & \vdots & \frac{1}{2} & \mathbf{0} & \mathbf{0} & \vdots & 1 \\ \mathbf{0} & 2 & 1 & \vdots & 1 & \mathbf{1} & \mathbf{0} & \vdots & 3 \\ \mathbf{0} & 1 & 0 & \vdots & -2 & \mathbf{0} & \mathbf{1} & \vdots & 1 \\ \hline 0 & -4 & -3 & \vdots & -2 & 0 & 0 & \vdots & f-4 \end{bmatrix}.$$

Note that certain interior columns are not used in this formation of I_3, and especially note that column three is omitted. The reason that the fifth column is selected as part of I_3 rather than the third column is that the last entry of the third column is not zero, and hence z_3 would not serve as a basic variable.

PART C: From the final matrix we read $-X^T = [-2 \quad 0 \quad 0]$,

therefore $X = \begin{bmatrix} 2 \\ 0 \\ 0 \end{bmatrix}$. Also $Z = \begin{bmatrix} 1 \\ 0 \\ 0 \end{bmatrix}$, and $f = 4$. See Fig. 12.5.

When one has some experience, Step V can be done mentally.

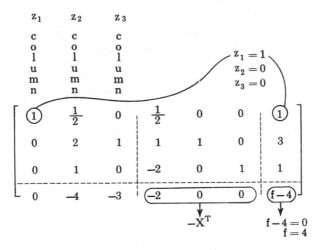

Figure 12.5

EXERCISES

Solve the following by the simplex method. Also determine the solution of the dual.

1. Maximize $f = z_1 + 2z_2$,

$$\text{subject to } \begin{cases} z_1 + z_2 \leq 4, \\ z_1 + 4z_2 \leq 7, \end{cases} \quad \text{and} \quad \begin{cases} z_1 \geq 0, \\ z_2 \geq 0. \end{cases}$$

2. Maximize $f = z_1 - 3z_2$,

$$\text{subject to } \begin{cases} z_1 - z_2 \geq -1, \\ z_1 + z_2 \leq 1, \end{cases} \quad \text{and} \quad \begin{cases} z_1 \geq 0, \\ z_2 \geq 0. \end{cases}$$

3. Maximize $f = 2z_1 + z_2 + 6z_3 + z_4$,

$$\text{subject to } \begin{cases} z_1 + 3z_2 + z_3 + z_4 \leq 4, \\ z_1 + z_3 + 2z_4 \leq 3, \\ z_2 + z_3 \leq 2, \end{cases} \quad \text{and} \quad \begin{cases} z_1 \geq 0, \\ z_2 \geq 0, \\ z_3 \geq 0, \\ z_4 \geq 0. \end{cases}$$

4. Maximize $f = 4z_1 - 6z_2 + 5z_3$,

$$\text{subject to} \quad \begin{cases} -z_1 + z_2 \leq 1, \\ z_2 + 2z_3 \leq 4, \\ 2z_1 + z_3 \leq 6, \\ 2z_2 + z_3 \leq 1, \end{cases} \quad \text{and} \quad \begin{cases} z_1 \geq 0, \\ z_2 \geq 0, \\ z_3 \geq 0. \end{cases}$$

5. Minimize $x_1 + x_2 + 4x_3$,

$$\text{subject to} \quad \begin{cases} -x_1 - x_2 + x_3 \geq 2, \\ -x_1 + x_2 + 2x_3 \geq 1, \end{cases} \quad \text{and} \quad \begin{cases} x_1 \geq 0, \\ x_2 \geq 0, \\ x_3 \geq 0. \end{cases}$$

6. Minimize $3x_1 + 5x_2 + 2x_3$,

$$\text{subject to} \quad \begin{cases} x_1 + x_2 + 3x_3 \geq 4, \\ x_1 + 2x_2 \geq 2, \\ x_1 + x_2 + x_3 \geq 6, \end{cases} \quad \text{and} \quad \begin{cases} x_1 \geq 0, \\ x_2 \geq 0, \\ x_3 \geq 0. \end{cases}$$

7. Show that the simplex method fails to provide a solution for the problem:
Maximize $2z_1 + z_2$,

$$\text{subject to} \quad \begin{cases} -z_1 + z_2 \leq 1, \\ z_1 - 2z_2 \leq 2, \end{cases} \quad \text{and} \quad \begin{cases} z_1 \geq 0, \\ z_2 \geq 0. \end{cases}$$

Then show graphically why there is no solution.

12.8 DEGENERACY

One complication that occasionally occurs will be introduced by means of an example. Remember that in Step II of the simplex method we formed certain ratios and selected the minimum in order to establish the pivot. You may have wondered: What if there is a tie for this minimum ratio? The following example illustrates how this situation may arise.

Example 1. Consider the minimum problem (Fig. 12.6):

Minimize $g = 2x_1 + x_2$,

subject to $\begin{cases} 2x_1 + x_2 \geq 2, \\ x_1 + 2x_2 \geq 2, \end{cases}$

and $X \geq 0$,

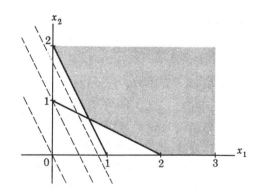

Figure 12.6

and its dual (Fig. 12.7):

Maximize $\quad f = 2z_1 + 2z_2,$

subject $\quad \begin{cases} 2z_1 + z_2 \le 2, \\ z_1 + 2z_2 \le 1, \end{cases}$
to

and $\qquad\qquad Z \ge 0.$

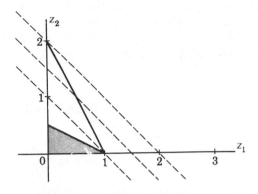

Figure 12.7

From Figure 12.6, notice that the minimum problem has more than one solution since one of the boundary lines of the feasible set is parallel to lines representing the function to be minimized. Beginning the simplex method we get

$$\begin{bmatrix} B & \vdots & I_2 & \vdots & C^T \\ \cdots & \vdots & \cdots & \vdots & \cdots \\ R^T & \vdots & 0 & \vdots & f \end{bmatrix} = \begin{bmatrix} 2 & 1 & \vdots & 1 & 0 & \vdots & 2 \\ 1 & 2^* & \vdots & 0 & 1 & \vdots & 1 \\ \cdots & \cdots & \vdots & \cdots & \cdots & \vdots & \cdots \\ 2 & 2 & \vdots & 0 & 0 & \vdots & f \end{bmatrix} \sim \begin{bmatrix} \frac{3}{2} & 0 & \vdots & 1 & -\frac{1}{2} & \vdots & \frac{3}{2} \\ 1 & 2 & \vdots & 0 & 1 & \vdots & 1 \\ \cdots & \cdots & \vdots & \cdots & \cdots & \vdots & \cdots \\ 1 & 0 & \vdots & 0 & -1 & \vdots & f-1 \end{bmatrix}.$$

At this stage, we must choose the first column and form the ratios $\frac{3}{2}/\frac{3}{2}$ and $1/1$; we notice that they are equal. We will finish the problem in two ways, first with the first entry as the pivot and next with the second entry as pivot.

$$\begin{bmatrix} \frac{3}{2}* & 0 & \vdots & 1 & -\frac{1}{2} & \vdots & \frac{3}{2} \\ 1 & 2 & \vdots & 0 & 1 & \vdots & 1 \\ \cdots & \cdots & \vdots & \cdots & \cdots & \vdots & \cdots \\ 1 & 0 & \vdots & 0 & -1 & \vdots & f-1 \end{bmatrix}$$

$$\underset{\substack{(-\frac{2}{3})R_1+R_2 \\ (-\frac{2}{3})R_1+R_3}}{\sim} \begin{bmatrix} \frac{3}{2} & 0 & \vdots & 1 & -\frac{1}{2} & \vdots & \frac{3}{2} \\ 0 & 2 & \vdots & -\frac{2}{3} & \frac{4}{3} & \vdots & 0 \\ \cdots & \cdots & \vdots & \cdots & \cdots & \vdots & \cdots \\ 0 & 0 & \vdots & -\frac{2}{3} & -\frac{2}{3} & \vdots & f-2 \end{bmatrix}$$

$$\underset{\substack{(\frac{2}{3})R_1 \\ (\frac{1}{2})R_2}}{\sim} \begin{bmatrix} 1 & 0 & \vdots & \frac{2}{3} & -\frac{1}{3} & \vdots & 1 \\ 0 & 1 & \vdots & -\frac{1}{3} & \frac{2}{3} & \vdots & 0 \\ \cdots & \cdots & \vdots & \cdots & \cdots & \vdots & \cdots \\ 0 & 0 & \vdots & -\frac{2}{3} & -\frac{2}{3} & \vdots & f-2 \end{bmatrix}$$

from which we read

$$X = \begin{bmatrix} \frac{2}{3} \\ \frac{2}{6} \end{bmatrix} \quad \text{and} \quad Z = \begin{bmatrix} 1 \\ 0 \end{bmatrix}.$$

$$\begin{bmatrix} \frac{3}{2} & 0 & \vdots & 1 & -\frac{1}{2} & \vdots & \frac{3}{2} \\ 1* & 2 & \vdots & 0 & 1 & \vdots & 1 \\ \cdots & \cdots & \vdots & \cdots & \cdots & \vdots & \cdots \\ 1 & 0 & \vdots & 0 & -1 & \vdots & f-1 \end{bmatrix}$$

$$\underset{\substack{(-\frac{3}{2})R_2+R_1 \\ -R_2+R_3}}{\sim} \begin{bmatrix} 0 & -3 & \vdots & 1 & -2 & \vdots & 0 \\ 1 & 2 & \vdots & 0 & 1 & \vdots & 1 \\ \cdots & \cdots & \vdots & \cdots & \cdots & \vdots & \cdots \\ 0 & -2 & \vdots & 0 & -2 & \vdots & f-2 \end{bmatrix}$$

$$\underset{R_1 \leftrightarrow R_2}{\sim} \begin{bmatrix} 1 & 2 & \vdots & 0 & 1 & \vdots & 1 \\ 0 & -3 & \vdots & 1 & -2 & \vdots & 0 \\ \cdots & \cdots & \vdots & \cdots & \cdots & \vdots & \cdots \\ 0 & -2 & \vdots & 0 & -2 & \vdots & f-2 \end{bmatrix}$$

from which we read

$$X = \begin{bmatrix} 0 \\ 2 \end{bmatrix} \quad \text{and} \quad Z = \begin{bmatrix} 1 \\ 0 \end{bmatrix}.$$

Notice that both of the answers are compatible with the geometric solutions shown above.

The situation described in the example above is known as *degeneracy*. In general, degeneracy occurs when the vector C^T can be expressed as a linear combination of fewer than r linearly independent columns of B where r is the rank of B. Although degeneracy can cause some theoretical complications, fortunately it usually does not cause trouble in finding solutions to practical problems.

EXERCISES

1. By the simplex method, solve:

   Maximize $f = 8z_1 + 9z_2$, subject to $\begin{cases} 4z_1 + z_2 \leq 2, \\ 6z_1 + 9z_2 \leq 3, \end{cases}$ and $\begin{cases} z_1 \geq 0, \\ z_2 \geq 0. \end{cases}$

When a tie is encountered in the ratios of Step II, finish the problem in two ways as was done in Example 1.

2. Solve the dual in Exercise 1 by the geometric method. What do you observe?

3. Show that in Exercise 1, C^T can be expressed as a linear combination of fewer than r (rank of B) columns of B.

4. Repeat Exercise 3 for the problem:

   Maximize $f = 4z_1 + 2z_2 + z_3$, subject to $\begin{cases} z_1 + z_2 + 2z_3 \leq 6, \\ z_1 + z_2 \qquad \leq 4, \\ 2z_1 + z_2 + z_3 \leq 9, \end{cases}$ and $\begin{cases} z_1 \geq 0, \\ z_2 \geq 0, \\ z_3 \geq 0. \end{cases}$

5. Solve the maximum problem in Exercise 4 by the simplex method.

12.9 DISCUSSION OF THE SIMPLEX METHOD

Now that the mechanical manipulations have been presented it will be enlightening to amplify the discussion begun in Section 12.6.

This discussion of the simplex method requires that $C \geq 0$ for the problems:

$$\text{Minimize } CX, \text{ subject to } AX \geq R, \text{ and } X \geq 0,$$

and

$$\text{Maximize } R^T Z, \text{ subject to } A^T Z \leq C^T, \text{ and } Z \geq 0.$$

As explained in Section 12.6, the matrix $\begin{bmatrix} B & I_m & C^T \\ \hline R^T & 0 & f \end{bmatrix}$, where $B = A^T$,

expressed two ideas simultaneously. First of all it was the augmented matrix for the system,

$$\begin{cases} b_{11}z_1 + \cdots + b_{1n}z_n + z_{n+1} = c_1, \\ \qquad \cdots \\ b_{m1}z_1 + \cdots + b_{mn}z_n + z_{n+m} = c_m, \\ r_1 z_1 + \cdots + r_n z_n = f. \end{cases}$$

This was the maximum problem. Secondly, it was the transpose of a matrix associated with the dual, minimum problem.

In performing the various steps on the matrix $\begin{bmatrix} B & \vdots & I_m & \vdots & C^T \\ \text{---} & \vdots & \text{---} & \vdots & \text{---} \\ R^T & \vdots & 0 & \vdots & f \end{bmatrix}$, we were

in essence doing two things at the same time. (For the sake of simplicity we will use Example 1 of Section 12.7. The ideas can be generalized easily.)

First: We were finding a complete solution of the system

$$8z_1 + z_2 + 2z_3 + z_4 \qquad = 1000,$$

$$2z_1 + z_2 + 7z_3 \qquad + z_5 = 2000,$$

and then a basic solution where the eventual parameters z_1, z_4, and z_5 of the complete solution were zero. This was accomplished by repeated applications of Step III and then Step V. The goal was to find that nonnegative basic solution which maximizes f.

Second: We were transforming the minimum problem to a form where it can be recognized immediately that the solution vector is $(0, 0)$. That is, the original problem was transformed into a new form by the introduction of new nonnegative variables. Then the minimum, in terms of the new variables, occurred when they were both zero. We interrupt our discussion to show how this was accomplished.

Example 1. Show that by a sequence of transformations we can transform the minimum problem of Example 1 of Section 12.7 into a problem where $(0, 0)$ is the obvious solution. *For restrictions $AX \geq R$, $X \geq 0$, the origin will be an obvious solution when the function to be minimized has nonnegative coefficients and the entries of R are all nonpositive.* The student should satisfy himself that this statement is true (Exercise 4, page 197). It is the motivation for the following work.

The minimum problem is:

Minimize $g = 1000x_1 + 2000x_2$,

subject to $\begin{cases} 8x_1 + 2x_2 \geq 16, \\ x_1 + x_2 \geq 5, \\ 2x_1 + 7x_2 \geq 20, \\ x_1 \qquad \geq 0, \\ x_2 \geq 0. \end{cases}$

The corresponding graph is Fig. 12.8.

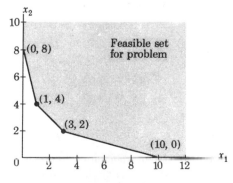

Figure 12.8

Introducing a new variable $\bar{x}_1$ where $\bar{x}_1 = x_1 + \frac{1}{4}x_2 - 2$ (this is in essence what is done by the first use of Steps I, II, III), we obtain a new problem: Call it transformation 1. The student should refer back to Section 10.2, and, in particular, to Examples 8 and 9 of that section for an explanation of this transformation.

Minimize $1000\bar{x}_1 + 1750x_2$,

subject to $\begin{cases} 8\bar{x}_1 & \geq & 0, \\ \bar{x}_1 + \frac{3}{4}x_2 & \geq & 3, \\ 2\bar{x}_1 + \frac{13}{2}x_2 & \geq & 16, \\ \bar{x}_1 - \frac{1}{4}x_2 & \geq & -2, \\ x_2 & \geq & 0. \end{cases}$

The corresponding graph is Fig. 12.9.

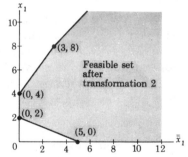

Figure 12.9

Introducing another variable $\bar{\bar{x}}_1$ where $\bar{\bar{x}}_1 = \bar{x}_1 + \frac{3}{4}x_2 - 3$, we obtain transformation 2 (Step IV).

Minimize $1000\bar{\bar{x}}_1 + 1000x_2$,

subject to $\begin{cases} 8\bar{\bar{x}}_1 - 6x_2 & \geq & -24, \\ \bar{\bar{x}}_1 & \geq & 0, \\ 2\bar{\bar{x}}_1 + 5x_2 & \geq & 10, \\ \bar{\bar{x}}_1 - x_2 & \geq & -5, \\ x_2 & \geq & 0. \end{cases}$

The corresponding graph is Fig. 12.10.

Figure 12.10

Finally transformation 3 is obtained by introducing the variable $\bar{x}_2$ where $\bar{x}_2 = \frac{2}{5}\bar{\bar{x}}_1 + x_2 - 2$.

Minimize $600\bar{\bar{x}}_1 + 1000\bar{x}_2$,

subject to $\begin{cases} \frac{52}{5}\bar{\bar{x}}_1 - 6\bar{x}_2 & \geq & -12, \\ \bar{\bar{x}}_1 & \geq & 0, \\ 5\bar{x}_2 & \geq & 0, \\ \frac{7}{5}\bar{\bar{x}}_1 - \bar{x}_2 & \geq & -3, \\ -\frac{2}{5}\bar{\bar{x}}_1 + \bar{x}_2 & \geq & -2. \end{cases}$

The graph is shown in Fig. 12.11.

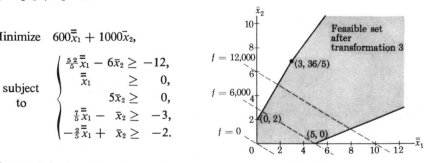

Figure 12.11

It is obvious that minimum $600\bar{\bar{x}}_1 + 1000\bar{x}_2$ occurs at $(0, 0)$. By using $\bar{\bar{x}}_1 = 0$ and $\bar{x}_2 = 0$ and retracing steps back, we find $x_1 = 3$ and $x_2 = 2$.

The iterative procedure has the convenient property that the solution can be read from the final matrix and in practice this eliminates the necessity of retracing our steps in the minimum problem. *Note the correspondence between the coefficients of the previous four systems and the first four matrices of Example 1 of Section 12.7.*

With the solution of the minimum problem and the corresponding minimum value of g we make use of the duality theorem to assert that the solution of the maximum problem is found by letting the resulting parameters of the newly found complete solution be zero (a basic solution). The preceding sentence is quite important and will be explained by an example.

Example 2. The final matrix of Example 1 of Section 12.7 was

$$\left[\begin{array}{ccc:cc:c} \frac{52}{5} & 1 & 0 & \frac{7}{5} & -\frac{2}{5} & 600 \\ -\frac{8}{5} & 0 & 1 & -\frac{1}{5} & \frac{1}{5} & 200 \\ \hdashline -12 & 0 & 0 & -3 & -2 & f - 7000 \end{array}\right].$$

This was the augmented matrix for the system,

$$\begin{cases} \frac{52}{5}z_1 + z_2 & + \frac{7}{5}z_4 - \frac{2}{5}z_5 = 600, \\ -\frac{8}{5}z_1 & + z_3 - \frac{1}{5}z_4 + \frac{1}{5}z_5 = 200, \\ -12z_1 & - 3z_4 - 2z_5 = f - 7000. \end{cases}$$

Now, since we know that $g = 7000$ from the solution of the minimum problem, then by the duality theorem, $f = 7000$ for the maximum problem. It should be evident from the last equation of the system that this can only occur when $z_1 = z_4 = z_5 = 0$ since $Z \geq 0$. Therefore the parameters of the complete solution,

$$\begin{cases} z_2 = 600 - \frac{52}{5}z_1 - \frac{7}{5}z_4 + \frac{2}{5}z_5, \\ z_3 = 200 + \frac{8}{5}z_1 + \frac{1}{5}z_4 - \frac{1}{5}z_5, \end{cases}$$

are zero and the resulting basic solution is $(0, 600, 200, 0, 0)$ from which we get the solution of the maximum problem.

We are now in a position to re-emphasize the purpose of the various steps. Step I was performed to begin the process of making the entries in the last row nonpositive. Step II assures that all new entries in the space originally occupied by C^T will be positive. Step III carries out a single transformation in the minimum problem and also starts the process of finding the desired basic solution in the maximum problem. Step IV repeats the transformations until all the entries of the last row are nonpositive. Step V performs the final step in making the values of basic variables of the maximum problem appear in order in the last column.

In the second example of Section 12.7, we found a complete solution of the system

$$\begin{cases} z_1 + 2z_2 + z_3 & = 6, \\ z_1 + z_2 + z_4 & = 4, \\ z_1 - z_2 + z_5 = 2, \end{cases}$$

and then a basic solution where the parameters z_4 and z_5 are zero. Simultaneously we were performing a sequence of transformations on the dual (minimum problem) in such a way that $(0,0,0)$ was the extreme point at which the *transformed* function assumed its minimum.

Not all linear programming problems will satisfy the restrictions that $C \geq 0$.

Example 3.

Maximize $z_1 - 2z_2$, subject to $\begin{cases} -z_1 - z_2 \leq -1, \\ z_2 \leq 1, \\ z_1 - z_2 \leq 1, \end{cases}$ and $\begin{cases} z_1 \geq 0, \\ z_2 \geq 0. \end{cases}$

Notice that $C = [-1 \quad 1 \quad 1]$ where the entries are not all nonnegative. The various steps in Section 12.7 will provide the solution of this problem; however, we have not shown that they will in general.

Example 4.

Maximize $2z_1 - z_2$, subject to $\begin{cases} -z_1 + z_2 \leq 4, \\ 3z_1 - z_2 \leq -3, \end{cases}$ and $\begin{cases} z_1 \geq 0, \\ z_2 \geq 0. \end{cases}$

Again notice that the entries of C are not all nonnegative. The various steps of Section 12.7 will *not* provide a solution of this problem.

For a discussion of problems such as those above, more detailed books on linear programming should be consulted.

12.10 FURTHER DISCUSSION OF THE SIMPLEX METHOD

When one has studied the concept of "a basis of a vector space" as presented in Section 9.3, an alternate discussion can be given for the simplex method.

To begin with we must understand that the dual linear programming problems

Minimize CX,

subject to $\begin{cases} AX \geq R, \\ X \geq 0, \end{cases}$

Maximize $R^T Z$,

subject to $\begin{cases} A^T Z \leq C^T, \\ Z \geq 0, \end{cases}$

can be rewritten by changing some of the inequalities to equalities.

Minimize CX,	Maximize $R^T Z$,
subject to $\begin{cases} AX - U = R, \\ X \geq 0, \\ U \geq 0. \end{cases}$	subject to $\begin{cases} A^T Z + W = C^T, \\ Z \geq 0, \\ W \geq 0. \end{cases}$

Note that this required the introduction of two sets of nonnegative variables U and W.

Remember that the solution of a linear programming problem occurs at an extreme point. The essence of the simplex method is that we start with one extreme point of the maximum problem, namely $Z = \begin{bmatrix} 0 \\ 0 \\ \vdots \\ 0 \end{bmatrix}$, and progress by a systematic process from one extreme point to an adjacent one and continue the process until we reach the one that yields a maximum.

Each successive extreme point used will yield a larger value (or at least as large a value) of $R^T Z$ until finally the maximum is reached.

When we start by taking $Z = 0$, the system of linear equations

$$A^T Z + W = C^T$$

becomes

$$A^T 0 + W - C^T \quad \text{or} \quad W = C^T;$$

thus we have a basic solution of the system. The components of W are then basic variables of this system. And simultaneously in the minimum problem when $X = 0$, the system of linear equations

$$AX - U = R$$

becomes

$$A0 - U = R \quad \text{or} \quad U = -R,$$

which produces a basic solution of that system. The components of U are then basic variables of this system. But unless R initially has all nonpositive entries, this last statement does *not* satisfy the restriction that $U \geq 0$, and therefore we do *not* have a solution of the maximum or minimum problem. Hence we perform certain linear transformations in such a way that we maintain nonnegative variables of the maximum problem and after passing through a finite number of extreme points of the maximum problem we make the variables of the corresponding minimum (dual) problem nonnegative. This is accomplished when the entries of the last row of the transformed matrix are nonpositive (because after each transformation the last row represents $[-U^T \mid -X^T \mid g - CX]$ and hence both $U \geq 0$ and $X \geq 0$ only when the last row is nonpositive).

The procedure used to accomplish these transformations will now be reexamined making use of the concept of "a basis of a vector space" as presented in Section 9.3. Again let us recall our paper problem of Section 12.7. The first restriction of the maximum problem was

$$A^T Z \leq C^T, \quad \text{or} \quad BZ \leq C^T, \quad \text{where} \quad A^T = B.$$

This can be rewritten as

$$BZ + W = C^T,$$

or specifically,

$$z_1 \begin{bmatrix} 8 \\ 2 \end{bmatrix} + z_2 \begin{bmatrix} 1 \\ 1 \end{bmatrix} + z_3 \begin{bmatrix} 2 \\ 7 \end{bmatrix} + w_1 \begin{bmatrix} 1 \\ 0 \end{bmatrix} + w_2 \begin{bmatrix} 0 \\ 1 \end{bmatrix} = \begin{bmatrix} 1000 \\ 2000 \end{bmatrix}.$$

(For the remainder of this section the student should refer back frequently to Example 1 of Section 12.7.) When initially we let $z_1 = 0$, $z_2 = 0$, $z_3 = 0$, we were finding a basic solution where w_1 and w_2 were the basic variables. From the augmented matrix of the above system,

$$\begin{bmatrix} 8 & 1 & 2 & 1 & 0 & \vdots & 1000 \\ 2 & 1 & 7 & 0 & 1 & \vdots & 2000 \end{bmatrix},$$

there results a vector space formed by the set of all linear combinations of the column vectors of this matrix. This vector space is called the column space of the matrix and has as a basis the vectors $\begin{bmatrix} 1 \\ 0 \end{bmatrix}$ and $\begin{bmatrix} 0 \\ 1 \end{bmatrix}$. Thus the last column of this matrix can be written as a linear combination of these basis vectors by letting $z_1 = 0$, $z_2 = 0$, $z_3 = 0$, $w_1 = 1000$, $w_2 = 2000$.

$$0 \begin{bmatrix} 8 \\ 2 \end{bmatrix} + 0 \begin{bmatrix} 1 \\ 1 \end{bmatrix} + 0 \begin{bmatrix} 2 \\ 7 \end{bmatrix} + 1000 \begin{bmatrix} 1 \\ 0 \end{bmatrix} + 2000 \begin{bmatrix} 0 \\ 1 \end{bmatrix} = \begin{bmatrix} 1000 \\ 2000 \end{bmatrix}.$$

Each time we performed Step III of the simplex method we were simply removing one of the basis vectors from the basis and introducing another in its place. For example after Step III had been performed one time in this problem (see Example 1, Section 12.7), we obtained

$$\begin{bmatrix} 8 & 1 & 2 & 1 & 0 & \vdots & 1000 \\ 0 & \frac{3}{4} & \frac{13}{2} & -\frac{1}{4} & 1 & \vdots & 1750 \end{bmatrix},$$

where the vector in the fourth column has been removed from the basis, and the vector $\begin{bmatrix} 8 \\ 0 \end{bmatrix}$ in the first column has been introduced. Thus the vector in the last column can be expressed as a linear combination of the basis vectors by letting $z_1 = 125$, $z_2 = 0$, $z_3 = 0$, $w_1 = 0$, $w_2 = 1750$.

$$125 \begin{bmatrix} 8 \\ 0 \end{bmatrix} + 0 \begin{bmatrix} 1 \\ \frac{3}{4} \end{bmatrix} + 0 \begin{bmatrix} 2 \\ \frac{13}{2} \end{bmatrix} + 0 \begin{bmatrix} 1 \\ -\frac{1}{4} \end{bmatrix} + 1750 \begin{bmatrix} 0 \\ 1 \end{bmatrix} = \begin{bmatrix} 1000 \\ 1750 \end{bmatrix}.$$

Moreover $z_1 = 125$, $z_2 = 0$, $z_3 = 0$, is an extreme point of the maximum problem. Step II saw to that. Now although the function to be maximized is larger than it was at the first extreme point, it is not as large as it can be made because there are still some positive entries in the last row of the transformed matrix. [From Example 1 in Section 12.7 these entries can be observed to be $(0, 3, 16, -2, 0)$ and thus $u_1 = 0$, $u_2 = -3$, $u_3 = -16$, $x_1 = 2$, $x_2 = 0$ at this stage.] Therefore we perform Step III again and introduce a new vector into the basis of our column space. We obtain

$$0 \begin{bmatrix} 8 \\ -6 \end{bmatrix} + 1000 \begin{bmatrix} 1 \\ 0 \end{bmatrix} + 0 \begin{bmatrix} 2 \\ 5 \end{bmatrix} + 0 \begin{bmatrix} 1 \\ -1 \end{bmatrix} + 1000 \begin{bmatrix} 0 \\ 1 \end{bmatrix} = \begin{bmatrix} 1000 \\ 1000 \end{bmatrix},$$

where the new basis consists of the second and fifth vectors of the column space. Here $z_1 = 0$, $z_2 = 1000$, $z_3 = 0$ is an extreme point which yields a larger value of $R^T Z$ but it is still not maximum. Finally applying Step III again we do arrive at the maximum by introducing the vector in the third column into the basis replacing the vector in the fifth column. The last column can then be expressed as a linear combination of the vectors of the basis.

$$0 \begin{bmatrix} \frac{52}{5} \\ -6 \end{bmatrix} + 600 \begin{bmatrix} 1 \\ 0 \end{bmatrix} + 200 \begin{bmatrix} 0 \\ 5 \end{bmatrix} + 0 \begin{bmatrix} \frac{7}{5} \\ -1 \end{bmatrix} + 0 \begin{bmatrix} -\frac{2}{5} \\ 1 \end{bmatrix} = \begin{bmatrix} 600 \\ 1000 \end{bmatrix}.$$

Therefore, by the duality theorem, $z_1 = 0$, $z_2 = 600$, $z_3 = 200$ is the solution of the maximum problem because all the entries of the last row of the matrix are now nonpositive (they are $(-12, 0, 0, -3, -2)$ and hence $u_1 = 12$, $u_2 = 0$, $u_3 = 0$, $x_1 = 3$, $x_2 = 2$ at this stage), and

$$CX_0 = \begin{bmatrix} 1000 & 2000 \end{bmatrix} \begin{bmatrix} 3 \\ 2 \end{bmatrix} = R^T Z_0 = \begin{bmatrix} 16 & 5 & 20 \end{bmatrix} \begin{bmatrix} 0 \\ 600 \\ 200 \end{bmatrix}.$$

The student should know that some of the finer points and some of the difficulties have not been discussed in this presentation of linear programming and the simplex method. We have restricted ourselves here to the more elementary and intuitive aspects. If, however, your interest has been aroused, there are many books which will give a more detailed and rigorous presentation.

The following books are listed for reference. The level and detail of these books vary considerably.

CHARNES, A., and COOPER, W. W., and HENDERSON, A., *An Introduction to Linear Programming*, John Wiley & Sons, New York, 1953.

DANTZIG, G. B., *Linear Programming and Extensions*, Princeton University Press, Princeton, New Jersey, 1963.

GASS, SAUL, *Linear Programming, Methods and Applications*, 2nd ed., McGraw-Hill Book Co., New York, 1964.

GLICKSMAN, A. M., *An Introduction to Linear Programming and the Theory of Games*, John Wiley & Sons, New York, 1963.

HADLEY, G., *Linear Programming*, Addison-Wesley Publishing Co., Reading, Mass., 1962.

KEMENY, J., SCHLEIFER, A., SNELL, J., and THOMPSON, G., *Finite Mathematics with Business Applications*, Prentice-Hall, Inc., Englewood Cliffs, N. J., 1962.

SPIVEY, W. A., *Linear Programming: An Introduction*, The Macmillan Co., New York, 1963.

EXERCISES

1. Use the numerical example of this section to:

(*a*) Illustrate that $AX - U = R$ after each transformation. Remember that the components of X and U change with every transformation and may be read from

the last row of the matrix which was originally $\begin{bmatrix} A^T & \vdots & I_2 & \vdots & C^T \\ --- & \vdots & --- & \vdots & --- \\ R^T & \vdots & 0 & \vdots & f \end{bmatrix}$.

(*b*) Illustrate that $A^T Z + W = C^T$ after each transformation.
(*c*) Illustrate that $CX = R^T Z$ after each transformation.

2. What determines which column vector is to be introduced into the basis in the three transformations of the example of this section?

NEW VOCABULARY

linear programming	12.1	shadow price	12.5
minimum of a linear		simplex method	12.6
function	12.1	slack variables	12.6
maximum of a linear		pivot	12.7
function	12.1	degeneracy	12.8
dual problem	12.5		

Answers to Odd-Numbered Exercises

1. (a) $2, -6, \sqrt{9}$; (b) $2, \frac{3}{4}, \pi, \sqrt{3}, \frac{9}{4},$
   $2 + \sqrt{3}, -6, \sqrt{9}$;

   (c) $2, \frac{3}{4}, \frac{9}{4}, -6, \sqrt{9}$; (d) $\pi, \sqrt{3}, 2 + \sqrt{3}$;

1. No.   The number of rows and columns are independent of each other.
3. (a) $a_{32} = 3$; (b) $a_{21} = 6$.
5. (a) $a_{13} = 6$; (b) $a_{23} = -7$; (c) a_{32} is not defined.
7. (a) 1 by 4; (b) 3 by 1; (c) 2 by 4;
   (d) 1 by 1; (e) 1 by 1.

1. (a) $x = 7$; (b) $y = \frac{5}{2}$;
   (c) Impossible; (d) $x = -1; y = 0$;
   (e) $x = -\frac{2}{3}; y = -\frac{1}{3}$; (f) t = any value;
   (g) $x > 8$; (h) Impossible;
   (i) Not of same order, hence impossible;
   (j) Impossible; (k) $w \geq 0$;
   (l) $x \geq 0$.

1. $\begin{bmatrix} 2 & 0 \\ -1 & -3 \end{bmatrix}$.

3. (a) $\begin{bmatrix} 4-i & 6-i \\ 4-i & -2+3i \end{bmatrix}$;   (b) Not of same order, hence impossible;

(c) $\begin{bmatrix} 5 & 4+\sqrt{2} & -5 \\ 2+\pi & 7+2x & x+1 \\ 3+i & -1 & -\frac{1}{3} \end{bmatrix}$;   (d) $\begin{bmatrix} [1 & -1] & [-0.25 & 11] \\ \begin{bmatrix} 71 \\ 5 \end{bmatrix} & \begin{bmatrix} -6 \\ -2 \end{bmatrix} \end{bmatrix}$;

(e) $\begin{bmatrix} 6 & 7 \\ 0 & 5 \end{bmatrix}$;   (f) $\begin{bmatrix} 6 & 4 \\ 3 & 2 \end{bmatrix}$.

1.5   Page 9

1. (a) $\begin{bmatrix} 6 & -3 \\ -9 & -12 \end{bmatrix}$;   (b) $\begin{bmatrix} 4 & 0 \\ 2 & -6 \end{bmatrix}$;   (c) $\begin{bmatrix} -2 & 1 \\ 3 & 4 \end{bmatrix}$;

(d) $\begin{bmatrix} -4 & -1 \\ -6 & 5 \end{bmatrix}$;   (e) $\begin{bmatrix} -5 & 2 \\ \frac{11}{2} & \frac{19}{2} \end{bmatrix}$;

(f) $\begin{bmatrix} 4 & -1 \\ -2 & -7 \end{bmatrix}$;   (g) $\begin{bmatrix} 3 & -\frac{1}{2} \\ -\frac{1}{2} & -5 \end{bmatrix}$.

3. $\begin{bmatrix} 1 & 2 & 4 \\ -13 & 3 & -2 \end{bmatrix}$.

5. No.

1.6   Page 14

1. $\begin{bmatrix} 2 & 1 \\ 8 & -1 \end{bmatrix}$.   3. $[8 \quad 2]$.

5. (a) $t = 4$;   (b) 3 by 5;   (c) BA does not exist.

7. (a) $\begin{bmatrix} 8 & -2 \\ 12 & -1 \end{bmatrix}$;   (b) $\begin{bmatrix} 5 & -1 \\ 6 & 2 \end{bmatrix}$;

(c) $\begin{bmatrix} 16 & -6 \\ 0 & 4 \end{bmatrix}$;   (d) $\begin{bmatrix} 64 & -28 \\ 0 & 8 \end{bmatrix}$;

(e) $\begin{bmatrix} 4 & -1 \\ 0 & 2 \end{bmatrix}$;   (f) $\begin{bmatrix} 0 & 0 \\ 0 & 0 \end{bmatrix}$;

(g) $\begin{bmatrix} 1 & 0 \\ 0 & 1 \end{bmatrix}$.

9. (a) Not possible — not conformable;   (b) $\begin{bmatrix} 13 & 3 \\ -1 & -4 \\ 5 & -8 \end{bmatrix}$;

(c) $[39]$;   (d) Not possible — not conformable;

(e) $\begin{bmatrix} 18 & 90 \\ 8 & 43 \end{bmatrix}$;   (f) $\begin{bmatrix} 6 & -2 \\ 0 & 0 \end{bmatrix}$;

(g) $\begin{bmatrix} (2x+y) \\ (4x+3y) \end{bmatrix}$.

1.7 Page 17

1. $1 + 2 + 3 + 4 + 5$.

3. $1^3 + 2^3 + 3^3$;

5. $a_{21}a_{13} + a_{22}a_{23} + a_{23}a_{33}$.

7. $\sum_{k=1}^{5} a_{2k}$.

9. $\left[\sum_{k=1}^{3} a_{ik}b_{kj} \right]_{(1,1)}$.

11. $\left[\sum_{k=1}^{2} a_{ik}b_{kj} \right]_{(2,3)}$.

13. $a_{11} + a_{21} + a_{12} + a_{22}$.

1.8 Page 19

1. $\begin{bmatrix} 3x_1 + 2x_2 + x_3 \\ 4x_2 + x_3 \\ 2x_1 + x_2 + 6x_3 \end{bmatrix}$.

3. $AX = B$ where $A = \begin{bmatrix} 1 & 1 & 1 & 1 \\ 1 & -1 & -2 & -1 \end{bmatrix}$, $B = \begin{bmatrix} 4 \\ 6 \end{bmatrix}$, $X = \begin{bmatrix} x_1 \\ x_2 \\ x_3 \\ x_4 \end{bmatrix}$

5. x_1 and x_2 represent the number of days the respective factories operate. The system $\begin{cases} 2x_1 + x_2 \geq 9, \\ 4x_1 + 3x_2 \geq 8, \end{cases}$ or $A \begin{bmatrix} x_1 \\ x_2 \end{bmatrix} \geq \begin{bmatrix} 9 \\ 8 \end{bmatrix}$ specifies that the number of units of the two products produced (at both factories) will be greater than or equal to 9 and 8 respectively.

2.1 Page 22

1. (a) $(4, -4, 3, 4 + x)$;
   (b) $(6, -9, 0, 12)$;
   (c) Only when $x \geq 4$;
   (d) $(-2, -3, -9, 8 - 3x)$;
   (e) $(10, -9, 9, 8 + 3x)$;
   (f) $(2, -3, 0, 4)$.

2.2 Page 28

1.

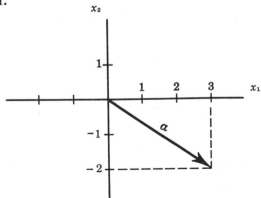

3. $|\alpha| = \sqrt{29}$
   $|\beta| = \sqrt{5}$.
   $|\gamma| = \sqrt{17}$

5.

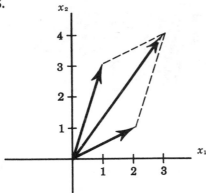

7.

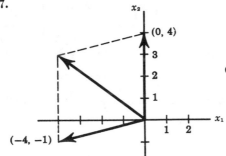

OR

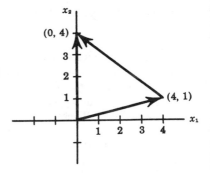

9. $\left(\dfrac{4}{5\sqrt{2}}, \ \dfrac{3}{5\sqrt{2}}, \ \dfrac{1}{\sqrt{2}}\right).$

11.

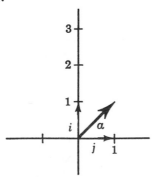

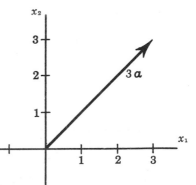

13. 30° East of North; speed $= 25(1 + \sqrt{3})$.

2.3   Page 32

1. (*a*) 10;   (*b*) 10;   (*c*) 0;   (*d*) 0;   (*e*) Not possible;   (*f*) -2.

3. $-1/5\sqrt{2}$; obtuse angle.   **5.** $|\alpha|^2$ or $a_1^2 + a_2^2 + \cdots + a_n^2$.

7. $x = -1$.   9. $-1/\sqrt{5}$; obtuse angle between
11. 14 units.   vectors.

2.4   Page 34

1. $43 profit for the refining industry;
   $20 profit for the utility industry.

3.1   Page 41

1. (a) No;   (b) No.
3. $(x \oplus y) \cdot (x \oplus z) = x \oplus (y \cdot z)$.
5. (a) No.   Neither the reflexive nor the symmetric properties hold.
   (b) Yes.   All properties hold.   (c) Yes.   All properties hold.
7. (a) No;   (b) No: (c) Yes;
   (d) Yes;   (e) $\geq$ and "is a multiple of" and many others.
9. (a) No;   (b) No;   (c) (a) would be yes and (b) would be no.

3.2   Page 43

1.
	(+)	(·)
commutative	yes	yes
associative	yes	yes
cancellation	yes	yes

3. commutative: no;
   associative: no;
   cancellation: yes.

distributive: (·) with respect to (+).

3.3   Page 47

7. (a) $(A + B) + C = A + (B + C) = \begin{bmatrix} 8 & 12 \\ 2 & -5 \end{bmatrix}$;

   (b) $A(BC) = (AB)C = \begin{bmatrix} -31 & -37 \\ 11 & 29 \end{bmatrix}$;

   (c) $A(B + C) = AB + AC = \begin{bmatrix} 6 & 48 \\ 2 & -6 \end{bmatrix}$;

   (d) $c(AB) = (cA)B = \begin{bmatrix} -3 & 87 \\ 9 & -15 \end{bmatrix}$;

   (e) $AB = \begin{bmatrix} -1 & 29 \\ 3 & -5 \end{bmatrix}$, $BA = \begin{bmatrix} 8 & -5 \\ 6 & -14 \end{bmatrix}$;

   (f) $(A + B)^2 = \begin{bmatrix} 48 & 8 \\ 6 & 28 \end{bmatrix} \neq A^2 + 2AB + B^2 = \begin{bmatrix} 39 & 42 \\ 3 & 37 \end{bmatrix}$;

   (g) $(AC)^2 = \begin{bmatrix} 30 & 114 \\ -6 & -18 \end{bmatrix} \neq A^2C^2 = \begin{bmatrix} -7 & 95 \\ -1 & -7 \end{bmatrix}$.

11. (a) Theorem 1;   (b) Theorem 2.
13. $(A - B)(A + B) = (A - B)A + (A - B)B$
$$= A^2 - BA + AB - B^2 \neq A^2 - B^2$$
      since $AB \neq BA$ in general.
17. No.

3.4 Page 50

1. (a) False; (b) False; (c) True; (d) True; (e) True; (f) True;
   (g) False. Neither side is defined; (h) True.
5. (d) No.   9. The resultant of $\alpha + \beta$ added to γ
                                           is the same as the resultant of $\beta + \gamma$
                                           added to α.

3.5 Page 53

1. (a) $a + 0 = 0 + a = a$ where a is any complex number;
   (b) $-2, -\frac{2}{3}, 0, -2 + 3i$ respectively;
   (c) $a \cdot 1 = 1 \cdot a = a$ where a is any complex number;
   (d) $\frac{1}{3}, -2$, no inverse, $\left| 1/\sqrt{2}, \frac{1}{5} - \frac{2}{5}i \right.$, respectively.
3. (a) 0; (b) None; (c) $-a$; (d) None.
5. (a) $\begin{bmatrix} 0 & 0 & 0 \\ 0 & 0 & 0 \end{bmatrix}$;   (b) We cannot multiply two 2 by 3
                                                matrices;
   (c) $-A$;   (d) There is no identity element.
7. The zero vector $(0, 0, 0, 0)$ is the identity for $+$. The vector $-\alpha$ is the inverse
   of α for $+$.
   There is no identity for the scalar product because any two vectors so multiplied
   will not yield a vector. There is no inverse for the scalar product because there
   is no identity.
9. I_3.   11. (a) 2; (b) 1.

3.6 Page 55

1. (a) Not a field because of postulate 4(b); (b) A field;
   (c) Not a field because the set is not closed under ($\cdot$); also postulates 3(a),
   3(b), 4(a), and 4(b) fail;
   (d) Not a field because the set is not closed under the dot product; also, postulates 2(b), 3(b), and 4(b) fail;
   (e) A field;
   (f) Not a field because postulates 1(b), 3(a), and 4(a) fail and we do not have
   closure under addition.

3.7 Page 57

1. (a) Not a ring because the set is not closed under $+$; also, postulates 3(a),
   and 4(a) fail;
   (b) A ring;
   (c) Not a ring because the set is not closed under ($\cdot$); also, postulates 3(a)
   and 4(a) fail;
   (d) A ring; (e) A ring; (f) A ring.
3. The requirements for an integral domain include the requirements for a ring
   plus postulates 1(b), 3(b), and the cancellation law for $\odot$. Thus any set that
   forms an integral domain must necessarily form a ring.
5. (a) Because all entries of the tables are elements of the set $\{w, u, v, x\}$;
   (b) $u \oplus v = v = v \oplus u$; $\oplus$ is a commutative operation;
   (c) To justify postulate 2(a) all possible arrangements of 4 elements taken 3 at
   a time would have to be verified. There would be 64 of these arrangements.

A similar situation would exist in the justification of postulates 2(b) and 5.
(d) Because for any element a in the set, $a \oplus u = u \oplus a = a$;
(e) x is its own inverse for $\oplus$; (f) Yes; (g) Yes, v;
(h) Consider the following counterexample: $x \odot x = x$ and $x \odot v = x$ but $v \neq x$; (i) Yes.

3.8   Page 59

1. (a) Not a group because the set is not closed under $+$; also, postulates (2) and (3) fail;
   (b) Not a group because of postulate (3);
   (c) A group;   (d) A group;
   (e) Not a group; postulates (2) and (3) fail;
   (f) Not a group; postulates (1), (2), and (3) fail;
   (g) A group;
   (h) Not a group because of postulate (3);
   (i) A group; (j) Not a group because postulate (3) fails; the element 0 has no inverse;   (k) A group;   (l) A group.

3. l and g.

5. The set is closed because in a field the product ($\odot$) of two elements is not ϵ_0 unless one of the elements was ϵ_0. The associative property, the existence of an identity element, and the existence of an inverse for each element were inherited from the field postulates. Thus the given set forms a group under $\odot$.

4.1   Page 63

1. (a) $\begin{bmatrix} 3 & 5 \\ -3 & 6 \end{bmatrix}$;   (b) $\begin{bmatrix} 3 \\ 4 \\ -2 \end{bmatrix}$;   (c) $\begin{bmatrix} 2 & 3 \\ -1 & 4 \\ 0 & 4 \end{bmatrix}$.

3. When F is a square matrix.

5. (b) $\begin{bmatrix} 2 & 0 \\ 7 & 4 \\ 6 & 8 \end{bmatrix} = (AB)^T = B^T A^T$.

9. No.   Given: $A = B^T$ and $B = C^T$;   by Theorem 1, $B^T = (C^T)^T = C$. Therefore $A = C$.

13. Yes.

15. $(A^T + 2B^T + C)^T = (A^T + 2B^T)^T + C^T$ by Theorem 2
$= (A^T)^T + (2B^T)^T + C^T$ by Theorem 2
$= (A^T)^T + 2(B^T)^T + C^T$ by Theorem 4
$= A + 2B + C^T$ by Theorem 1.

4.2   Page 64

1. (a) Symmetric;
   (b) Not symmetric because the matrix is not square and cannot equal its transpose;
   (c) Not symmetric because the matrix does *not* equal its transpose.

3. Not possible.

11. Yes.   An explanation would consist of showing that the postulates of a group are valid for the set of all 2 by 2 symmetric matrices.

4.3   Page 65

1. (a) No; (b) Yes; (c) No; (d) Yes.

3. $\begin{bmatrix} 0 & 0 \\ 0 & 0 \end{bmatrix}$.

7. (a) $\begin{bmatrix} 9 & \frac{13}{2} \\ \frac{13}{2} & -2 \end{bmatrix} + \begin{bmatrix} 0 & \frac{1}{2} \\ -\frac{1}{2} & 0 \end{bmatrix}$; (b) $\begin{bmatrix} 3 & \frac{3}{2} & -1 \\ \frac{3}{2} & 3 & 0 \\ -1 & 0 & 2 \end{bmatrix} + \begin{bmatrix} 0 & \frac{3}{2} & 0 \\ -\frac{3}{2} & 0 & -2 \\ 0 & 2 & 0 \end{bmatrix}$.

9. Each entry of the diagonal of the product is equal to the sum of squares of the entries of the corresponding row (or column) of the original matrix.   This can also be stated:
   Let $D = AA^T$,
   The diagonal entries of D
   are $d_{ii} = (a_{i1})^2 + (a_{i2})^2 + \ldots + (a_{in})^2$
   or $d_{jj} = (a_{1j})^2 + (a_{2j})^2 + \ldots + (a_{nj})^2$.

11. Yes.

4.4   Page 67

1. (a) The conjugate matrix is $\begin{bmatrix} -i & 2+i & 2 \\ 0 & -3i & 4 \end{bmatrix}$;

   The tranjugate matrix is $\begin{bmatrix} -i & 0 \\ 2+i & -3i \\ 2 & 4 \end{bmatrix}$;

   (b) The conjugate matrix is $\begin{bmatrix} 2 & 2-i \\ -i & -2i \end{bmatrix}$;

   The tranjugate matrix is $\begin{bmatrix} 2 & -i \\ 2-i & -2i \end{bmatrix}$;

   (c) The tranjugate matrix is $\begin{bmatrix} 0 & 3+i \\ 3-i & 2 \end{bmatrix}$;

   (d) The conjugate and tranjugate matrices equal original matrix;

   (e) The conjugate matrix is $\begin{bmatrix} 0 & -i & -2i \\ -i & 0 & -4 \\ -2i & 4 & 0 \end{bmatrix}$;

   The tranjugate matrix is $\begin{bmatrix} 0 & -i & -2i \\ -i & 0 & 4 \\ -2i & -4 & 0 \end{bmatrix}$.

11. Yes.

4.5   Page 69

1. (a) Not either;   (b) Triangular, echelon;
   (c) Echelon;   (d) Triangular;
   (e) Triangular, echelon;   (f) Echelon;
   (g) Triangular;   (h) Triangular;

(i) Triangular;   (j) Triangular;
(k) Echelon.

3. Yes.

5. No.   The set is not closed under addition.   For example,

$$\begin{bmatrix} 1 & 1 & 1 \\ 0 & 1 & 1 \\ 0 & 0 & 1 \end{bmatrix} + \begin{bmatrix} 1 & 0 & 0 \\ 1 & 1 & 0 \\ 1 & 1 & 1 \end{bmatrix} \text{ is not a triangular matrix.}$$

4.6   Page 71

1. (a) True;   (b) False;   (c) True;   (d) False;
   (e) True;   (f) False;   (g) True.

5. Yes, because all the postulates for a field are satisfied.

7. (a) $\begin{bmatrix} -1 & 0 & 0 \\ 0 & -1 & 0 \\ 0 & 0 & -1 \end{bmatrix}$ or $\begin{bmatrix} -2 & 0 & 0 \\ 0 & -2 & 0 \\ 0 & 0 & -2 \end{bmatrix}$;

   (b) $\begin{bmatrix} -2 & 0 & 0 \\ 0 & -2 & 0 \\ 0 & 0 & -2 \end{bmatrix}$ or $\begin{bmatrix} 2 & 0 & 0 \\ 0 & 2 & 0 \\ 0 & 0 & 2 \end{bmatrix}$;

   (c) $\begin{bmatrix} -1 & 0 & 0 \\ 0 & -1 & 0 \\ 0 & 0 & -1 \end{bmatrix}$ or $\begin{bmatrix} \sqrt{2}i & 0 & 0 \\ 0 & \sqrt{2}i & 0 \\ 0 & 0 & \sqrt{2}i \end{bmatrix}$

   or $\begin{bmatrix} -\sqrt{2}i & 0 & 0 \\ 0 & -\sqrt{2}i & 0 \\ 0 & 0 & -\sqrt{2}i \end{bmatrix}$.

4.7   Page 73

1. (a) $\begin{bmatrix} 0 & \vdots & 8 \\ \cdots & \vdots & \cdots \\ 4 & \vdots & 20 \\ 2 & \vdots & 8 \end{bmatrix}$; (b) $\begin{bmatrix} 8 & 0 & 4 \\ 16 & 8 & 6 \end{bmatrix}$; (c) $\begin{bmatrix} 23 & \vdots & 4 \\ \cdots & \vdots & \cdots \\ 16 & \vdots & 7 \\ 26 & \vdots & 12 \end{bmatrix}$.

3. $\begin{bmatrix} 1 & 0 & -2 \\ 4 & 5 & 3 \end{bmatrix}, \begin{bmatrix} 1 & 0 \\ 4 & 5 \end{bmatrix}, \begin{bmatrix} 1 & -2 \\ 4 & 3 \end{bmatrix}, \begin{bmatrix} 0 & -2 \\ 5 & 3 \end{bmatrix}, \begin{bmatrix} 1 \\ 4 \end{bmatrix}, \begin{bmatrix} 0 \\ 5 \end{bmatrix}, \begin{bmatrix} -2 \\ 3 \end{bmatrix},$

   $[1 \ 0 \ -2], [4 \ 5 \ 3], [1 \ 0], [4 \ 5], [1 \ -2],$
   $[4 \ 3], [0 \ -2], [5 \ 3], [1], [0], [-2], [4], [5], [3].$

5. (a) $\begin{bmatrix} 2 & 3 & 2 & \vdots & 1 & 0 & 0 \\ 1 & 4 & 6 & \vdots & 0 & 1 & 0 \\ 2 & 1 & 0 & \vdots & 0 & 0 & 1 \end{bmatrix}$;

   (b) $\begin{bmatrix} 2 & 3 & 2 & \vdots & 1 & 0 & 0 & \vdots & 2 \\ 1 & 4 & 6 & \vdots & 0 & 1 & 0 & \vdots & 0 \\ 2 & 1 & 0 & \vdots & 0 & 0 & 1 & \vdots & 1 \\ \cdots & \cdots & \cdots & \vdots & \cdots & \cdots & \cdots & \vdots & \cdots \\ 3 & 2 & 1 & \vdots & 0 & 0 & 0 & \vdots & f \end{bmatrix}$.

4.8   Page 75

1. (a) $\begin{bmatrix} 1 & -1 & 1 & 4 \\ 2 & 0 & 1 & 2 \\ 0 & 1 & 2 & 1 \end{bmatrix}$ and $\begin{bmatrix} 1 & -1 & 1 \\ 2 & 0 & 1 \\ 0 & 1 & 2 \end{bmatrix}$;

(b) $\begin{bmatrix} 1 & 1 & 1 & -1 & 2 \\ 1 & 0 & 1 & 2 & 1 \end{bmatrix}$ and $\begin{bmatrix} 1 & 1 & 1 & -1 \\ 1 & 0 & 1 & 2 \end{bmatrix}$;

(c) $\begin{bmatrix} 1 & 1 & 2 \\ 1 & 2 & 4 \\ 2 & -1 & -2 \end{bmatrix}$ and $\begin{bmatrix} 1 & 1 \\ 1 & 2 \\ 2 & -1 \end{bmatrix}$;

(d) $\begin{bmatrix} 1 & 1 & -1 \\ -1 & 1 & 0 \end{bmatrix}$ and $\begin{bmatrix} 1 & 1 \\ -1 & 1 \end{bmatrix}$.

3. $\begin{bmatrix} \dfrac{b_1}{d_{11}} \\ \dfrac{b_2}{d_{22}} \\ \cdot \\ \cdot \\ \cdot \\ \dfrac{b_n}{d_{nn}} \end{bmatrix}$ Where D is the coefficient matrix, and $[D \vdots B]$ is the augmented matrix.

5.1   Page 79

1. (a) 20;   (b) -2;   (c) $-1 + 2i$ (d) $-3t$.
3. $4! = 24, n!$ 5. t is odd but not unique.

5.2   Page 81

1. (a) $2\begin{vmatrix} 2 & 2 \\ 4 & 0 \end{vmatrix} - 3\begin{vmatrix} 3 & 0 \\ 4 & 0 \end{vmatrix} + (-1)\begin{vmatrix} 3 & 0 \\ 2 & 2 \end{vmatrix} = -22$;

(b) $(-1)\begin{vmatrix} 3 & 0 \\ 2 & 2 \end{vmatrix} - 4\begin{vmatrix} 2 & 0 \\ 3 & 2 \end{vmatrix} + 0 = -22$;

(c) $0 - 2\begin{vmatrix} 2 & 3 \\ -1 & 4 \end{vmatrix} + 0 = -22$;

(d) $(-1)^{3+2}\begin{vmatrix} 2 & 0 \\ 3 & 2 \end{vmatrix} = -4$;   (e) $\begin{vmatrix} 3 & 2 \\ -1 & 0 \end{vmatrix} = 2$.

3. $+4$.
5. (a) $a_{11} \cdot a_{22} \cdot a_{33}$;   (b) $a_{11} \cdot a_{22} \cdot \ldots \cdot a_{nn}$;   (c) 16.

5.3   Page 86

1. (a) True;   (b) True;   (c) False.   3. -8.
5. 108 by application of Theorem 8 three times.

9. 15.   **11.** (a) $612 = |AB| = |A| |B|$;   (b) $14 = |AB| = |A| |B|$
15. (a) -17;   (b) -5;   (c) 0;   (d) -13;   (e) 39.

5.5   Page 93

1. (a) $x = 4, y = 1$;   (b) $x = \frac{11}{2}, y = -5, z = -\frac{1}{2}$
(c) $x = 1, y = -1, z = -3, t = 3$.

5.6   Page 94

1. (a) False.   If the determinant of every fourth order submatrix is zero, then the rank is 3 or less.
(b) True; $|A| = |A^T|$ (Theorem 3, Section 5.3).
(c) True; if $A_3 = -A_3^T$ then $|A_3| = |-A_3^T| = (-1)^3|A_3^T|$, and $|A_3| = -|A_3^T|$ only if $|A| = 0$.
3. (a) two;   (b) three;   (c) one;   (d) zero;   (e) one.
5. Rank of A is 2; rank of $[A \vdots B]$ is 3.
7. The rank is two or less.

6.2   Page 97

1. (a) $\begin{bmatrix} 1 & -3 \\ 4 & 2 \end{bmatrix}$;   (b) $\begin{bmatrix} 2 & 1 & 0 \\ -2 & -1 & 0 \\ -2 & -1 & 0 \end{bmatrix}$;

(c) $\begin{bmatrix} -1 & 3 & 0 \\ 2 & -1 & 0 \\ 2 & -1 & -5 \end{bmatrix}$;   (d) $\begin{bmatrix} -4 & 0 & 0 & 2 \\ 0 & 0 & -2 & 0 \\ 0 & -4 & 0 & 0 \\ 0 & 0 & 0 & -2 \end{bmatrix}$.

5. (a) Rank is 3;   (b) Rank is less than 3.
7. They are equal.

6.3   Page 101

1. (a) $\frac{1}{14}\begin{bmatrix} 1 & -3 \\ 4 & 2 \end{bmatrix}$;   (b) No inverse because det $B = 0$;

(c) $\frac{1}{5}\begin{bmatrix} -1 & 3 & 0 \\ 2 & -1 & 0 \\ 2 & -1 & -5 \end{bmatrix}$;   (d) $\begin{bmatrix} 1 & 0 & 0 & -\frac{1}{2} \\ 0 & 0 & \frac{1}{2} & 0 \\ 0 & 1 & 0 & 0 \\ 0 & 0 & 0 & \frac{1}{2} \end{bmatrix}$.

3. In order for a matrix A to have an inverse B, AB must equal BA which must equal I. If, however, A is not square, it is impossible for AB to equal BA.
5. No.   "B" is not a square matrix.   Therefore B^{-1} does not exist, and hence B^{-3} does not exist.
9. (a) Because A^{-1} must exist.

6.4   Page 104

5. $(A^T)(A^{-1})^T$ $\quad = (A^{-1}A)^T$ $\qquad$ By Theorem 3 of Chapter 4.
$\qquad\qquad\qquad\qquad = I^T.$ $\qquad\qquad\qquad\quad$ By definition of inverse.
$\qquad\qquad\qquad\qquad = I.$
Likewise $(A^{-1})^T A^T = I.$ $\qquad\qquad$ By Theorem 3 of Chapter 6.
Therefore $(A^{-1})^T = (A^T)^{-1}.$ $\qquad$ By Theorem 2 of Chapter 6.

13. Rank of $A =$ Rank of $B = 1.$

6.5   Page 107

1. (a) $\begin{cases} x_1 = \frac{13}{4} \\ x_2 = \frac{1}{4} \end{cases}$; (b) $\begin{cases} x_1 = \frac{2}{3} \\ x_2 = -\frac{1}{3} \end{cases}$;

(c) $x_1 = \frac{9}{2}$; $x_2 = -\frac{1}{2}$; $x_3 = -\frac{7}{2}$;
(d) $x_1 = -\frac{1}{2}$; $x_2 = -\frac{1}{2}$; $x_3 = \frac{3}{2}$.

3. B and C are nonsingular. $X = B^{-1}AC^{-1}.$

7.1   Page 111

1. (a) The third elementary operation. $(-2R_1 + R_2.)$
(b) The second elementary operation. $(\frac{1}{2}R_1.)$
(c) The first elementary operation. $(R_2 \leftrightarrow R_1,$ then $R_2 \leftrightarrow R_3.)$

3. (a) $\begin{bmatrix} 2 & 1 & 6 \\ 2 & 4 & 9 \end{bmatrix} \sim \begin{bmatrix} 1 & \frac{1}{2} & 3 \\ 0 & 1 & 1 \end{bmatrix}$, $\begin{cases} x + \frac{1}{2}y = 3 \\ \quad\quad y = 1 \end{cases}$, $x = \frac{5}{2}, y = 1$;

(b) $\begin{bmatrix} 1 & 1 & 1 & 4 \\ 0 & 1 & 1 & 6 \\ 3 & -1 & -2 & 9 \end{bmatrix} \sim \begin{bmatrix} 1 & 1 & 1 & 4 \\ 0 & 1 & 1 & 6 \\ 0 & 0 & 1 & -21 \end{bmatrix}$,

$\begin{cases} x + y + z = 4, \\ \quad\quad y + z = 6, \\ \quad\quad\quad\quad z = -21. \end{cases}$ $\qquad x = -2,\ \ y = 27,\ \ z = -21.$

5. (a) No. The augmented matrices are not row equivalent.
(b) Yes. The augmented matrices are row equivalent.

7. Order of $A =$ Order of B.

7.2   Page 114

1. Rank 2. **3.** Rank 2. **5.** Rank 2.

7. $\begin{bmatrix} I_2 & \vdots & 0 \\ \cdots & \vdots & \cdots \\ 0 & \vdots & 0 \end{bmatrix}_{(4,6)}.$ $\qquad\qquad$ **9.** $A \sim G,\ \ B \sim E.$

11. Their normal forms are equal; or one can be transformed into the other by elementary operations; or the ranks are equal and the order is the same.

7.3   Page 117

1. $E = \begin{bmatrix} 0 & 1 \\ 1 & 0 \end{bmatrix}.$ $\qquad$ **3.** $E = \begin{bmatrix} 1 & 0 \\ 0 & 9 \end{bmatrix}.$ $\qquad$ **5.** $E = \begin{bmatrix} 1 & 0 \\ 4 & 1 \end{bmatrix}.$

7. P and Q are not unique but a P and Q which will satisfy Theorem 2 are

$$P = \begin{bmatrix} -2 & 1 \\ -3 & 1 \end{bmatrix} \quad \text{and} \quad Q = \begin{bmatrix} 1 & 0 \\ 0 & -\frac{1}{2} \end{bmatrix}.$$

P is the product of the two elementary matrices

$$\begin{bmatrix} 1 & 1 \\ 0 & 1 \end{bmatrix}, \quad \text{and} \quad \begin{bmatrix} 1 & 0 \\ -3 & 1 \end{bmatrix}.$$

Q is an elementary matrix.

9. P and Q are not unique but a P and Q which will satisfy Theorem 2 are

$$P = \begin{bmatrix} 1 & 0 & 0 \\ 0 & 1 & 0 \\ -1 & 0 & 1 \end{bmatrix} \quad \text{and} \quad Q = \begin{bmatrix} 1 & 0 & 0 \\ 0 & 1 & 0 \\ 0 & 0 & 1 \end{bmatrix}.$$

11. $E = \begin{bmatrix} 1 & 0 \\ 2 & 1 \end{bmatrix}, \quad E^{-1} = \begin{bmatrix} 1 & 0 \\ -2 & 1 \end{bmatrix}, \quad A = \begin{bmatrix} -1 & 2 \\ -7 & 4 \\ 6 & 0 \end{bmatrix}.$

13. $E = \begin{bmatrix} 1 & 0 \\ 2 & 1 \end{bmatrix}, \quad E^{-1} = \begin{bmatrix} 1 & 0 \\ -2 & 1 \end{bmatrix}, \quad A = \begin{bmatrix} 1 & 0 \\ -2 & 1 \end{bmatrix}.$

Yes, because $AE = I$ and by Theorem 3 of Chapter 6, $EA = I$, therefore E is the inverse of A.

7.4   Page 119

1. $A^{-1} = \begin{bmatrix} 0 & \frac{1}{4} \\ \frac{1}{3} & -\frac{1}{12} \end{bmatrix}.$

3. $\begin{bmatrix} 0 & 0 & 1 \\ 0 & 1 & -3 \\ 1 & 0 & -1 \end{bmatrix}.$

5. $A^{-1} = \frac{1}{9} \begin{bmatrix} -4 & 5 & 4 \\ 1 & 1 & -1 \\ 10 & -8 & -1 \end{bmatrix}.$

7. $B = kA^{-1}.$

9. A could not be transformed to I by elementary row operations. If A is singular, A is not equivalent to I.

8.1   Page 124

1. (a) The system is inconsistent; the rank of A does not equal the rank of $[A \mid B]$. Therefore r doesn't exist.

(b) The system is consistent and $r = 2 = n$; therefore there is a unique solution.

(c) Consistent. $r = 3 = n$, therefore there exists a unique solution.

(d) Consistent. $r = 2$, $n = 3$, $r < n$. There are an infinite number of solutions.

(e) It is a homogeneous system because $B = 0$; therefore the system is consistent. $r = 2 < n$ hence there are an infinite number of solutions.

(f) It is a homogeneous system because $B = 0$; therefore the system is consistent. $r = 3 = n$ hence there is a unique solution.

(g) Consistent. $r = 3 < n$ hence there are an infinite number of solutions.

(h) It is an inconsistent system because the rank of A does not equal the rank of $[A \mid B]$.

3. (*a*) (Rank of augmented matrix) = (rank of coefficient matrix) = 6.   (Theorem 2).
   (*b*) There must be at least 6 equations because *r* is 6.
5. Unique solution; moreover the solution is the trivial solution.
7. *r* is the order of a submatrix of *A*, and the order of *A* is *m* by *n*, hence $r \leq n$ and $r \leq m$.

8.2   Page 126

1. (*a*) Rank of coefficient matrix = 2;   (*b*) Rank of *A* is 2;
        Rank of augmented matrix = 3;   Rank of [*A* ⦙ *B*] is 3;

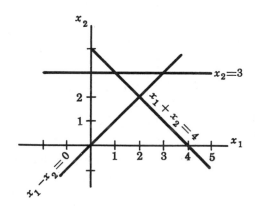 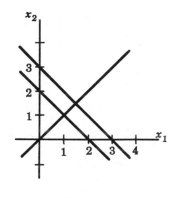

(*c*) Rank of *A* is 1;   (*d*) Rank of *A* is 1;
     Rank of [*A* ⦙ *B*] is 2;   Rank of [*A* ⦙ *B*] is 2.

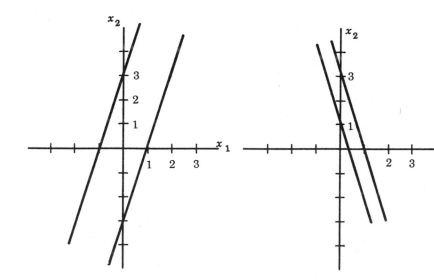

3. The rank of $[A \mid B]$ is 3. The most that the rank of A could be is 2, therefore r cannot exist.

5. If $b = 4$, any point along the line $x_1 + x_2 = 4$ will satisfy the system. If $b \neq 4$, the system is inconsistent. Geometrically we would have two parallel lines.

8.3   Page 130

1. (a) The solution is $(2, 1)$.   (b) The solution is $(0, 0)$.
   (c) The system is inconsistent.   (d) The system is inconsistent.
   (e) The solution is $(1, 3)$.   (f) The system is inconsistent.

3. The last row which does not contain all zeros will have a nonzero entry only in the last column.

5. 4 type 1 trucks; 6 type 2 trucks; 2 type 3 trucks.

7. $I_1 = \frac{3}{140}E_0$, $I_2 = \frac{1}{140}E_0$, $I_3 = \frac{1}{70}E_0$.

8.4   Page 136

1. (a) Infinite number of solutions;
   (b) Infinite number of solutions;
   (c) Inconsistent, no solution;   (d) Unique solution, $(0, 0)$.

3. The number of rows which do not consist of all zeros is less than the number of unknowns, and the last of these rows has two or more nonzero entries.

5. No.   Theorem 3.

7. (a) Let $x_1 = x_2 = 0$.
      A basic solution would be $(0, 0, 4, 5)$.
   (b) Any two unknowns can be found in terms of any other two, except x_1 and x_2 cannot be found in terms of x_3 and x_4.

11. (a) There is no unique answer; 4 type 1 trucks must be sent, and if k type 3 trucks are sent, then $(8 - k)$ type 2 trucks must be sent.
    (b) There will be exactly 9 solutions because in order to send fully loaded trucks, k must be an integer such that $0 \leq k \leq 8$.

8.5   Page 139

1.	No Solution	There are m lines. At least 2 intersect at a point. At least one other line does not pass through that point.
	Unique Solution	m lines pass through a single point.
	Infinite Number of Solutions	m lines intersect along a line.

8.6   Page 140

1. (a) No, because rank of A is 2 which does not equal the rank of $[A \mid B]$.

3. (a) Yes, because the rank of A equals the rank of $[A \mid B]$.
   (b) Yes, because $r = 2 = n$.

9.1   Page 143

3. Part (1) of the definition of a vector space is valid because set is closed under matrix addition.   Part (2) is valid because a scalar times a matrix of the set yields a matrix which also belongs to the set.   Part (3) is valid because of: Theorem 1 of Chapter III, the existence of O_2 and $-A_2$, Theorems 6 and 7 of Chapter III, and the existence of the scalar, 1, such that $1 \cdot A_2 = A_2$.

5. Yes.   To show why, the student should verify that each of the three parts of the definition are valid for the given set and operations.

9. No, because, among other reasons, the set would not be closed under addition.

9.2   Page 147

1. (a) Linearly dependent;   (b) Linearly independent;
   (c) Linearly independent;   (d) Linearly dependent;
   (e) Linearly dependent;   (f) Linearly independent;
   (g) Linearly independent;   (h) Linearly dependent.

3. $(a, b, c) = a(1, 0, 0) + b(0, 1, 0) + c(0, 0, 1)$.

5. No, any vector, which does not lie in the plane of the two given vectors, cannot be expressed as a linear combination of the two given vectors.

7. (a) No;   (b) Yes;   (c) Yes;   (d) Yes.

9. (a) 3-space;   (b) One of the coordinate planes in 3-space;
   (c) The plane in 3-space in which the two given vectors lie.

11. The set $\{(0, 0)\}$ is linearly dependent.
    The set $\{(1, 2)\}$ is linearly independent.

9.3   Page 151

3. The sets of parts (a), (b), (d), and (e) are not a basis.
   (a) Because the set does not span the space, nor is the set linearly independent;
   (b) Because the set does not span the space;
   (d) Because the set is not linearly independent;
   (e) Because the set does not span the space nor is the set linearly independent.

5. No, because all three vectors could be colinear or coplanar, and hence not span the space nor be linearly independent.

7. The dimension is three or less.

9. (a) 1;   (b) 2;   (c) 1;   (d) 2;   (e) 3;   (f) 4.

10.1   Page 156

1. (a) $\begin{bmatrix} -2 \\ 4 \end{bmatrix}$;   (b) $\begin{bmatrix} 0 \\ -6 \end{bmatrix}$;   (c) $\begin{bmatrix} 4 \\ 4 \end{bmatrix}$.

3. Domain: The set of real numbers.
   Range: The set of 2-dimensional vectors with real components and with a second component which is twice the first.

5. Domain: The set of 2-dimensional vectors with real components.
   Range: The set of vectors with zero as the first component and any real number as the second component.

7. Domain: The set of real numbers.
   Range: The set of pure imaginary numbers bi where $b > 0$ and the set of real numbers between 0 and 1 inclusive.

9. Domain: The set of real numbers.
   Range: The set of complex numbers $1 + bi$ where $0 < b \le 1$ and the set of
            real numbers greater than or equal to one.

11. A stretching (twice the magnitude) of a reflection through the origin.

13. A shear parallel to the x_1-axis.

15. A stretching (twice the magnitude) of a rotation of 90°.

10.2   Page 162

1. $A = \begin{bmatrix} k & 0 \\ 0 & k \end{bmatrix}$.

3. (a) $A = \begin{bmatrix} 1 & 0 \\ 0 & 0 \end{bmatrix}$;   (b) $A = \begin{bmatrix} 2 & 0 \\ 0 & -2 \end{bmatrix}$;   (c) $A = \begin{bmatrix} \dfrac{\sqrt{2}}{2} & -\dfrac{\sqrt{2}}{2} \\ \dfrac{\sqrt{2}}{2} & \dfrac{\sqrt{2}}{2} \end{bmatrix}$.

10.3   Page 164

1. $T\{(a_1, b_1) + (a_2, b_2)\} = (a_1 + a_2, 2)$,
   whereas $T(a_1, b_1) + T(a_2, b_2) = (a_1 + a_2, 4)$,
   and they are not equal.
   Also, $T(ka_1, kb_1) = (ka_1, 2)$,
   whereas $k[T(a_1, b_1)] = (ka_1, 2k)$,
   and they are not equal.

3. $T\{(a_1, b_1) + (a_2, b_2)\} = T(a_1, b_1) + T(a_2, b_2)$
                    $= (-2[a_1 + a_2], 2[b_1 + b_2])$
   Also, $T\{k(a, b)\} = kT(a, b)$
                    $= (-2ka, 2kb)$.

11.1   Page 170

1. $x \le -2$

3.   5.

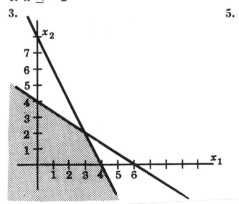

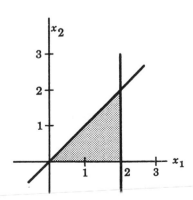

7.

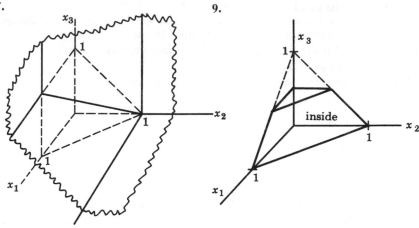

9.

11. $x_1 + 2x_2 - 3x_3 + x_4 > 2.$

13. $x > 1, x < 0.$

15. (a)

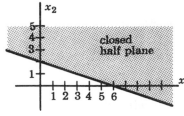

(b) Same as part (a) except that the line is not included — open half plane.

(c)

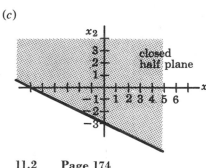

(d)

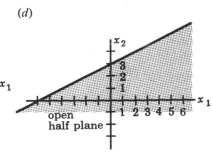

11.2   Page 174

1. Parts (a), (b), (c), and (d) represent convex sets.   Parts (a), (c), (d) represent polyhedral convex sets.

3. Two of the many examples are:

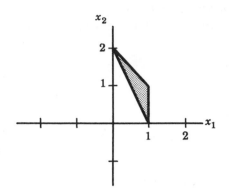

and

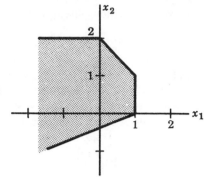

5. The convex set is the solution
of the system

$$\begin{cases} x_1 + 2x_2 \geq 12, \\ x_1 \qquad \geq 6, \\ \qquad x_2 \geq 0. \end{cases}$$

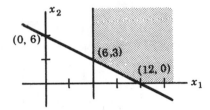

The extreme points are $(6, 3)$ and $(12, 0)$.

7. The convex set is the solution
of the system

$$\begin{cases} x_1 \qquad \geq 200, \\ \qquad x_2 \geq 100, \\ x_1 + x_2 \geq 600, \\ x_1 + x_2 \leq 800. \end{cases}$$

The Extreme points are
$(500, 100, 200)$,
$(200, 400, 200)$,
$(200, 600, 0)$,
$(700, 100, 0)$.

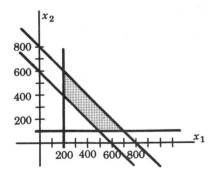

11.3   Page 179

3. $1 - \frac{1}{3}$.

12.1   Page 182

1. Minimum $f = 9$ at $(6, 3)$.   3. Maximum $f = 8$ at $(4, 0)$.
5. Minimum f along line $x_1 + 2x_2 = 9$ from extreme points $(3, 3)$ to $(9, 0)$.

12.2   Page 185

1. Operate refinery 1 one hundred times.
   Operate refinery 2 ten times.
3. Use two type A trucks.   Use six type B trucks.
5. Program A twice.   Program B four times.

12.3   Page 188

1. Minimize CX, subject to $AX \geq R$ and $x_2 \geq 0$, where

$$X = \begin{bmatrix} x_1 \\ x_2 \end{bmatrix}, \quad A = \begin{bmatrix} 1 & 2 \\ 1 & 0 \end{bmatrix}, \quad R = \begin{bmatrix} 12 \\ 6 \end{bmatrix}, \quad C = [1 \ \ 1].$$

3. Maximize CX, subject to $AX \leq R$ and $x_2 \geq 0$, where

$$X = \begin{bmatrix} x_1 \\ x_2 \end{bmatrix}, \quad A = \begin{bmatrix} -1 & -1 \\ -1 & 1 \\ 1 & 2 \end{bmatrix}, \quad R = \begin{bmatrix} -1 \\ 1 \\ 4 \end{bmatrix}, \quad C = [2 \ \ 1].$$

5. Minimize CX, subject to $AX \geq R$ and $X \geq 0$, where

$$A = \begin{bmatrix} 2 & 1 \\ 1 & 1 \\ 1 & 2 \end{bmatrix}, \quad X = \begin{bmatrix} x_1 \\ x_2 \end{bmatrix}, \quad R = \begin{bmatrix} 8 \\ 6 \\ 9 \end{bmatrix}, \quad C = [1 \ \ 2].$$

7. Minimize CX, subject to $AX \geq R$ and $X \geq 0$, where

$$X = \begin{bmatrix} x_1 \\ x_2 \end{bmatrix}, \quad A = \begin{bmatrix} 1 & 1 \\ 3 & 4 \\ 1 & 5 \end{bmatrix}, \quad R = \begin{bmatrix} 100 \\ 340 \\ 150 \end{bmatrix}, \quad C = [300 \ \ 500].$$

9. Minimize CX, subject to $AX \geq R$ and $X \geq 0$, where

$$A = \begin{bmatrix} 20 & 20 \\ 30 & 10 \end{bmatrix}, \quad X = \begin{bmatrix} x_1 \\ x_2 \end{bmatrix}, \quad R = \begin{bmatrix} 160 \\ 120 \end{bmatrix}, \quad C = [300 \ \ 200].$$

11. Maximize CX, subject to $AX \leq R$ and $X \geq 0$, where

$$X = \begin{bmatrix} x_1 \\ x_2 \end{bmatrix}, \quad A = \begin{bmatrix} 20 & 10 \\ -1 & -1 \end{bmatrix}, \quad R = \begin{bmatrix} 80 \\ -6 \end{bmatrix}, \quad C = [30{,}000 \ \ 10{,}000].$$

12.5   Page 192

1. Maximize $g = 12z_1 + 6z_2$,

   subject to $\begin{cases} z_1 + z_2 \leq 1, \\ 2z_1 + 3z_2 \leq 1, \end{cases}$ and $\begin{cases} z_1 \geq 0, \\ z_2 \geq 0. \end{cases}$

3. Minimize $f = -x_1 + x_2 + 4x_3$,

$$\text{subject to} \begin{cases} -x_1 - x_2 + x_3 \geq 2, \\ -x_1 + x_2 + 2x_3 \geq 1, \end{cases} \quad \text{and} \quad \begin{cases} x_1 \geq 0, \\ x_2 \geq 0, \\ x_3 \geq 0. \end{cases}$$

5. Maximize $g = 2z_1 + 3z_2$,

$$\text{subject to} \begin{cases} 2z_1 + 2z_2 \leq 16, \\ 3z_1 + 5z_2 \leq 30, \end{cases} \quad \text{and} \quad \begin{cases} z_1 \geq 0, \\ z_2 \geq 0. \end{cases}$$

Maximum g is 19 at $(5, 3)$.

7. Maximize $g = 6z_1 + 2z_2 + 4z_3$,

$$\text{subject to} \begin{cases} z_1 + z_2 + z_3 \leq 3, \\ 3z_1 \quad\ + z_3 \leq 4, \end{cases} \quad \text{and} \quad \begin{cases} z_1 \geq 0, \\ z_2 \geq 0, \\ z_3 \geq 0. \end{cases}$$

Let z_1 = hypothetical number of hours to make one unit of G_1.
z_2 = hypothetical number of hours to make one unit of G_2.
z_3 = hypothetical number of hours to make one unit of G_3.
g represents the hypothetical number of hours to meet the order. The company wishes to maximize this number to justify prices.
$z_1 + z_2 + z_3$ represents the total hypothetical number of hours required in M_1. This naturally must be less than or equal to 3 which is the actual time of production in M_1. Likewise $3z_1 + z_3$ represents the total hypothetical number of hours required in M_2 and must be less than or equal to 4.

9. The supplier is faced with this problem
Maximize $g = 80z_1 + 60z_2$,

$$\text{subject to} \begin{cases} 2z_1 + 5z_2 \leq 100, \\ 4z_1 + 2z_2 \leq\ \ 80, \end{cases} \quad \text{and} \quad \begin{cases} z_1 \geq 0, \\ z_2 \geq 0. \end{cases}$$

Let z_1 = shadow price of vitamins per unit;
z_2 = shadow price of minerals per unit;
g represents the shadow price of the order which supplier wishes to maximize to show that the greatest value is obtained. $2z_1 + 5z_2$ and $4z_1 + 2z_2$ represent the shadow prices of F_1 and F_2 which, of course, must remain less than or equal to the cost because no one would believe that the supplier would sell at a loss.

12.6   Page 197

1. (a) $\begin{cases} z_1 + 2z_2 + z_3 \quad\quad\ = 5, \\ z_1 + 3z_2 \quad\ + z_4 = 7; \end{cases}$

(b) $\begin{cases} z_1 + z_2 + z_3 \quad\quad\quad = 4, \\ z_1 + 4z_2 \quad\ + z_4 \quad\quad = 7, \\ \quad\ + 2z_2 \quad\quad\ + z_5 = 3. \end{cases}$

3. (a) The augmented matrix for the system
$$\begin{cases} 3z_1 + 4z_2 + 2z_3 + z_4 \quad\quad = 6, \\ z_1 + 3z_2 + z_3 \quad\ + z_5 = 8; \end{cases}$$

(b) The augmented matrix for the system
$$\begin{cases} 3z_1 + 4z_2 + 2z_3 + z_4 \quad\quad = 6, \\ z_1 + 3z_2 + z_3 \quad\ + z_5 = 8, \\ 7z_1 + 8z_2 + 9z_3 \quad\quad\quad = f. \end{cases}$$

12.7   Page 205

1. Maximum $f = 5$ at $(3, 1)$.
   Dual: Minimum $g = 5$ at $(\frac{2}{3}, \frac{1}{3})$.
3. Maximum $f = 16$ at $(2, 0, 2, 0)$.
   Dual: Minimum $g = 16$ at $(2, 0, 4)$.
5. Minimum $x_1 + x_2 + 4x_3 = 8$ at $(0, 0, 2)$.
   Dual: Maximum is 8 at $(4, 0)$.

12.8   Page 208

1. Maximum $f = 4$ at $(\frac{1}{2}, 0)$.
   Dual: Minimum $g = 4$ at $(0, \frac{4}{3})$ or $(\frac{3}{5}, \frac{14}{15})$.

3. $C^T = \begin{bmatrix} 2 \\ 3 \end{bmatrix}$,   and $\begin{bmatrix} 2 \\ 3 \end{bmatrix} = \frac{1}{2} \begin{bmatrix} 4 \\ 6 \end{bmatrix}$ where $\begin{bmatrix} 4 \\ 6 \end{bmatrix}$ is the first column of B.

   The rank of B is 2.
5. Maximum $f = 17$ at $(4, 0, 1)$.
   Dual: Minimum $g = 17$ at $(\frac{1}{2}, \frac{7}{4})$ or $(0, 2, 1)$.

Index